REFLECTIONS IN A TARNISHED MIRROR
THE USE AND ABUSE OF THE GREAT LAKES

Photographs by Jim Legault
Text by Tom Kuchenberg
Illustrations by Mary Ellen Sisulak

Acknowledgements

It is obvious that a great deal of help was needed in the preparation of this book. It would not have been possible without the cooperation of Vernon Applegate, Harold Harvey, K. H. Loftus, Henry Regier, Mrs. Paul Pirtle, Stanford Smith, Claude VerDuin, and Wayne Willford.

We would also like to extend special thanks to Senator William Proxmire and his staff for their continuing interest and assistance in this project.

If this book is found useful, a major reason will be the candor of those who allowed their views to be quoted directly. We are indebted to Jim Addis, Charles R. Burrows, Delano Graff, Nino Green, Ralph Hile, Jim Janetta, Bob Koch, Bill Shepherd, David Schindler, Wayne Tody, Tom Washington, and Asa Wright.

The following people also provided vital information, contacts, and comments; Carl Baker, Carlos Fetterolf, Adele Hurley, Girard LeTendre, Warren Lougheed, Norma Gibson MacDonald, Victor Malarek, Bud Nagelvoort, D. R. Rosenberger, Keta Steebs, Robert W. Wells, and Paul Vidal.

One of our major themes has been the commercial fishing industry. Those connected with the industry who gave of their time were Alvin Anderson, Dan Burnett, Russell Devroy, Steve Fleischel, Raymond Halberg, Dennis Hickey, Jeff Hickey, Clayton Johnson, Elaine Johnson, Bob Maricque, Jim Maricque, Jack Schmirler, Clarence Sellman, Raymond Tuttle, Marvin Weborg, Jeff Weborg, and Francis Wenniger.

Jim LeGault would also like to thank Thomas Uttech, NOAA, Vernon Applegate, and Woodrow Jarvis for photo contributions. The Fish and Wildlife Dvision of the Ontario Ministry of Natural Resources graciously permitted publication of the net drawings used in this book.

In addition, there were those who gave freely of their time and support in the preparation of materials. Chan Harris, Margret Kuchenberg, Bob and Ruth LeGault, and Bill and Nancy Skadden all gave freely of their time during particularly difficult periods.

Much of this manuscript was written in Fairbanks, Alaska. I would like to especially thank Bob and Loretta LeRude, Patsy Turner, and Mr. and Mrs. Wally Turner for their support and encouragement. I am also grateful to Shirley, Jim, Sandy, and Sue who provided ideas and early morning inspiration.

This book is dedicated to Madeline Tourtelot and Joseph Jachna. Without their many influences this collaboration would have never taken place.

Jim Legault   Tom Kuchenberg

Contents

THE GREAT LAKES

|||||||||| Niagara Escarpment
— - — - Laurentian Highlands

MINNESOTA

Thunder Bay

Pink Salmon

Isle Royale

Lake Superior

Silver Bay

Keweenaw Peninsula

Duluth

MICHIGAN

LAURENTIAN HIGHLANDS

ONTARIO

White Fish Bay

Soo Locks

North Channel

La Cloche

Sudbury

NIAGARA

SUPERIOR HIGHLANDS

WISCONSIN

Green Bay

Hammond Bay

Manitoulin Is.

Georgian Bay

Sea Lamprey ?

Door Peninsula

Green Bay

Fox R.

Traverse Bay

Crystal Lake

Smelt

Lake Huron

Bruce Peninsula

ESCARPMENT

Bay of Quinte

Saginaw Bay

Lake Michigan

MICHIGAN

Toronto

Lake Ontario

Alewife ?

ERIE CANAL

Milwaukee

Alewife

LAKE ST. CLAIR

Detroit

ONTARIO

NIAGARA FALLS
(LOVE CANAL)

WELLAND CANAL

Buffalo

NEW YORK

Chicago

Chicago Sanitary Canal

Toledo

Lake Erie

ILLINOIS

INDIANA

OHIO

Cleveland

PENNSYLVANIA

Introduction

The main focus of this book is on the fish of the Great Lakes. It is important to understand that they are only a focus. The great debate over use and abuse of the Lakes raises questions of priorities and basic values. We chose these living creatures because through the years they have reflected the effects of man-made changes in the environment and centered the conflict over what has been finally understood as a limited resource.

Geologically the lakes are recent. They were formed, or perhaps reformed in the wake of the retreating Wisconsin glacier five to twenty thousand years ago. Their present shape was preceded by the formation of earlier lakes and proto-lakes. Drainage patterns changed, sometimes rapidly, as the glacier retreated, readvanced, and retreated in its flickering decline.

When the first European settlers reached the Great Lakes, their shorelines and watersheds were dominated by climax forests. Shaded streams delivered cool water to the lakes; consequently, in midsummer, streams, rivers, and the near-shore areas of the lake were much cooler than they are at present. Organic sediments, now extensive on lake bottoms in some places, were confined to bays and marshes. The general wetland area of swamp and marsh was far more extensive than it is today, and provided habitat for birds and refuge, spawning, and feeding areas for some fish.

The fish community was dominated by older, bigger fish which constituted a far larger percentage of the biomass than they do at present. There were certain species and sub-species of fish that have since disappeared. In addition, there were certain locally adapted stocks of the same species which tended to spawn in specific locations. Finally, there were no Pacific salmon, brown or rainbow trout, carp, smelt, alewife, white perch, or goldfish. There may also have been no lampreys or, if there were, they were confined to Lake Ontario.

The first Europeans were far more aware of the unique nature of the lakes than many of their present descendents. Then the lakes were the main, often dangerous, highways to the interior of North America. Here the Indians fought each other, the French, and the English. The Empires of France and England contested the region until England's victory in the French and Indian War. Finally, there was the War of 1812 between the United States and England, centered mainly in the lower lakes region.

In recent times the Great Lakes have been less celebrated than other spectacular features of North America. Comprehension of the Lakes as a unit has been slow in coming, and this factor has contributed greatly to the ecological disasters which have enveloped the area. In many respects this is difficult to understand for they are truly awesome features. Over 90,000 square miles of surface overlay the largest concentration of fresh water in the world. It is perhaps the designation of ''lake'' that carries with it the diminutive concept of a watery interruption of the landscape. In fact, these waters dominate the surrounding land, bringing a marine element deep into the heart of the continent.

When the violent continental storms encounter the three hundred mile lengths of Michigan and Superior, waves of forty feet can snap steel vessels in two and ravage lee shores. When strong fronts or summer squalls sweep the lakes, sudden pressure differences can cause tide-like seiches to move swiftly across the waters. On June 26, 1954, such a seiche formed into a wave that reached ten feet. Seven lives were lost as it crashed into the Chicago waterfront. In the summer of 1977, a Wisconsin fishing community witnessed a six foot fluctuation that alternately raised vessels above dock level, then set them on suddenly exposed lake bottom. The whole event took place in twenty minutes.

The longer range climatic effects are profound. A journey of only one hundred miles northwest from the western shore of Green Bay witnesses a reduction in the growing season from 155 to 90 days. The waters, slower to cool or warm than the surrounding land, moderate the heat of summer and the cold of winter. The vast surface areas of the Lakes seldom freeze. In winter the sub-zero air masses moving south from the Arctic pass over the warmer waters of these inland seas. Bottom layers of the air mass are warmed and charged with moisture. Temperatures drop again on lee shores and massive snowfalls are precipitated, some areas averaging over one hundred inches a year. The marine effects are most noticeable during the transition seasons. Cold and damp, Spring is in many respects the least pleasant lakeside season. Popular enthusiasm for this time of the year, reflected in prose, poem, and popular song, is apt to mystify those who have never traveled far from the lakes. Autumn, by contrast, is often magnificent with the warm lakes prolonging the frost-free season. This effect has made possible the orchards of Michigan and Ontario, as well as the vineyards of northern Ohio.

The Lakes have also allowed ships to penetrate deeply into the continent. Deepwater ports have facilitated grain shipments from the plains to major markets and the movement of lumber and mineral wealth to manufacturing centers. People have used the lake basins for agriculture, industry, food, transportation, recreation, and waste disposal. For several centuries it seemed that the great mass of water could accommodate all of these uses. The fact that this was not so, is the subject of this book.

Winter storm, Marinette, Wis.

11

Courtesy of The Division of Fish and Wildlife Canadian Ministry of Natural Resources

This sturgeon, caught in 1922, was 7 feet long, weighed 310 pounds and had a girth of 3' 9''.

SECTION 1:
THE LAKES TO 1940

"The Peshtigo River had been alive with pickerel, bass, sturgeon, suckers, and other fish. Each spring before the fire, farmers had driven down to the banks with poles and nets. By evening they had a wagonload of fish to take home, where it was salted or smoked for use the following winter. But that fall of 1871, after the Great Fire had passed, the streams in the burned-over area were full of dead fish and for weeks afterward the water tasted of lye." (1)

". . . 'Indian John' Buschow is quoted as saying that on April 12, 1878, with a canoe and dipnet, he caught 1,800 whitefish; on the 13th, over 1,300; and on the 14th, about 1,000, and for six weeks following an average of 250 per day of an average weight of four pounds each. In 1885 his daily catch averaged 200 three pound fish." (2)

"On April 15, 1935, Mr. Clarence Mertz, a commercial fisherman at Rogers City, Michigan, forwarded to the Department of Conservation, Lansing, Michigan, a specimen which was later identified as the alewife. So far as I know this is the first record of this species reported for the State of Michigan and the second for Lake Huron. . . ."

". . . The occurrence of the alewife in Lake Erie is not entirely unexpected since it now has access to this lake from Lake Ontario through the Welland Canal, but its isolated occurrence in northern Lake Huron is more difficult to explain. . . . (3)

Chapter 1:
Lake Ontario

"The extinction or near extinction of salmonid species prior to the present generation contributed to the lack of public and professional interest in intensive fish management. Few people could recall this fishery and, therefore, were not interested in it. In the upper lakes, the demise of salmonids was relatively recent; therefore the public was aware of the problem and demanded a solution." (3a)

Each of the lakes has a separate personality, but Ontario is probably the most profoundly different, isolated from the upper lakes by Niagara Falls and connected more intimately with the Atlantic by the St. Lawrence River.

The end of the Wisconsin glacier was staggered over a fifteen thousand year span with the ice generally retreating, but re-advancing briefly on at least six occasions. In succession the forerunners of Lake Ontario emptied east and south via the Hudson and Mohawk Rivers to the Atlantic, and at one time to the *west* through Lake Erie, Huron, and Michigan, the Des Plaines River, the Mississippi, and eventually the Gulf of Mexico.

The most singular event in the history of the lake, is that for a period of approximately two thousand years it was connected to the sea. Briefly, this is what is believed to have happened:

1. As the glacier retreated north of the Ontario basin two things occurred. The land, freed of the weight of the ice, began rising slowly. The immense amount of water liberated from the retreating ice cap caused the level of the oceans to rise rapidly.

2. About 8,000 years ago the ocean level rose sufficiently to invade the St. Lawrence valley and reach the Ontario basin.

3. About 6,000 years ago the land had risen so far that the Ontario outlet to the east rose above sea level. The Gulf of St. Lawrence retreated to its present location and outflowing fresh water refilled the St. Lawrence River.

It is important the lakes be perceived in three dimensions. Ontario has the smallest surface area of the lakes, 7,520 square miles, but its central-western basin plunges to 778 feet, deeper than anything found in either Erie or Huron. Further, it is second only to Superior in average depth. The volume of water it contains, 393 cubic miles, is far greater than Erie's 116 cubic miles.

Ontario has been the least productive of the lake fisheries in total volume for nearly a hundred years. It has been the lowest producer on a per acre basis since the 1930's when it fell behind Lake Superior. The western-central basin is a deep trough with only a relatively narrow zone that is shallower than 130 feet, the area of greatest fish accessibility and concentration. Only a relatively small portion of the lake, mainly its northeastern segment, contains over 70 percent of the coastline. It is in these relatively shallow areas, primarily centered around the Bay of Quinte, that the bulk of the commercial and sport fishing is conducted.

Native species

In the early years of the last century the Lake Ontario fisherman had an abundant choice of magnificent fish. There was the often gigantic and long lived sturgeon, the Atlantic salmon, the lake trout, the whitefish, and a variety of chubs. Fishing was good almost everywhere. In the years prior to 1870; the Ontario commercial fishery may have produced between 3.5 and 4.0 pounds per acre. In the 1930's this had fallen to .79 pounds per acre. Gillnetting was almost the only method used in the central and western basin. In the more productive eastern area, setlines were used as well. The pound net was never extensively utilized in Lake Ontario.

The first to go was the Atlantic salmon. It was a landlocked native species that spawned and, for a period of time, lived in the streams surrounding the lake. It was a staple of early residents, abundantly available in the streams before the onset of winter. Beginning in the 1830's or 40's the species began to deteriorate.

This was the first alarm of its kind on the lakes, and a pattern was established which would be followed with monotonous regularity. First, fishing was restricted. In 1866 there was an attempt at restocking that was almost thwarted by the difficulty in obtaining enough fish for a hatchery operation. A temporary recovery in the 1870's led to the belief that the hatchery move had been successful, but in the next decade the fish went into final collapse. A stark sentence describes the first Great Lakes species obliteration: ''The last record we have of Atlantic salmon in Lake Ontario is that of one netted in April 1898 off Scarborough.'' (4)

Historians have argued over the cause of this first species disaster. What happened? Overfishing is the official explanation for the decline or disappearance of most species. Not with the Atlantic salmon. It was too early for the commercial fishery to have had the primary impact and even those predisposed to this

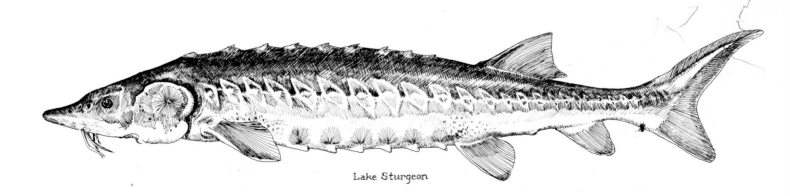

Lake Sturgeon

explanation have looked elsewhere. Settlement of the Ontario Basin had proceeded rapidly during the first half of the 19th century. Land had been cleared for farming and an increasing number of dams had been constructed to support sawmills, gristmills, and later woolen mills. The first impact of settlement produced a number of factors likely to have destroyed the salmon:

1. Some dams at the mouth of rivers blocked entry into streams for spawning. Others, further upstream, limited spawning areas.

2. The clearing of the land changed the watershed. Destruction of cover led to greater amounts of silt and loosened soil invading the spawning areas.

3. The clearing of land created swifter runoff. This meant a lower stream level in the autumn leading to reduced spawning areas and formation of anchor ice in the winter. During spring break-up the moving ice scoured stream bed gravel and destroyed incubating eggs.

4. Land clearance meant destruction of the shade which kept small streams cool in summer. These higher stream temperatures could have been harmful.

5. The effects of sawmills were extremely damaging to stream environments. Waste products were discharged in massive amounts into the streams in this early period, smothering spawning areas with bark and sawdust. This activity and its resulting damage affected all the lakes during their respective lumbering eras.

6. The effects of the sawmills may have been concentrated by a phenomenon known as the thermal bar:

"... The inshore areas of the Great Lakes, because of the higher surface-to-volume ratio, warm more rapidly than the open lake. The creation of a strong temperature gradient between the inshore and open lake waters is an effective horizontal mixing barrier, which may persist as long as 6 weeks. During this period silt, pollutants, and nutrients from the watershed become concentrated on the inshore side of this barrier while the central portion of the lake remains less affected.... The implications for spawning grounds are alarming." (5)

The lake sturgeon was the second fish to go into decline. Though pushed to the edge, it has not followed the Atlantic salmon into extinction. It is a magnificent creature, reaching lengths of 8 feet and weights of 300 pounds. Potentially, it has an incredible life span that may reach 150 years. Ironically this life span may have been its chief difficulty, for it does not reach spawning age for a leisurely 14 to 23 years and does not spawn in every year. Its near disappearance presents the strongest case for overfishing. It was first regarded as a nuisance because of low market value and the destruction of nets the giant caused when trapped. So plentiful and lightly regarded was the fish, that it is reported to have been used as fuel under the boilers of early Great Lakes steamboats. The deliberate destruction of the fish must have been considerable. Compounding the problem was the discovery of a number of uses for the sturgeon. This led to an upsurge in harvesting that in Lake Ontario led to a catch of 581,000 pounds in 1890. The fish thereupon became increasingly rare, reaching levels of less than 10,000 pounds by the early 1920's.

The great length of time required to reach sexual maturity made these fish exceptionally vulnerable. Once stocks had been reduced it was extremely difficult for them to regenerate. Protective measures helped preserve a remnant of the stock, and as late as 1976 a thousand pounds were taken from the lake.

The most desirable species in the Lake Ontario fishery were the lake trout, whitefish, lake herring, and chub. These fish all went through considerable fluctuations during this early period.

In 1879 over a million pounds of trout were harvested. There is a swift drop from this peak. By 1890, less than 200,000 pounds were being taken and from 1900 to 1905, less than 100,000. The twenties saw the second peak of the trout fishery, again cresting at over a million pounds in 1925.

Whitefish roughly paralleled this cycle, going from 1.8 million pounds in 1879, to less than a hundred thousand in 1902, and rising to a million in 1909. After a brief dip, production rose again to a million pounds and annually remained above that figure until 1929, peaking at 2.8 million in 1924.

The catch records of chub and lake herring were combined during the era being discussed, and it is difficult to differentiate relative abundance. Except for a brief period (1910-13) combined catches exceeded a million pounds from 1889 to 1921, peaking at five million in 1889. After a second period of less than a million pounds (1922-27), they were above or near that figure until 1945.

Students of the fisheries believe that hidden in the combined statistics is the fact that chubs were diminishing from 1900 to the 1920's and that there was a resurgence thereafter, It is also believed that two of the larger species of chub fell to insignificance sometime between the turn of the century and the 1940's.

Sketchy catch records indicate that yellow perch were fairly important in the lake by 1890. In 1899, 636,000 pounds of the fish were taken. It was a record that was to last for seventy years. It is likely that perch were taken primarily in years when other fish were not abundant. Thus in the 20's, the halcyon period for the trout-whitefish fisheries, production dropped below 100,000 pounds for the first time since 1908. Since they were basically a 'consolation' fish, perch records are unreliable as to total abundance. In terms of tonnage, however, it has periodically been important since before the turn of the century.

Alien Species

No other fish is as noticeable to the casual observer as the alewife. The spring die-off of this species litters the shoreline with rotting carcasses. This gift to the lakes apparently made its way to Ontario from the Atlantic via the Erie Barge Canal in the 1860's.

A second theme was thus introduced into the alteration of fish stocks in the lakes. A commercial demand led to the barge canal, opening a connection between habitats that had been separated for a long period of time. The alewife, finding the Ontario basin congenial, flourished. Some observers believe that the alewife invasion was the primary cause of the subsequent disasters that overtook fish stocks in the lake. Desirable species fluctuated in abundance, however, long after introduction of the alewife. It was, in fact, a favored food of trout and whitefish. It may have been that the alewife interacted as a food competitor with certain other species and led to their decline. All speculation is limited by lack of reliable information on their abundance.

One clue to the durability of the fish is its utilization of vast sections of the lake in the course of its life span. The die-offs may be related to climatic factors and occur when the fish move out of the deeper waters of the lake to spawn. Smaller fish spend some time in the shallower waters. In summer adults range down to about twenty fathoms. As winter approaches and surface waters cool, the alewife moves to warmer deep waters where it spends the winter.

At least the alewife invaded the lakes. Carp were planted. It is difficult to understand why but, at the time, they were regarded as a highly desirable delicacy. The following passage recaptures some of the enthusiasm of another era and palate:

"... In the 1870's, for example, the carp was introduced widely into American waters from Europe. Today, American anglers regard carp as an unmitigated nuisance. Not only are they held in low esteem as a food fish, they also crowd out native fish far more desirable, both by competition and by damaging effects on the environment. But 75 years ago their introduction was hailed with joy. The man chiefly responsible received a governmental decoration. Arrival of shipments of carp for release was hailed at railroad stations by local deputations in holiday mood, complete with flags and village bands. In fact an early volume of the *Transactions of the American Fisheries Society* contains comments by the Fish Commissioner of Colorado of that time in which he outlined his plan for throwing low dams across the mountain streams where, as he said, carp could be cultured 'after extermination of the inferior native trout' ..." (6)

The carp may have moved into the food chain position previously occupied by the sturgeon. Its effect on the existing community is unknown but numbers increased steadily. Supply has almost always exceeded demand for the fish and catch records do not reflect the size of the population.

There were other attempts in the early years to plant fish. The effort to save the Atlantic salmon has been described. Between 1870 and 1873 there was an attempt to establish American shad. Chinook salmon were stocked in the period 1878-82 and again in the 1920's. Although some specimens of these fish were sighted long after the plantings, the efforts eventually failed.

What caused the lake trout and whitefish stocks to decline during the last century and then rebound during the second and third decades of this century? Fish management explanation generally lays the main stress on overfishing, but this is far from certain. The spectacular catch of 1879 appears as an isolated event. Lake trout catches remained low until 1909. With greater fluctuation, whitefish catches are generally lower from 1882 to 1908.

It is interesting that this is the same period that saw the final disappearance of the Atlantic salmon and the invasion of alewives and carp. It was also just after the era of maximum land clearance and sawmilling activity. There may well have been a negative change in water quality, especially in shallow spawning areas, that was reversed when land clearance was completed and stable farm and pasture regimes were established.

Thus in Lake Ontario we have seen the major themes laid out. Alteration of the surrounding landscape that probably led to the extinction of the Atlantic salmon, overfishing that probably led to the decline of the sturgeon, and the introduction of new species by design and by accident coincident to an expanding commerce. It is a good introduction to the disasters and dislocations that were to follow.

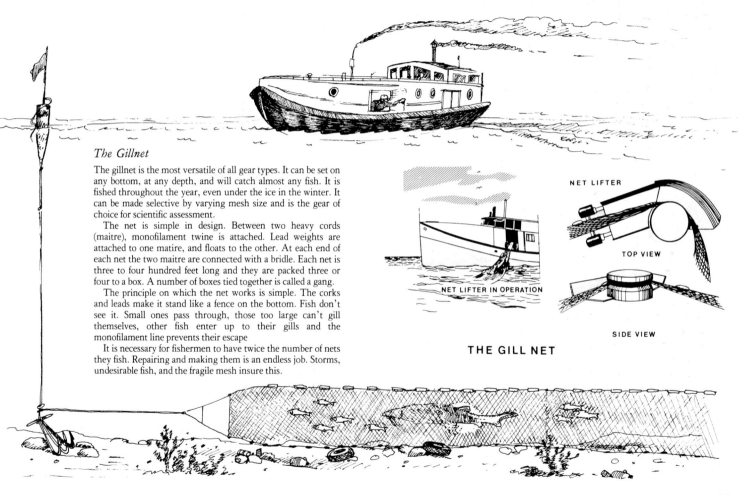

The Gillnet

The gillnet is the most versatile of all gear types. It can be set on any bottom, at any depth, and will catch almost any fish. It is fished throughout the year, even under the ice in the winter. It can be made selective by varying mesh size and is the gear of choice for scientific assessment.

The net is simple in design. Between two heavy cords (maitre), monofilament twine is attached. Lead weights are attached to one matire, and floats to the other. At each end of each net the two maitre are connected with a bridle. Each net is three to four hundred feet long and they are packed three or four to a box. A number of boxes tied together is called a gang.

The principle on which the net works is simple. The corks and leads make it stand like a fence on the bottom. Fish don't see it. Small ones pass through, those too large can't gill themselves, other fish enter up to their gills and the monofilament line prevents their escape

It is necessary for fishermen to have twice the number of nets they fish. Repairing and making them is an endless job. Storms, undesirable fish, and the fragile mesh insure this.

NET LIFTER

TOP VIEW

NET LIFTER IN OPERATION

SIDE VIEW

THE GILL NET

Chapter 2:
Lake Erie

"No other lake as large as Lake Erie . . . has been subjected to such extensive changes in the drainage basin, the lake environment, and the fish populations over the last 150 years . . ." (7)

The ancestor lakes of Erie were some of the first to appear. Their character was determined by the shifts of the ice margin and drainage patterns. Lake Maumee drained south through the Fort Wayne River to the Wabash River, and eventually to the Mississippi. Lake Arkona formed a single lake out of an enlarged area that included parts of what is now western Erie, southern Huron, Lake St. Clair, and Saginaw Bay. It discharged through Saginaw Bay and westward across lower Michigan to the Michigan basin. Lake Grassmere, at one point, discharged north through the Huron basin. Following the ice margin the waters flowed in an arc close to the present Straits of Mackinac before turning south into the Michigan basin. At another phase waters emptied into the Ontario basin and then south via the Mowhawk-Hudson river systems.

These are a few of the names given to the rapidly shifting bodies of water and rivers that drained them. The remains of glacial forces are left across the landscapes of the Province Ontario and the bordering lake states. The effects of drumlins, moraines, eskers, and ancient shores give a variety to the landscape that produces a vague boredom when residents travel through areas with a steadier geologic past.

Modern Erie is the shallowest, warmest, and most productive of the Great Lakes. It lies on the border between the northern continental climate (microthermal) and that of the warmer mid-continent (mesothermal).

The lake basin is divided into three areas. The western is extremely shallow with most of the depths between 25 and 30 feet. It comprises 13 percent of the surface area but only 5 percent of its volume. The central is generally deeper, with 63 percent of both surface and volume. The eastern basin is the deepest, reaching the lake maximum of 210 feet. This relatively small area has 24 percent of Erie's surface area but 32 percent of its volume.

The surface waters can reach 80°F in the summer. The shallow western basin usually freezes over in winter and is uniformly warm in summer. The central and eastern basins seldom freeze and are more like the other Great Lakes with warm surface water over much cooler deep waters in the summer and cooler surface water over warmer deep water in the winter. Temperatures are generally uniform in the spring and fall. The most interesting thing about the temperature of the lake is evidence that it may have warmed by 2°F between the early 1920's and the 1950's. This may have had a strong effect on some species.

The fish production of Erie is awesome. Since the end of the last century it has often equalled or surpassed the combined production of the other Great Lakes. It has averaged between 6.5 and 10 pounds per acre since 1900, making it the consistent champion. For instance, the total harvest of Lake Ontario in 1940 was 4.4 million pounds. In the same year Erie produced 32.7 million pounds, considered a poor year on the Lake. Unlike Ontario, which showed an irregular but persistent downward trend in total production to 1940, Erie continued to produce fish at a consistent rate. The point is that the fish being caught at the end of the period were not the ones being caught at its beginning.

To the territorially, socially, and resource restricted European immigrant of the last century, North America was a heady place. It appeared that the vast continent contained limitless supplies of everything needed for human comfort. The general attitude is summed up in the frequent references to the 'taming' of the land and its native inhabitants. The prevailing philosophy of the period sanctified this goal. Whatever its merits as a general economic concept, the extension of laissez-faire mentality to the natural environment produced devastating results. In the extreme case, if one resource hindered access to one considered more valuable, it was removed. In the fisheries, the systematic destruction of the sturgeon was a good example.

More subtle was the role of technological development. When a new fishing technique proved superior, it was adopted by other fishermen as a matter of economic survival. This was true whether or not the long term effect was destructive to the total resource. It is important to note that this connection was recognized by perceptive individuals in the Great Lakes fisheries long before it was recognized as a general principle relating to the environment as a whole. These few included some early conservationists, biologists and some of those most intimately connected with the resource, the commercial fishermen. It is easy to forget that until recent decades the battles over potentially destructive fishing technologies were fought within the commercial community itself.

A hook and line commercial fishery developed in Lake Erie about 1795 around the early settlement of Presque Isle, Pennsylvania. In the western part of the lake seining started in Maumee Bay and the Maumee River. Sauger, walleye, and smallmouth bass were the principal species caught, though the most desired was whitefish. Seining spread along the coasts of Ohio and Michigan and into the Detroit River, peaking between 1850 and 1860. (8)

Ice fishing with dogs, Munsing, Mich.

This early fishery, confined before 1850 to seines, brush weirs, spears, and trotlines, was limited to the spring months. In the middle of the century the development of water powered mills required damming of many of the area streams. Fish were trapped, or at least concentrated, in the pools below the dams and mill owners leased seining rights to commercial fishermen.

The first technological jump came with the development of the pound net around 1850 in bays of the south shore. Tended by small rowboats, these early pound nets lacked tunnels into the hearts and were generally constructed from remnants of seine nets. Over the next two decades the net evolved as tunnels were added and the improved gear set in deeper water. This, in turn, required bigger boats and the development of pile driving and stake driving equipment. Soon strings of pound nets extended into the lake intercepting fish that might have gone to the seiners. Their discontent was somewhat appeased by the fact that the pound nets also helped to intercept the hated

A steam powered gillnet tug

sturgeon. It was asserted that the destruction of the giant fish spared both seine nets and the spawn of desirable fish, thus more than compensating for the reduced number of whitefish reaching the shore. It is not recorded whether this represented the actual state of affairs or was an early example of skillful public relations work on the part of the pound netters.

Soon it was the turn of the pound netters to be distressed. Gill nets were first fished in the 1850's in the New York waters of Erie. These early homemade nets were developed from coarse cotton twine produced by the wives and daughters of the fishermen. Efficiency increased with the use of linen in the late 1850's, and by 1870 improved cotton and linen nets were being manufactured by professionals. Trout and whitefish were caught in six-inch mesh but this soon shrank to 4½ inches. Herring were caught with still smaller mesh. Herring and whitefish often shoaled together and young whitefish were reportedly killed in this manner. By 1880, western pound

netters were complaining of a decreasing whitefish harvest.

There were vast improvements during this period in the technologies supporting fishing. Freezing became increasingly widespread, and improved transport promoted swift delivery to the expanding lakeside cities. A massive advance came with the introduction of the steamboat. The increased speed and maneuverability of steam power made possible the development of the steam net lifter at the turn of the century. Now it was possible to set far more gillnets, and the gear was rapidly extended.

Toward the end of the nineteenth century the first species changes became apparent. Lake trout collapsed early. There are reports from the French explorers of Indians catching the fish and early settlers sought it in the eastern basin. From the beginning, they were reported to be rare in the western and central areas of the lake. The Province of Ontario reported a catch of 171,000 pounds in 1885, but a steady decline set in and the fish was seldom seen after the mid 1930's. Unlike the other lakes, Erie may never have had a substantial population. The lake is at the southern edge of the lake trout range and may have presented them with marginal conditions from the beginning. Artificial warming of the climate through removal of the forest cover, perhaps magnified by natural increases, may have left the fish extremely vulnerable.

Other man-made changes in the habitat may have furthered the destruction of the sturgeon. While the primary cause of its decline was probably overfishing or deliberate elimination, the early and intensive alteration of marsh and river spawning grounds may have contributed to its near disappearance. In 1885 over five million pounds were lifted from the lake. After 1916, totals slipped below 100,000 pounds and never exceeded that mark again.

The increasing rarity of the sturgeon may have combined with the first impact of land settlement to increase the numbers of other lake species. Land clearing and farming led to increased erosion and turbidity. The runoff of fertilizers and human wastes increased nutrients along the rapidly developing south shore. The changed environment favored such fish as herring, sauger, and blue pike, and the fishery began to turn to these species, previously regarded as "rough" fish.

It is one of the many ironies of lake history that the Canadian fishery of this period was both less developed and more strictly managed than its U.S. counterpart. The provincial government refused for a long while to permit either the fyke or trap net. It was felt that these nets were too destructive to small fish and too readily hidden from enforcement officers.

The decline of valued species had already produced the management fad of the nineteenth century—the hatchery. These operations were originally promoted by private entrepreneurs but quickly caught the fancy of governments. Fish were disappearing and artificial augmentation of stocks was a welcome alternative to restrictions on the fishery.

What restrictions were imposed stemmed from the popular hatchery program. The fish culturists were pursuing programs to limit fishing activity in spawning seasons. In Canada they were successful for a few years in the 1880's in stopping fishing during walleye and whitefish spawning periods, while in the United States the major breakthrough was regulation of mesh size. An Ohio attempt at closed seasons failed because of poorly drafted laws.

All the U.S. jurisdictions, the U.S. Federal government, and Canada got into the hatchery act. Whitefish, walleye, herring, and perch were propagated, as were carp. One feels a cautionary chill when one reads that the original introduction of this fish had followed a detailed study by biologists, presumably the best and brightest of their day. It is even more amazing to learn that at least one Great Lakes hatchery was still turning out the fish as late as 1924.

By the 1890's some observers were pointing out that the programs had not noticeably increased the abundance of fish. It was, however, convenient to believe otherwise. Who wanted to get into the political hornet's nest of restrictions? Continuous and confident reports, encouraged by the fishermen, emanated from the hatchery program which had spread throughout the Great Lakes during this period. After the first decade of this century many regulations on the U.S. side were dismantled. In the next ten years Canadian regulations were also seriously reduced.

The actual impact of this first round of plantings is lost. It is known from modern experience that artificial propagation can maintain stocks in certain circumstances. It may have helped more than critics now admit or less than supporters will concede. The serious problem with early stocking was the fact that it was often regarded as a general solution. It promoted the idea that as long as the hatcheries were producing full time, there need be no limitations placed on the harvest of mature fish during the spawning season. As important, no one today knows how successful these planted fish were at reproduction. There were originally a number of walleye stocks in Erie that were distinguished, in part, by their spawning locations. What happened to fish whose parents had spawned at one end of the lake when they were planted in the opposite end? On the other hand what was the genetic effect of mixing stocks from different areas? No one is certain and at the time the question was apparently not examined in any depth.

There were further gear innovations after the turn of the century. Gill nets are normally set on the bottom. It was discovered, some reports say by accident, that nets could be "canned" or floated at intermediate depths to intercept desired fish according to their seasonally preferred location. This concept was expanded around 1905 into the bull net, designed to take advantage of a whole range of lake depths. Net heights increased four or five times and, instead of presenting a relatively small curtain of mesh along the bottom, became mesh walls capable of intercepting greater numbers of lake herring. The net also caught many young whitefish and trout and a battle divided the fishing community for several decades.

Around 1915 the northern pike went into abrupt decline. Here the evidence points to the destruction of spawning grounds through continued dam building, draining of marshes to create farm land, and diking of marshes to create bird hunting preserves. It is possible that by the 1920's the northern had been denied access to areas favored for reproduction.

Something quite different happened to the blue pike. It had been consistently abundant from the 1880's to about 1910. Then, rather than declining, it began a nearly fifty-year period characterized by wild oscillations in abundance. Catches would soar above twenty million pounds yer year, then slump to around five million a few years later, whereupon the process would be repeated. In a 1969 report it was suggested that these undulations themselves were reflections of an over intensive fishery. The blue pike preys on small organisms, presumably including the young of its own species. If fishing intensity were high, many of these young fish would escape predation, and survival in that year would be very high. This large group would, however, subject succeeding year classes to greater predation and they would be small. Finally, the large year class would be extensively fished and the cycle would repeat:

"The regular spacing of the peaks of blue pike production . . . at periods of about twice the length of time required for a year class of blue pike to achieve peak reproductive capacity and also be decimated by the fishery, is what we would expect in an oscillating system in which the major predator is cannibalistic and is itself oscillating in abundance. We believe, therefore, that cannibalism on fry

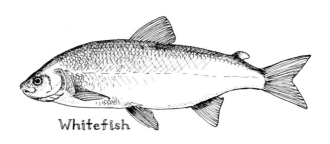
Whitefish

and fingerlings was the major mechanism responsible for these fluctuations from 1910 to 1950 . . ." (9)

The name lake herring is misleading. It resembles ocean herring but, along with the chub, is closely related to the lake whitefish. Catches of lake herring were as wildly cyclical as those of the blue pike in the early fishery. For instance, the catch soared from fourteen to forty-nine million pounds per year between 1916 and 1918. Then came a decline which spread across the lake in a west to east pattern that was highlighted by the great collapse of 1924-25 when production fell from 32.2 million pounds to 5.7 million. This time there was no recovery of significance for decades. What happened between 1924 and 1925? There is no single accepted answer though suggested explanations look to the years preceding this period. Some possibilities:

1. During this time the bull net was at its peak and use of the gill net was rapidly increasing in Canadian waters. The herring migrated eastward in the early summer and westward in early autumn. There is evidence that some fishermen had begun following the migrating fall stocks, using their knowledge of fish habits to repeatedly intercept the moving population. One of the pioneering fish managers, John Van Oosten, suggested that unusual storms in the spring of 1923 concentrated the fish in the eastern basin and led to excessively heavy fishing during the next two years. (10)

2. The catch of herring declined in the western basin before it declined in the central and eastern sections. The small portion of Michigan that borders Erie recorded a catch of 1.4 million in 1890. This dropped sharply the following year and by 1925 only 4,000 pounds were taken from this area. After 1924 the fish was unimportant in the Michigan waters of the lake. It is known that pollution first became significant in the shallow and vulnerable western basin, in the direct path of Detroit and Toledo. One explanation sees the fish being reduced in range by the constricting effects of pollution spreading from west to east. The smaller, more concentrated, populations were therefore more vulnerable to fishing.

This theme of environmental degradation assumes increasing importance, and it is likely that its effects were advanced in the western basin by the 1920's. It is also possible that the destruction of spawning areas led more directly to the disappearance of the herring than over-fishing remnant stocks.

3. Lake herring are noted throughout the Great Lakes for extreme fluctuations in abundance. Lake herring that hatch at 4° to 11°C starve within eighteen days without food. Thus some investigators concluded that an unusually warm spring could have led to an early hatching. This hatching may have preceded the food supply and resulted in the starvation of an enormous number of fish. Only the passage of years would gradually reveal the extent of the destruction. (11)

This theory might offer some explanation for the volatile nature of lake herring, but it may also combine with the other causes to result in a permanent reduction of stocks.

The collapse accelerated the controversy over the bull net. It became the first innovation in gear technology to be limited in U.S. waters. It was outlawed in 1929 in Ohio and five years later in New York and Pennsylvania. Another gear disappeared, not by prohibition, but by evolution. In the face of the greater mobility of the trap net, the pound net fell into disuse. By the mid 30's it had largely disappeared from the south shore of the lake.

Like the herring, whitefish early lost their hold in the western basin. Michigan records show 411,000 pounds in 1913. After 1920 there were never more than twenty thousand pounds caught in any one year. Lakewide, while production varied sharply from year to year, it fell below a million pounds only once between 1908 and 1940.

The sauger was once an important commercial fish in Erie with a catch peaking at 6.1 million pounds in 1916. From 1921 the fish began to decline and again this slide shows up earlier and more significantly in Michigan records. Added to the commonly suggested factors of environmental decay and overfishing is evidence that the sauger's fall may have been accelerated by interbreeding with the walleye.

Perch were an important part of the Erie harvest from the latter part of the last century, but they were far from the first choice of the commercial industry. There is some correlation between perch and whitefish catches, reflecting the tendency to transfer effort to less valuable species when whitefish stocks were low.

The alewife probably moved into Erie by the Welland Canal. It caused little stir. Walleyes and blue pike added it to their diets but conditions for real abundance were lacking. Ironically a large part of the Erie basin, so warm in summer, is not deep enough to have the warmer bottom waters favored by the alewife in winter, and this may have kept the population small.

Erie was hard hit by the full effects of the first phase of pollution. This first phase was a direct result of the settlement of the land by the Europeans. It involved the following:

    1. Changes to the land: clearing of the forests, draining of the land, and resulting erosion and silting.

    2. Changes to the watershed: damming of streams, sawdust from mills, and organic wastes from slaughterhouses and breweries.

    3. Effects of urbanization and industrialization: the swift growth of cities and the poor disposal of human and industrial waste.

The third element in this list is the bridge to the more generalized industrial and municipal pollution of our time that I refer to as 'second stage' pollution. In Erie there was little separation between the two phases, and by 1940 we can already see localized effects of this factor on the more sensitive deep-water fish.

26

Sturgeon

The Trawl

The trawl is a large double bag of netting that tapers to a point. The outside bag is added for extra strength when necessary. The large end of the opening is weighted on the bottom and has floats on the top to keep the net open from top to bottom. The net is attached to *doors* which ride along the bottom and are angled in such a way as to keep the net spread left to right. Metal cables connect the doors to the power winches.

The net is released off the back of the boat and is dragged slowly along the bottom. Recording depth sounders are used to locate fish and help determine when to haul in the net. The power winches haul the catch on board with an assist from a hydraulically operated platform. This is lowered into the water to help the net slide on board more easily. The end of the bag is untied, the fish dumped on the deck and shoveled onto a conveyor which transports them to a storage area forward. In the trawler fishery for smelt, fish are iced and boxed after each drag.

On the Great Lakes trawls have been used mainly for smelt and alewife and occasionally, with a special permit, for whitefish. Trawling is the most mechanized of the commercial techniques. Record catches of alewife are over a hundred thousand pounds for a single trawler in a day.

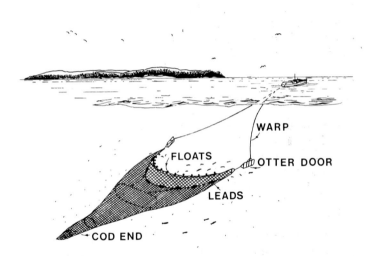

WARP

FLOATS

OTTER DOOR

LEADS

COD END

Chapter 3:
Lake Huron

"In the Saginaw valley of Michigan alone at its 1880 peak, sixty large sawmills scented the air above the twin industry capitals, Bay City and Saginaw.

"A lumber camp grown into a lumber town was like no other type of settlement. The air vibrated with snarling saws that forced conversations to a shout. The fragrance was strong, especially on hot or rainy days. The whole town was originally unpainted wood. The roads were corduroy logs, the sidewalks duckboards, the houses squared timbers. Along the Huron shore the very ground was a heavily piled carpet of sawdust and shavings." (12)

Huron has, perhaps, a greater environmental variety than any of the lakes. Its irregular basin plunges to 750 feet in one place but overall the lake is second only to Erie in the proportion of water less than a hundred feet deep. Its surface area is marginally greater than that of Michigan but is divided into three nearly separate bodies of water.

The Niagaran Cuesta, which forms Niagara Falls on its southeastern edge, cuts a broad limestone arc across the lake. The southerly outthrust forms the Bruce Peninsula dividing the main lake basin from Georgian Bay. A string of islands continues this northwestward sweep and the largest of these, Manitoulin, almost cuts off the third and smallest part of the lake, North Channel. Manitoulin is the largest lake island in the world and contains the largest lake within a lake. One hesitates to go further. In addition, there is the broad, shallow, and productive Saginaw Bay off the southwestern portion of the main basin.

Superior contributes two-thirds of the 122 thousand cubic feet per second inflow to the lake, Michigan the remainder. Additional waters from Huron result in an outflow of 177 thousand cubic feet per second.

During the course of post glacial formation, lakes occupying portions of the Huron basin discharged in various directions; at times west through the Grand River to the Michigan basin, at others north to the North Bay-Ottawa-St. Lawrence River route, and south through the present St. Clair-Detroit River exit into Erie.

Huron has generally been the third lake in production of fish. The central basin was habitat for chubs and trout. The northern straits and islands were the homes of trout and whitefish. The southern basin shoreline supported perch, herring, walleye, and suckers inshore, and whitefish offshore. Saginaw Bay's shallows provided an Erie-like environment for perch, walleye, herring, suckers, catfish and, eventually, smelt.

With the exception of Superior, this is the most lightly populated of the Great Lakes basins. Thus the impact of farming and land clearing was slower and less extensive than that which engulfed Erie and Ontario. As indicated by the opening quotation, however, there was another aspect of the first stage of settlement that strongly affected Huron:

"Forest products industries have had a significant effect upon the ecology of Lake Huron. Sawdust pollution was known to have adversely affected the spawning of lake whitefish . . . in the Saginaw Bay area as early as 1845 . . . Large rafts of logs traversed Georgian Bay during the period 1885-1900 and bark from these rafts undoubtedly littered a considerable portion of the lake bottom. . . .

Rafting of logs has only recently been discontinued on the open waters of the lake, but logs are still driven on tributary streams, and bark litter is known to be a problem to the operation of commercial fishing gear in the North Channel. The discharge of wood fibers from pulp mills has also polluted some tributary streams. Chemical contaminants from pulp mills are known to adversely affect the quality of fish products. . . .'' (13)

The very first settlements in the northern lakes areas tended to group around strategic points and the first Huron fishery developed around Michilimackinac, producing a flourishing local trade by 1800. Seine nets appeared off the Bruce Peninsula in 1831 and in U.S. waters about 1841. Gill nets of cotton or linen mesh were fished from canoes and small boats in Georgian Bay, starting about 1834 and the next year they appeared in Michigan waters near Alpena. Much of the early catch was preserved by salting and was shipped in barrels to developing markets.

By 1850 the gill net had spread to the open lake waters on the Michigan side where it was used to catch trout, whitefish, perch, and suckers. Schooners hauled fish from the Georgian Bay area to various U.S. markets. That area grew rapidly with the arrival of a railroad line at Collingwood, on the southwestern end of the bay, in 1855. A direct line was thus provided to the developing Toronto area. The gill net fisheries grew further with the advent of the steam tug in the 1870's and the steam net lifter in the 1890's.

Fyke nets were used during this period in ice fishing on the Saginaw River for perch, suckers, and catfish. Pound nets first made their appearance off Michigan about 1854 and by the 1860's they were in general use on the U.S. side. Three quarters of these nets were concentrated in Saginaw Bay by 1885. The pound net appeared in Georgian Bay and North Channel in the 1880's. The number of these nets in Canadian waters grew from seventy in 1885 to over three hundred in the 1930's. Trap nets made their appearance in Saginaw Bay and St. Mary's River in the 1890's. Pound and trap nets accounted for more than 75 percent of the landings on the U.S. side by the turn of the century. Baited hooks hung at varying depths from lines strung in the water were called night lines on Huron. Between 1915 and 1925 the number of hooks increased from five to sixty thousand, after which time the technique gradually disappeared.

The battle over use of the bull net on Lake Erie culminated in the first major success in controlling a potentially destructive fishing technique. The effects of that gear are, however, difficult to isolate from other forces acting on the Erie fishery. Such is not the case with another innovation that sparked a controversy, raging across Lakes Huron and Michigan with such fury that it is still vividly remembered by older fishermen. That the deep trap net was a destructive and short sighted piece of technology is readily conceded by almost everyone today. At the time, the battle divided the commercial fishing community and prompted the intervention of a team of federal and state investigators.

It all began on Lake Ontario when a fisherman named John Howard conducted a number of experiments aimed at developing a more efficient trap net. In 1924 he began testing some of his designs in the area of Cape Vincent, New York. The straightforward result of his research was the discovery that ''the bigger the trap the bigger was the catch of fish taken.'' (14) The enlarged net, increased in depth from twelve to as much as thirty feet, was adopted by some other fishermen of the Cape Vincent area. Although the gear did not spread beyond this area, negative effects were noted in Lake Ontario:

''The deep water trap nets appear to have been used first

in Lake Ontario, where according to Mr. J. P. Snyder, Superintendent of the U.S. Bureau of Fisheries Station, Cape Vincent, New York, they "cleaned" up the pike and whitefish at Cape Vincent and in Chaumont Bay. To quote him briefly: 'Two or three men could hardly move and reset a pound net in a couple days, but the same crew will change the position of half a dozen trap nets in a day. It is this mobility and the fact that they can be set in any depth of water, even to a hundred feet or more, that makes them so effective.' " (15)

Nonetheless the effect of the net was limited to a small area of the Lake Ontario fishery. Quite a different result followed in 1928 when Howard and his brother set the net off Alpena, Michigan, in Lake Huron. It was reported that some of the resulting catches ran as high as *two thousand dollars per week.* (16) That is a not insignificant sum in 1978 but in 1928 it was phenomenal. Word spread rapidly through lake ports so that by 1930 the gear was spreading along the U.S. shores of Huron and into the important whitefish grounds of Lakes Michigan and Superior.

Howard had developed a variation of the traditional pound net which, because of the stakes involved, requires areas of suitable bottom and depth. The deep trap could be set in greater depths, on a variety of bottoms, and handled easier than the static pound gear. It was strictly a whitefish net aimed at capturing the fish in their deeper summer range.

As early as the first year of its introduction complaints were finding their way to conservation officials. In 1929 and 1930 these turned into a torrent as some fishermen scrambled to convert to the new gear. Gill netters protested that it had invaded and usurped their traditional grounds and had even been deliberately set across their nets. Pound netters complained that the traps were set in such a way as to block access to their equipment.

The effect on whitefish production was abrupt, as catches doubled from the 1.5 million pounds of 1929 to 2.9 million in 1930. Fishermen were torn between joining the rush to conversion and common sense which dictated that this vastly increased intensity could have disastrous consequences in the long run. The clamor prompted a wide ranging investigation in the summer of 1931 as the U.S. Bureau of Fisheries and the Wisconsin and Michigan Departments of Conservation attempted to measure the impact of the net in northern Huron and Michigan. That year the whitefish catch soared to 4.1 million pounds.

In 1932 the Michigan Conservation Department submitted a questionnaire to licensed fishermen. Answers were received from 492 operators, a return of about forty percent. Of the 174 comments on deep traps, 142 registered disapproval and only 32 favored continued use of the net. A blunt note accompanied one license application of the period:

" 'If (deep water) trap nets are not outlawed, fishing in Lake Huron will be history in five years. This boat is for deep traps, but we would gladly quit, if they were outlawed.' " (17)

Investigators, headed by Dr. John Van Oosten, later reported that the lakewide statistics masked a southerly sweep of "submarine" trap netters through Lake Huron.

"A peculiar feature of the production of whitefish in Lake Huron, 1930-1935, lay in the circumstance that a high level of yield was maintained by a successive rather than a simultaneous exploitation of the stocks in the various portions of the lake. . . . In each area the catch of whitefish followed a typical cycle after the introduction of the deep trap net. Production was raised to tremendous

Whitefish

heights for about two years, only to fall away sharply. Since the use of the deep trap net spread gradually throughout the lake, first one area and then another bore the burden of heavy fishing.'' (18)

Whitefish were disappearing from the more northerly grounds but remained abundant in southerly areas. The research team's task had been complicated by considerable evidence that there was a true increase in the number of the fish in the late 1920's. Deep trap netters insisted that northern grounds had not been depleted; the whitefish had simply migrated from one part of the lake to another. Researchers were profoundly unimpressed by this explanation. ''The assumption of a mass migration of whitefish proceeding in the same direction year after year runs counter to all known facts concerning the species.'' (19)

Pressures in the fishing community reached the boiling point in 1934. When deep trappers from Lake Huron attempted to enter southerly waters of Lake Michigan, pound netters and gill netters resorted to self help and drove them out of the area. It was also in 1934 that lakewide totals in Huron began declining. In May of that year a trap net operator submitted the following comments with his monthly report:

> ''*No production.* If the continuation of deep sub-fishing is allowed, it will not be long before the daily report of all fisheries on the Great Lakes and especially on Lake Huron, will be such as this. Immediate action should be taken to prevent such a catastrophe and this action should consist in the elimination of deep trap nets commonly known as deep subs.'' (20)

By 1935 damage was becoming apparent. In Saginaw Bay production declined to 213 thousand pounds from a 1932 high of 2.4 million. Regulations were enacted that banned use of the nets in all waters of Lakes Michigan and Superior. In Huron the slide had just begun. Between 1935 and 1940, catches on the U.S. side of the lake dropped from 1.9 million to 188 thousand pounds. Other forces were at work and Canadian totals also fell during this time but nowhere near to the extent of the Michigan collapse. The net had not been used in the Canadian waters and the extremes of both boom and bust were avoided by the provincial fishermen.

The end of the deep trap was less dramatic than its rise. It was gradually tamed by size and depth restrictions into the more selective gear of today. It is notable that the crusade against the net was initiated and supported by the commercial fishermen themselves. Some of the opposition undoubtedly stemmed from jealousy, but a good portion came from the simple recognition that the resource could be destroyed by shortsighted technology. Even the massive production of the peak years had been considerably offset by declining prices as the whitefish market reached saturation.

The struggle had produced a certain bias against the whole concept of trap and pound nets. During this period one finds frequent reference to the superior selectivity of the gill net. Irony is commonplace in the history of the Great Lakes fisheries.

Native Species

This early period on Huron saw the near disappearance of two species, sturgeon and sauger. Over a million pounds of sturgeon were taken from Huron in 1885, but the amount fell below 100,000 pounds by 1904, and by the 1930's the fish had become a curiosity. A small sauger fishery developed on the U.S. side in the 1920's but was largely discontinued by the 30's because of the increasing rarity of the fish. This occurred in the absence of intensive fishing but at the same that water quality was deteriorating in Saginaw Bay. Heavy settlement and development may have early affected this bay which is generally less than sixty feet in depth.

Trout production was high through most of this period. Incomplete records show a high of over 7.4 million pounds in the early 1890's. From 1911 through 1939, catches remained over four million pounds per year. An ominous development occurred in the late 30's that was masked by lakewide statistics. Trout production was dropping in the southern part of the lake, particularly in Saginaw Bay. Landings in the bay in 1940 were a fifth of what they had been in 1930. In 1940 this decrease was reflected in figures for the lake as a whole when production fell below four million for the first time since the late nineteenth century.

Lake herring was second only to trout in production during the early part of this century. It was more important to the U.S.

than to the Canadian fishery. Lakewide totals ranged from two to 8 million pounds in the years for which figures are available and there were the characteristic wide swings from year to year though nothing like the great collapse of the Erie fishery.

Perch and walleye were two other important commercial fish. The perch fishery was centered in Michigan waters, especially in Saginaw Bay. Early records indicate that the U.S. catch was often ten times the Canadian. The catch of both fish tended to fall after the early years of this century.

Alien Species

Of all the species introduced to the Great Lakes, the most welcome have been the rainbow and brown trout. The rainbow, native to the Pacific coast, was planted first in Lake Superior and by 1904 had spread to Huron. The brown trout came from Lake Michigan, where it had first been introduced. Both species are considered highly desirable game fish.

Another migrant from Lake Michigan was less welcome. Smelt showed up in the main part of Huron by 1925, and by the 30's their numbers were increasingly noticeable during spring spawning runs.

There was the same dependence on hatchery reared fish as has been described on Erie. Billions of eggs, fry, and fingerlings were released by U.S. agencies alone. Distinct forms of trout and whitefish recognized by early fishermen disappeared during this period. It is pointed out that the widespread mixing of Huron and Erie stocks might have destroyed distinctive racial characteristics that had developed in each lake. (21)

The Trap Net

The trap net works in much the same way as the pound net. A number of differences in design make it a more flexible gear. The net uses anchors, not stakes, and has a covered pot and heart. This allows it to be set below the surface, on a greater variety of bottoms and at a greater depth.

To lift the net a special boat is required. It has a broad flat deck with low smooth railings and a cabin forward. The main offshore anchor line (King line) is lifted over the low railing and attached to a winch. The pot is literally moved across the back of the boat until the fish are concentrated. A string that secures the pot opening is undone, and the fish are scooped out. Resetting requires closing of the pot, moving it back into the water, and sliding the king line off the stern. Setting the net initially is quite complex and moving and resetting a net takes about a day.

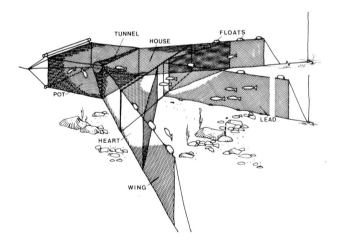

The Fyke Net

The fyke net is a shallow water impoundment gear most often used for perch. It consists of two hooped pots connected by a lead. Fish running along the lead in either direction stand a chance of being caught. The hearts are smaller than in other impoundment gear and are kept in place with spreader sticks. Anchors are used instead of stakes, and buoys mark their position. A fish entering the net travels through a series of tunnels until the pot is reached.

Both the lifting and the setting of the fyke net is done entirely by hand. The anchor is removed and tied off. The anchor line is lifted until the pot is reached. Then with a mighty heave, usually by three or more fishermen, the pot is rolled over the side of the boat. Once on the boat, the knot on the end of the pot is untied and the fish are released on the deck, sorted, measured, boxed and iced. It is not unusual for thirty pots to be lifted in a day.

33

Chapter 4:
Lake Michigan

"The effect of accelerated eutrophication and other pollution, although not always as easy to identify as the influences of other factors, were nevertheless clearly important as early as the mid-1800's. The first conspicuous contamination of Lake Michigan was by sawmill wastes, which covered spawning grounds in streams and around stream mouths. This type of pollution was particularly destructive to whitefish. Other forms of stream degradation (e.g., dams, deforestation of watersheds) although not strictly 'pollution' must also have been detrimental to stream spawners . . ." (22)

Lake Michigan stretches just over 300 miles north to south from the massively developed industrial heartland, through the farm country of the middle shores, and to the lightly populated and forested northern shore.

The southern half of the lake is relatively regular, lacking bays and islands, and progressing gradually from either shore to a depth of over 500 feet. The northern portion is chaotic, punctuated by numerous islands, surrounded by an irregular shoreline, and plunging to depths of over 900 feet. Although the surface area of the lake, 22,400 square miles, is smaller than Huron's 23,000, Michigan holds a much greater volume of water because of its greater average depth. There are approximately 1,180 cubic miles of water in Michigan as opposed to 849 cubic miles in Huron.

The Niagaran Cuesta, moving in a great arc from Huron, forms part of Upper Michigan, pushes southeast into Lake Michigan as the Garden Peninsula and a series of islands, and emerges finally as the Door Peninsula. The Door forms a mirror image of Huron's Bruce Peninsula. The limestone ridge of the Bruce divides Georgian Bay from Huron proper; the limestone ridge of the Door divides Green Bay from Lake Michigan. The shallow, productive waters of Green Bay, however, bear more resemblance to Saginaw than to Georgian Bay. The other major bay, Grand Traverse, offers a startling contrast with depths of three to six hundred feet.

The southern portion of the basin was, along with southwestern Erie, among the first areas to be freed of glacial ice. At various stages the basin received the west flowing waters of Erie and Huron via the Grand River crossing lower Michigan. In other phases Erie-Huron waters flowed northwestward, then turned southwest to the Michigan basin.

During the Lake Chippewa stage, waters in the Michigan basin shrank to a fraction of their present volume. A river system drained the reduced lake through the Straits of Mackinac. The submerged canyon of this river is clearly evident in topographic maps.

For much of its geologic history Michigan emptied south through the Des Plaines River into the Mississippi system. There is only a low ridge separating the two watersheds, and in 1848 a navigation canal was constructed through the ridge to the Illinois River. In 1900 the Sanitary District of Chicago repeated the old drainage pattern on a modest scale with a canal from the Chicago to Des Plaines River. This diversion is a source of great distress during every low water cycle on the lakes and was the subject of a Supreme Court suit in 1929. During periods of high water, as in the early 70's, there are equally vigorous cries for increased diversion by Chicago.

Michigan is the only one of the Great Lakes completely within the United States. The north-south orientation spans three fairly distinct zones. Significant population growth around the southern lake was evident by 1850. It has resulted in the megalopolis that now extends from Milwaukee on the eastern shore to the massive industrial concentrations on the Indiana shore to the south. This is one of the most intensely populated areas of the United States and the cumulative effect on the lake was increasingly detrimental through the period being discussed. By 1885 few fish entered the Milwaukee River.

The second zone extends on the western shore from north of Milwaukee to Marinette-Menominee and on the eastern from Michigan City to the Traverse City area. It is a mixed region with industrial and urban pockets alternating with intensive agricultural areas.

The third zone was once the home of magnificent hardwood and pine forests, and a portion of the area has been reforested since the thirties. There is also farming in this zone and in recent years it has become the scene of a growing tourist industry.

Technical development of the commercial fishing industry followed the same pattern discussed in connection with the other lakes. Fishing started before 1850 and was at first conducted in shoreline areas with haul seines. Gill nets were introduced in the 1840's, pound nets before 1860, and trap nets by 1885. Set lines were used and fyke nets have been of particular importance in the perch fisheries of Green Bay.

Native Species

Sturgeon were probably already in decline by the time the first catch statistics appeared in 1879. The large fish, prior to 1875, was thought to have no commercial value. It was either thrown in heaps on the shore or removed from nets, killed, and

Charlevoix, Mich.

dumped back in the water. Later, however, the flesh became more highly regarded, the eggs desired for caviar, the air bladder important in the manufacture of isinglass, and the oil useful for a variety of purposes. It is recorded that 3.8 million pounds of the fish were taken in 1879. This dropped to 1.4 million in 1885, 138 thousand in 1897, 14 thousand in 1911, and to near oblivion thereafter.

Whitefish was apparently the much favored food fish of the early European settlers of the Lake Michigan shoreline. They were initially easily caught near shore but by the 1860's certain areas were already depleted. J. W. Milner estimated that trout and whitefish abundance on the western shore of Green Bay had dropped by 50 percent from 1860 to 1872. In 1879, 12 million pounds of chubs, round whitefish, and whitefish were harvested. This combination of statistics of the various species creates some confusion, but it is believed that three-fourths of the catch was whitefish. Combined statistics dropped to 8.6

million in 1885 and 2.4 million in 1893. It is obvious from these figures that a decline was in progress and other information indicated it may have been going on for fifty years.

The Green Bay shoreline was the site of a savage series of environmental dislocations between 1850 and 1910. Intense land clearing and development along the Fox River and an early, and persistent, attitude that it was a convenient sewer led to substantial pollution in the shallow southern bay by no later than the 1870's. Development of the western shore was explosive. Clear cutting of lumber developed rapidly and both farmers and rail building crews disposed of unwanted cover by setting it on fire. Drought in the summer and early fall of 1871 was severe. By early October smoke from smoldering fires had reduced visibility throughout the area. On the night of October 8th southwest winds gathered the scattered fires into a single massive blaze.

It ravaged the eastern and western shores of Green Bay in one of the most destructive conflagrations recorded in North America. The massive burn created its own circulation as heated air soared upwards and surface air moved in at increasing velocity to the center of the holocaust. It became a fire storm, a hurricane of flame, as it moved north on the western shore. Approaching Peshtigo, it was burning along a forty to fifty mile front. Over a thousand people died that night.

The destructive effects on the environment lasted for decades. An area the size of Rhode Island burned along a 110-mile stretch from just north of the city of Green Bay to just south of Escanaba in the Upper Peninsula of Michigan. Streams and rivers were instantly polluted, former forest areas became swamps as the supporting root systems collapsed, and runoff patterns were altered.

In the period from 1850 to 1910 the northern and central areas of the Michigan basin were subject to intensive first stage pollution. The land clearing and siltation typical of the phase, was supplemented by a lumbering operation that reached gargantuan proportions from 1880 to 1910. One of the eyewitness reports comes from J. W. Milner who examined the Great Lakes fisheries in the early 1870's:

"Regarding sawmill pollution, Milner wrote 'The refuse from the sawmills is thrown into the streams in immense quantities to float out and sink in the lake. It is having a very injurious effect on the fisheries. The water-logged slabs . . . tear and carry away the nets. The sawdust covers the feeding and spawning grounds of the fish . . .' Complaints about sawdust were common on both sides of the lake; many of the whitefish spawning areas in streams (some, particularly in Green Bay, were entered for spawning in the early days) and in the lake near river mouths must have been destroyed. Although not specifically mentioned by investigators, other forms of stream degradation must have been locally detrimental to whitefish." (23)

Early reports stress the importance of Green Bay in whitefish production and separate statistics, kept since 1953, show that it has sometimes contributed half of the total lake production. In short there were changes in a limited but extremely productive area that may have led to the seemingly precipitous decrease in whitefish.

The fishery was relatively stable between 1894 and 1927, generally ranging from one to three million pounds. There was a strong resurgence in the late 1920's with production peaking at 5.4 million in 1930. This roughly corresponds with the similar increase in Huron and may well have been due to the combined effects of the deep trap net and a series of strong year classes. During the 1930's there was a steady descent and the 1939-1940 catches were the second and third lowest since the beginning of record keeping.

Lake trout were less desirable than whitefish in the early years. They did not become a highly sought after species until after the whitefish decline. The first year of record, 1879, shows that only 2.6 million pounds were harvested. The trout began a fifty-year domination of the lake fishery in 1890 when production reached 8.3 million. Catches were in excess of 8 million pounds for seven of the years from 1890 to 1911. In the latter year a period of stability began that lasted through 1940.

Early chub and herring figures are combined, but it is believed that the bulk of these figures represent herring. Evidence indicates that the majority of these fish were taken from Green Bay. As noted earlier, vast fluctuation in herring production was not unusual. Spectacular catches occurred at the turn of the century. There were 25.8 million pounds of herring and chub taken in 1896 and 27.2 million in 1908 and combined catches in excess of 20 million occurred in a number of years during this period. After 1910 there was apparently a swift decline in abundance. Complete figures for herring only, are available from 1927 and show wide, irregular changes from 2.6 million (1940) to 6.4 million (1934).

There were originally seven species of chub in Lake Michigan. As noted, the early catch statistics not only do not differentiate these types, but often grouped chubs with other fish. Apparently the larger species disappeared first as nets, originally 4½ inches, decreased steadily as the larger fish vanished. It is difficult to determine when these changes occurred. Moreover, in the earlier years the smaller chubs were not sold, while in later years they were, making catch statistics particularly unreliable for indications of abundance. Scientific surveys were not begun until the early 1930's. Figures do indicate a range from 6.2 million pounds (1934) to 1.6 million (1940). Catches were low in the early 20's and 40's.

The walleye was centered almost exclusively in Green Bay.

Marinette, Wis.

In this period it was not an important commercial species but was usually taken incidentally with preferred fish. It is nonetheless important that harvests declined sharply from the 500 to 750 thousand pounds per year in the first scattered statistics of the 1880's and 90's to less than 50 thousand by the late 1930's. The whitefish and walleye both declined at the same time they disappeared from southern Green Bay.

This all relates directly to the perch. It was apparently not abundant in Lake Michigan prior to 1880 but became so in southern Green Bay when whitefish and walleye became scarce and in the southern lake proper with the decline of whitefish and sturgeon. There was a period of strong harvests in the 1890's (6.5 million pounds in 1894) followed by a long period of stability. Production ranged from 1 to 3 million pounds in all but three years from 1911 to 1940.

Three other native species formed a less important part of lake commercial production. All varied greatly depending on the demand and availability of other fish. Over four million

Charlevoix, Mich

suckers were taken in 1917 and harvests were over a million pounds in the few years for which statistics are available. Round whitefish, (also known as Menominee, pilot fish, and frost fish) were apparently larger and more abundant in the early years. Burbot, also known as lawyer, were never very important to the fishery. Until the 1930's, catch records for species of minor commercial importance appeared sporadically.

Alien Species

Rainbow trout were stocked as early as 1880. Steelheads were stocked from 1896 to 1915. Brown trout were planted in 1883. All of these popular fish are generally caught in tributary streams.

Carp appeared in Lake Michigan commercial records in the 1890's. Their greater ability to tolerate pollution allowed them to move into the areas abandoned by other fish. They have

38

flourished in southern and western Green Bay since the turn of the century.

Early attempts to stock salmon were not successful. Between 1873 and 1880, 813 chinook salmon were released and in 1920 two thousand Masu salmon were introduced. The major effort was made with Atlantic salmon and from 1872 to 1932, 645,000 of these fish were released.

Another planting was frighteningly successful. It was intended to provide a food for the salmon that were being stocked. The salmon did not make it, but the smelt prospered with a vengeance. The first planting, in the St. Mary's River in 1906, was unsuccessful. Another effort placed the fish in Crystal Lake, Michigan, in 1912 where they were first observed spawning in 1918. The first commercial catch in Lake Michigan was recorded in 1923. The fish made it to Green Bay in 1924 and were found throughout the lake by 1936.

If the results of the carp planting frenzy was a strong indication that it is not wise to disturb the species balance, the smelt experience was final confirmation. No special imagination is required to recapture the feeling of apprehension that must have moved through fish management officials as they watched commercial smelt production rise from 86 thousand in 1931 to 4.2 million in 1940. The effects of this explosion were to become apparent in later years.

A Smelt

The Pound Net

The pound net works on the principle that fish will go to deeper water to avoid an obstacle. The obstacle placed in their way is the *lead*. It is made of a large mesh netting (large enough to allow fish to pass through) and is tapered to the slope of the bank. Floats keep the top of the net on the surface while lead weights hold the bottom down. In deep water it is secured with anchors. In shallow water it may be held in place with stakes (see illustration).

Fish move along the lead until they enter a small opening between the *wings* (hearts). From the heart, fish must either find their way back through the narrow opening or pass through the cone shaped tunnel into the pot. Once in the pot there is little chance for escape.

To remove the fish from the pot, a boat designed for the purpose is moved up to the outside of the net. The line holding the tunnel open is released. At each corner the net is held in place by a rope and pulley. These must be released and the corners raised. The side of the net is lowered temporarily and the boat, with motor off, is pulled over the pot.

After raising the inside corners the gathering begins. At least two, and usually three, fishermen are needed to pull the boat. As they move the boat, the fish are bunched toward the outside of the net. Scoop nets are used to bring the fish on board.

The size and weight of the pound net is awe inspiring. The stakes can be as long as ninety feet and are usually over fifty. The leads range from a thousand to eighteen hundred feet with a slope from shore to forty or fifty feet. The hearts are 175 feet long. The pot is forty feet square. Approximately thirty-five claw anchors hold the net in place.

It takes a full day to set the stakes and a day to set the twine. Every three months the twine has to be pulled out, loaded on a boat, brought to shore, washed, reloaded and reset. The stakes have to be pulled at the end of the season. They can be set only on sand or mud bottoms.

The vast majority of this work is done with back and muscle, only occasionally by power and hydraulics. During the off season considerable time, money and energy is devoted to repair and construction of nets.

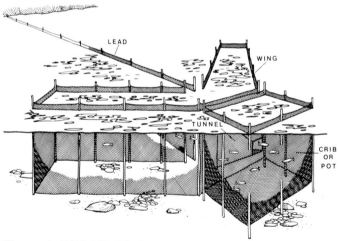

Figure 2: THE POUND NET

Chapter 5:
Lake Superior

". . . Superior sings in the rooms of her icewater mansion . . ." (24)

Superior inspires superlatives. It is the largest body of fresh water in the world, 31,820 square miles, slightly larger than South Carolina. It reaches an impressive depth of 1,333 feet and its volume of 2,935 cubic miles of water is two and a half times that of Michigan's 1,180.

Ferocious cyclonic storms, often occurring in the autumn, have 350 miles of east-west water surface in which to mount seas against lee shores. The lake is cold and the ridge of the Keweenaw Peninsula extends 75 miles into the lake and another climatic world. In some winters over 200 inches of snow falls on Houghton, Michigan. Its July average temperature of 60°F and persistent cloud cover can make summer inconspicuous.

Superior lies almost completely in the glacier scoured Canadian shield. The northwestern shore features spectacular cliffs which rise two to five hundred feet above the water. The highlands are remnants of pre-glacial mountains.

Isle Royale, now a National Park, lies in the west central part of the lake, offering a glimpse of how vast sections of the Great Lakes may have appeared before the coming of the white man. It is 45 miles long, has some 30 inland lakes, a moose herd, and a pack of timber wolves. Other significant islands are Ontario's Michipicoten and Wisconsin's Apostle group. Important bay areas are Thunder Bay on the northwest shore, Whitefish in the extreme east, and Keweenaw to the east of the peninsula.

The southwest portion of the present lake was the first to emerge from the ice and, as Lake Duluth, drained south to the St. Croix and Mississippi systems. At a later stage waters emptied south across eastern Upper Michigan to Green Bay. Still later, they flowed to an enlarged Georgian Bay which discharged at North Bay and flowed to the St. Lawrence via the Ottawa River across Ontario. This pattern completely bypassed Lakes Huron and Michigan, and it was during this period that they sank to fractions of their present size.

It was the Ottawa River route that allowed French explorers to bypass the hostile Indians of the lower lakes and reach Superior a quarter century before they reached Erie. There they found people already living off the resources of the lake:

". . . The Jesuit Relation of 1669-1671 notes that '. . . a single fisherman will catch in one night twenty large sturgeon, or a hundred and fifty whitefish, or eight hundred herring in one net.' Elsewhere in the same source the fishery in the Ontonagon River was said to be '. . . carried on, day and night, from spring until autumn and it is there that the savages go to lay in their provision.' " (25)

Early trading companies were the first commercial operations in many areas of western and northern North America. They used lake and river transport for their operation whenever possible. One of these, the Northwest Company, established headquarters at Fort William on Lake Superior at the end of the 18th century. Trout and whitefish were caught, salted, and shipped to outlying posts as well as being consumed by the local population. In 1835 a competitor, the American Fur Company, established a series of fishing stations. The mesh size used by

Whitefish Point, Mich.

Marquette, Mich.

the fishermen was a considerable six inches and'' . . . It is a reasonable inference that the average whitefish and trout in 1839 were considerably larger than their 1.4 kg (3 lb) modern equivalent.'' (26) The company failed in 1842.

Population growth of the basin area was spurred by the discovery of iron ore in Upper Michigan in 1844. Copper had been mined by the Indians and there were fabulously rich deposits in the Keweenaw Peninsula. Transportation problems were solved by the opening of the canal at Sault St. Marie. It is important to note that the vast bulk of economic enterprises which drew settlers to the southern and western shores of Superior were transient. The poor soil and climate confined agriculture to scattered areas. A tragically vulnerable economy was built on the exploitation of natural resources.

''In the rapacious exploitation of these forests there was no element of sound forest management or of general conservation. Clear cutting was the rule, tops and limbs were left where they had been cut, and fire was a common sequel, so that the understory was often destroyed, the forest litter burned away and the exposed soils leeched and eroded. As with the pulp log industry on the Canadian north shore, the timber was taken to the sawmills by 'driving' the rivers so that extensive scouring of stream beds and the introduction of allocthonous materials must have occurred. Moreover, as in the pulp log industry the sawmills were located at the shore, often on the estuaries of major rivers down which the logs were brought, and their operations resulted in the introduction of large quantities of sawdust and coarser woody materials to the neighboring areas of the lake . . .'' (27)

Native Species

The effects of the pollution may be reflected in the whitefish statistics. In 1885 5.1 million pounds of whitefish were harvested. The figure declined steadily until by 1911 it was less than a million pounds and except for two years production remained low through the 1920's. A marked recovery began in the thirties that resulted in a million pound catch by 1940, a revival that would last into the 50's. The SCOL report for Superior comments on a possible connection:

"... Certainly it was a common complaint of commercial fishermen that deep drifts of sawdust blanket many whitefish spawning beds in the lake and they believed that these both inhibited spawning and suffocated such eggs as were deposited ...."

"... It may be ... that the environment recovered somewhat following the marked reduction in lumbering activities early in this century." (28)

Trout, the second aristocrat of the early fisheries, are recorded in scattered and intermittent fashion. Nonetheless, the period from 1885 to about 1910 appear to have been the glory years. Yields were often in the 5 to 7 million pound range with the highest, 7.3 million, in 1903. From 1910 until 1940 the fishery enjoyed a long period of stability. Production ranged from a low of 3.1 to a high of 5.2 million.

It may have been 1926 that saw the birth of the commercial charter boat on the Great Lakes. A fisherman decided to try the trolling method he had used to catch salmon on the west coast, to catch trout. After five hours of trolling near Munising, he is said to have returned with nearly 1,500 pounds of trout. The implications of this experiment were not lost on entrepreneurs who began taking individuals and parties on a search for the "big ones." The outlines of a tourist industry thus took shape in the 30's, adding a source of income to an economy suffering from the combined effects of the collapse of the lumber industry and national depression.

Statistics for herring and chub were combined until 1940. It

appears that in the latter years of this period the overwhelming majority were herring. As early as 1896, five million pounds of herring were caught off the Wisconsin portion of the coastline. By 1915 the tonnage of these two fish passed that of trout and whitefish. Harvests followed the now familiar pattern of wide yearly fluctuations. Production dropped to a low of 4.3 million in 1922. A corresponding increase occurred in the 1930's, culminating in a mammoth 19.2 million in 1941.

The history of the chub in Lake Superior is similar to that in Lake Michigan. The larger species became progressively scarce and the mesh size decreased to accommodate the next species. The following recounts the overfishing theory:

"The first major change in the chub populations of Lake Superior occurred between 1893 and 1910. C. nigripinnis (blackfin-ed) was probably the most desirable table fish of the lot. Koelz (1929) stated that they were in short supply in Lake Michigan in the late 1800's and that, therefore, production was shifted to Lake Superior. This large chub was fished there for about ten years and was reported to be commercially extinct by 1907. The diary of one commercial fish tug from Marquette, Michigan, showed a further decline in catch-per-unit-effort of C. nigripinnis from ... (151 lb per 100,000 ft) of net to only ... (4 lb per 100,000 ft) in 1915. ... There is no evidence of anything besides the fishery which could have affected its abundance during this period." (29)

The fishery then shifted to the shortjaw (C. Zenithicus) and there are indications that in the 20's and 30's it comprised the overwhelming majority of chub populations.

Other fish played a minor role on Superior. Sturgeon catches follow the familiar curve, declining into obscurity by the 1920's. Walleye has been of local importance in some island and bay areas.

Chapter 6:
Management Policies

We have seen that the periodic attempts to manage the fisheries during this long period were frequently unsuccessful. Around the turn of the century efforts were made to impose controls on the fisheries. While some restrictions were established, most conservation initiatives faded in the atmosphere of continued faith in the stocking concept. These planting efforts followed two lines. One involved the introduction of exotic species. Here the results were either unsuccessful, as with the many attempts to establish salmon, or successful in the manner of Dr. Frankenstein, as with carp and smelt.

The second line was the continuing dependence on hatchery stocking of native fish. We have seen how these exercises shifted attention from the plight of valued fish stocks. As the century wore on, confidence in this approach steadily eroded. The major gear restrictions imposed during this time came from pressures within the commercial community. In the 20's and 30's the bull and deep trap nets were stopped when fishermen complaints were seconded by research. Generally, research activities were occasional and incomplete. Further, there was no baseline from which to measure changes as the variety and abundance of fish stocks in the Indian and early European period were unknown. The starting point for statistical analysis is the scattered and incomplete catch records of the mid-nineteenth century. By this time major changes had already altered much of the original environment. Some species were apparently already greatly reduced by 1860.

Canadian management practices were far more conservative than those of the United States jurisdictions. The agencies involved took a dim view of many gear innovations and, as we have seen, avoided the deep trap net completely. Moreover, Canadian fishermen were often integrated into the U.S. fishery.

U.S. controls were imposed on a state-by-state basis. It early dawned on a number of people that regulations passed were of limited value if a neighboring jurisdiction followed a conflicting policy. The situation was inherently chaotic. Boundary settlements had given eight states a share of the U.S. shoreline. Imagine the politics of the situation. Suppose a majority of the fishermen in one state agreed on the need for certain controls and, as we shall see, a surprising number of them did by the end of this period. The state legislature is encouraged to pass restrictive legislation. The fishermen then notice that no such legislation is upcoming in neighboring jurisdictions. It is obvious to them that competitors across the state line are going to attain an advantage and they successfully oppose the restrictions.

The torturous search for coordination and uniformity on the lakes stretches back to 1883 when representatives of Minnesota, Wisconsin, Ohio, and Michigan and the U.S. Fish and Game Commission, met in Detroit and passed thirteen recommendations. None was adopted by the states. A script was thus established which was faithfully followed for over fifty years. Meetings were called, resolutions were passed, delegates went home, and little or nothing was done. Over and over this pattern was repeated. In all, twenty-seven interstate or international conferences were held between 1883 and 1941.

Some people quickly understood the limitations of the single jurisdiction approach. At one conference in 1904, officials of the lake states met and, in an attempt to promote uniform regulations, recommended passage of state resolutions ceding control of the commercial fisheries to the U.S. Government. The legislatures of Wisconsin and Minnesota actually passed such measures. The search for a common regulatory framework resulted in a spectacular fiasco in the early 1930's. In 1931 New York initiated an attempt to establish uniform laws for Lake Erie. In February of 1933 it seemed that at last a breakthrough had been achieved when, at Toronto, the heads of the Fish and Game or Conservation Departments of the Erie jurisdictions signed a formal agreement and four of the five recommended regulations were subsequently signed into law. It lasted less than a year:

> "Due to political pressure, however, in the fall of 1933 one of the states found it impossible to enforce the adopted closed season. The result was that a third meeting of the committee was held at Columbus, Ohio, which resulted in the complete abrogation of the Toronto agreement and dissolution of the Lake Erie Advisory Committee. Thus, this formal contract signed by representatives of four Great Lakes states and the Province of Ontario for the purpose of providing uniform regulation of their commercial fisheries ended in failure and led to endless controversy and even to the disruption of friendly relations among the representatives charged with its enforcement." (30)

Dr. John Van Oosten had become increasingly disturbed by the failure of the states to face the difficult decisions involved in controlling the commercial fisheries. In 1936 he stated,

> "Unless some firm action is taken, and taken soon, the important fisheries of all the Great Lakes are doomed to commercial extinction. We know what should be done but the Great Lakes fisheries are not under federal

control, and thus far the several state legislatures have failed to follow our recommendations. I have no reason to believe that these legislatures will change their apathetic attitude toward the problem of conserving their commercial fisheries." (31)

Finally, in February of 1938, a meeting, attended by representatives of all the lake states, by Ontario, and by the state department, called for an International Board of Inquiry to explore various means of establishing coordination. This board was set up and Van Oosten was one of the four members appointed to it.

The Board examined interstate agreements and compacts. Basically this was the approach that had failed over and over through the years. The U.S. Congress had even gone so far as to approve compacts in advance. The formulation and passage of such compacts are massive operations. They had to be passed by both houses of each state legislature in exactly the same form or they broke down. Any changes likewise had to be approved by everyone and were similar to a renegotiation of the whole agreement. Further, a state could withdraw at any time and nullify the whole procedure. The Board's report recommended a different approach:

> "... The preceding pages of this report have described the obstacles, in fact almost insurmountable obstacles, in the path of securing ratification of a compact by the Great Lakes states, and emphasis has been placed on the fact that even if a compact were ratified international questions would remain unsettled because the Province of Ontario would still be outside the compass or jurisdiction of such a compact. Confronted with these practical considerations the United States members of the Board have given their attention to an international treaty as the best possible solution to the problem." (32)

The Board also solicited the opinions of commercial fishermen on the state of the Great Lakes fisheries. Fishermen were asked what they thought were the major factors in the decline of favored species. The response is illuminating for even as early as the time of this survey, 1939, pollution was the factor mentioned most often. Small mesh in nets and over-fishing were the second and third most frequent replies. Effects of the deep trap controversy were apparent as trap nets were listed in fourth place. Fishing during the spawning season was the fifth crucial concern. (33)

The fishermen were then asked for recommendations for specific measures for controlling the fisheries. There were close to 6,500 specific suggestions received from U.S. commercial operators. Here the five most frequent replies were: (34)

1. Maintenance of strictly closed seasons during the spawning of fish.
2. Elimination of the habitual violator.
3. Prevention of pollution.
4. Planting of more fry.
5. Planting of more large fish.

In addition the Board tested the political waters surrounding a potential treaty. They found that most fishermen favored coordinated control of the Great Lakes. While not the first choice of many, a majority of fishermen felt that if it were the only means available, an international treaty would be an acceptable means to this end:

"Sixty-eight percent of the fishermen who replied or a total of 342 men would not oppose control by an international commission established by treaty with Canada if that were the only means of obtaining uniform laws on the Great Lakes; 32 percent or 159 fishermen would oppose such control." (35)

These replies demonstrate a degree of concern and perception by pre-war commercial fishermen that contrasts sharply with the image later presented by sport and conservation groups. The allocation conflict was already developing and commercial fishermen were being warned as early as 1936 to prepare for it with sufficient organization:

"The threat of closing commercial waters to commercial operations and opening them to sport fishing applies to practically all of the lake states. If the commercial fishermen are to hold their own against the sportsmen, they will have to forget some of their petty grievances and unite in some, one strong organization that will be able to exert enough influence to protect them against the advances of the sportsmen." (36)

A treaty was drawn up, signed, and submitted to the U.S. Senate for ratification. It was eventually withdrawn by President Eisenhower. Politely, it can be said that it floundered in the changed post-war environment. Actually the commercial fishermen showed a rare burst of organizational skill that was the major factor in defeat of the treaty. Some lived to deeply regret this opposition, which was based on the fear of stringent, distant, and politically motivated controls. It was felt that there was greater protection under state Departments of Conservation. It was to take a crowning ecological disaster to produce a degree of international cooperation.

Setting back gillnets

48

Gillnet spreader

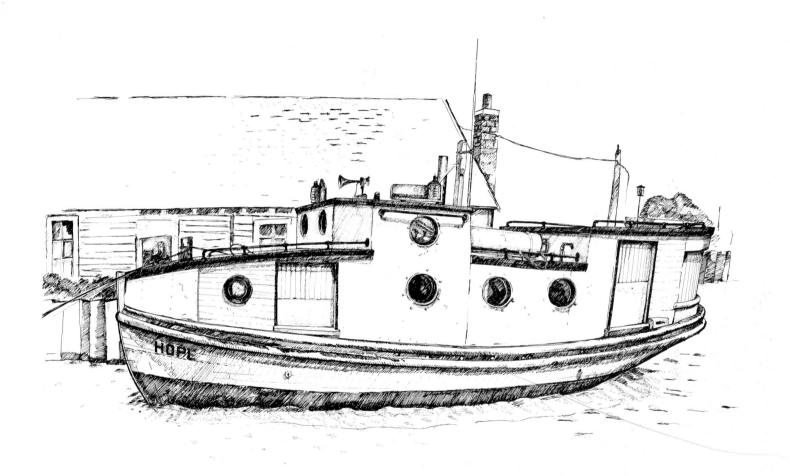

SECTION 2:
THE NIGHTMARE

"I never met Creaser. I had a letter from him in which he said that he had run across a copy of my publication and commended me for getting it out. He thought it would serve a need in the industry. He noted that from the copies he'd seen, and *The Fisherman* was only a year or so old at the time, that we carried technical articles.

He said that he had a rather interesting paper, on a more or less popular level, about a problem that could cause a complete collapse of the fisheries of the upper Great Lakes.

As soon as I heard that I got in touch with him and we published it. That was in 1933, the year the first specimen was taken from Huron, and three years before the first sighting in Lake Michigan." (1a)

"The Atlantic sea lamprey now becomes of interest to all commercial fishermen of the Great Lakes because it has recently appeared in Lake Erie, presumably by passing the Niagara barrier by way of the Welland Canal. It is already well established in Lake Erie, having been first recorded in 1921 and now not uncommon throughout the lake. Last spring it was found well up the Huron River at Flat Rock, in the state of Michigan where it probably is establishing a spawning ground. The way is now open for a further penetration into Lake St. Clair and Lake Huron. In the not too distant future, it will no doubt be encountered throughout the Great Lakes waters. Knowing its record of destruction among the food fishes of Cayuga Lake, we must consider it as one more source of further depletion of the fishes of the Great Lakes. The Atlantic sea lamprey and the fast spreading smelt will act as great disturbers of the natural balance and will have an important influence on the large fisheries of these extremely productive lakes, which are already in much distress." (1b)

Chapter 1:
The Siege

The Lamprey. In the space of twenty years this parasite devastated the fish stocks of the upper lakes and completely changed the species balance in their waters. It destroyed a large segment of the commercial fishing industry, and the resulting economic dislocations affected scores of small communities. It destroyed or severely reduced predator species, leading to an explosion of smaller native and colonizing species that disrupted the food chain. In short, it produced a chaotic ecosystem and left aftershocks which persist to this day.

It is a parasite of marine origin. Adults gather in the river estuaries during late winter and begin their nocturnal migrations when spring temperatures exceed forty degrees Fahrenheit. The migrations are sometimes awesome, with as many as 25,000 adults entering a single modest sized river. Rapids are navigated by alternately swimming and attaching to stones. The lamprey can surmount near vertical barriers by creeping over them on the sucking disc. Males use this same sucking disc to remove stones as nest building begins. Lighter material is cleared by a thrashing action of the body. As much as twenty-five pounds of gravel and other materials can be displaced in constructing the nest, which ranges from ten to forty inches in diameter. The displaced materials form a crescent on the downstream side of the nest, which may be as much as ten inches high. The female lays an average of sixty to sixty-five thousand eggs. Both males and females die shortly after the completion of spawning.

It is estimated that 1.1 percent of the eggs produce larvae. These larvae burrow out of the nest eighteen to twenty-one days after spawning is completed, the small larvae drifting downstream to eddies or pools where they dig themselves a U-shaped nest. They remain in these nests for up to seven years. It is now known that transformation to the parasitic phase takes place in the summer of the fifth to eight year, depending on environmental conditions. External changes are completed within one to two weeks, and during the following autumn, winter, and spring transformed parasitic adults drift downstream to the lakes.

The lamprey is not truly an eel. Eels have hard and separated bones in the back, while the lamprey has a spinal column composed of cartilage. Its mouth is a round sucking disc which the adult attaches to a prey, and using the tooth-like appendage to cut into its victim, proceeds to suck out blood and body fluids. This prey cycle lasts from twelve to twenty-two months, after which the adults return to streams, spawn, and die.

The lamprey is extremely destructive in its parasitic phase. A single adult lamprey can kill 19.6 pounds of fish, sometimes growing to over thirty inches in the process. It is estimated that during their peak abundance in Lake Michigan they destroyed over five million pounds of fish annually. In addition to the fish destroyed, some observers stated that 85 percent of various species of fish not killed by the lampreys had been attacked from one to five times and somehow survived.

There is an abiding mystery about the lamprey. Did it exist in Lake Ontario for thousands of years with species it was nearly to obliterate in the upper lakes? Many modern writers believe that it entered the lake sometime in the early post-glacial period, possibly during the time of the St. Lawrence embayment when the Atlantic reached the Ontario basin. There is another argument that claims the lamprey reached the lake through the Erie Barge Canal. In either case it was in the lake no later than 1850. Scarring was not reported until the 1880's and 90's, after which stocks of large fish collapsed. Nonetheless, stock depletion was not as calamitous as that which occurred in the upper lakes. What maintained this relative stability?

A number of possibilities have been suggested:

1. The genetic argument: This view holds that two strains of lake trout developed in the post-glacial lakes. That of the Ontario basin developed over the centuries of contact as resistant to lamprey attack. Those of the upper lakes developed without such resistance and were decimated when finally exposed. The Atlantic salmon apparently developed such a resistance from sharing their original marine environment with the predator. The problem is that no scarred salmon or trout were seen prior to the 1880's.

2. The balance argument: The heart of this explanation is that the predator-prey ratio shifted drastically due to either habitat degradation or overfishing. In this view a large, healthy individual is capable of withstanding a lamprey attack. The lamprey is able to inflict damage only when both the abundance and size of the fish decline.

3. The spawning argument: Lampreys spawn in streams. Where access to streams is absent they are held in check. During the early period of settlement main streams and rivers in the Ontario basin were dammed for sawmills and gristmills. These dams decayed or were removed as increasing numbers of these mills ceased operating. Thus as this century passed, more and more streams were opened for spawning. This argument is particularly interesting if the lamprey entered by way of the Erie Barge Canal as the predators were not observed in streams in the century before the dams were built (2).

Whatever the reason, the parasite was on the increase in Lake Ontario by the 1920's. The decline of lake trout was apparent by the 30's, and during the 40's it became an irreversible spiral. In 1940, 201 thousand pounds of trout were harvested; in 1945, 106 thousand, in 1950, 15 thousand; and in 1955, 4 thousand. In 1962 the New York State fishery was closed and the Province of Ontario reduced its fishermen to "quotas sufficient only to provide adequate samples for assessments."

The lamprey moved into Lake Erie, apparently via the Welland Canal, and was first reported in Lake Erie in 1921. The Welland began as a small ditch in 1824. What then took the lamprey close to a century to appear in the neighboring lake? The early canal was enlarged and reconstructed a number of times in the nineteenth century. Throughout this early period, however, water was supplied to the canal from a stream that had originally flowed from the Niagaran Escarpment. The engineers diverted a portion of the water so that it flowed through the lock system to Lake Ontario. The original stream bed provided the pathway for the canal water to Lake Erie. Thus water from a common source flowed *downward* from the escarpment into *each* lake. The significance of all this is the manner in which it relates to the lamprey's spawning habits. The lamprey's instinct drives it upstream to spawn. It is believed that spawners from Lake Ontario that entered the canal pursued its course only as long as the movement was upstream. Thus the point of diversion provided a natural, if not consciously intended, barrier to movement of the creature.

Demands for shipping increased drastically in World War I and a major overhaul of the canal was begun. This third reconstruction provided a downstream flow through which Erie waters were directly channeled to Lake Ontario. The largely rebuilt canal was completed in 1919, and two years later the first lamprey specimen was discovered in the now directly upstream Lake Erie (3). The natural barrier of Niagara Falls had separated the two lower lakes for millenia. Now the demands of commerce tied the two environments together with increasing efficiency.

The alarms would certainly have been out if the lamprey had reduced the extremely productive fish harvests of Erie. The irony is that its residence in that lake made even less of an impression than it had in Ontario. Why? A number of factors have been suggested. There may well have been a lack of desirable spawning streams for the parasite. Constant erosion along tributary streams and a subsequent wash of sediments contrasts sharply to the preferred spawning areas. Further the warm and shallow waters of the western basin might well have provided an environmental barrier that kept them in the deeper eastern basin.

In all, human activities may have produced an interesting cancelling effect that limited the early impact of the potentially dangerous creature. The technology of the early canal opened a waterway between the lower lakes but inadvertently barred migration. The reconstructed canal removed this bar, but man-made alteration of the Erie watershed masked the lamprey's potential harm as stream damming may have done in Lake Ontario. It is known, for instance, that pre-settlement Erie had streams of clean sand and gravel bottoms.

The lamprey spread slowly across Erie, reaching the western margins in the late 20's. It then moved up the Detroit River, through Lake St. Clair, and reached the river of the same name in 1930. By 1933 it was moving into Lake Huron.

Now began the nightmare. Even in 1933 some of the fishermen became alarmed at the numbers of the ugly eel-like creatures. Professor of zoology, Dr. Charles Creaser, issued the first written warnings that something very dangerous was happening. In 1936 the fishermen of the Rogers City, Michigan area, on northern Lake Huron, complained of badly marked

fish, and in the next three years their production dropped sharply. Massive spawning runs were observed in the nearby Ocqueoc River. It was a group of sportsmen from Rogers City that suggested an experimental weir to catch the lampreys on their upstream spawning runs. The commercial fishermen organized under the aegis of the Michigan Fish Producer's Association in May of 1940, and plans were made to enlist the aid of the federal government. The situation grew more alarming. Trout catches on Huron dropped from five million pounds annually, a figure they had maintained through most of the 30's, to 3.7 million in 1941.

With rationed meat during World War II, every possible source of protein was assiduously cultivated. Fish production was encouraged but most other projects were suspended for the "duration." Nonetheless, the lamprey situation worsened and it was during the war that the Michigan Conservation Department aided the sport groups in constructing a weir on the Ocqueoc River. After World War II a grateful Michigan Legislature officially commended the commercial fishermen for their cooperation with the war effort. The fishermen were interested in more tangible aid at this point and appealed to the federal government for help in fighting the lamprey.

This produced a further series of frustrations. In 1946, House Joint Resolution 366 was pushed through Congress and authorized the modest sum of $20,000 per year to be used by the Fish and Wildlife Service for a ten-year investigation of the problem. The Resolution was signed by President Truman, but Congress neglected to appropriate the money. The Fish and Wildlife Service tried to set up a cooperative program between various lake states and the Province of Ontario. Of all the states, Michigan was the only one to move on the problem. In 1946 the state legislature appropriated $40,000 to be spent over a four-year period for study of the lamprey with a view to possible control or eradication. These funds were assigned to the Michigan Conservation Department which, in turn, made them available to its research arm, the Michigan Institute for Fisheries Research. Finally an appropriation came out of Congress and closer liaison was established between the U.S. Fish and Wildlife Service and the Michigan Conservation Department so that the limited federal funds could, for the moment, support the efforts of state biologists in studying the life cycle of the lamprey. This study began in January 1947.

At last, in the summer of 1948, an experimental weir was set up near the site of the one originally constructed nearly five years earlier. The small federal staff turned this facility over to the Michigan Conservation Department to use in its study of the lamprey. The Michigan study followed several earlier efforts. A Department of Conservation employee, Matt Patterson, had operated a weir on Hibbard's Creek in Door County, Wisconsin, from 1945 to 1949. There was a similar effort on the Thessalon River off of North Channel, Lake Huron in Ontario starting in about 1946. Both weirs provided valuable information but neither completely blocked movement of the lamprey. The first lamprey proof weir was constructed on Carp Creek, twenty miles from Rogers City in the spring of 1947. It was in this area of northern Michigan that the vital Michigan study was centered.

It is difficult to overestimate the importance of this pioneering Michigan research. It made possible an understanding of the heavy dependence of the sea lamprey on its stream existence. It was here that the conditions favorable to spawning lamprey, length of larval residence in streams, and parasitic development were revealed or confirmed. Of equal importance, it was demonstrated that the life cycle ends with the completion of a single spawning run. Finally, it was understood what type of obstacle presented an effective barrier to the migrating lamprey.

For Lake Huron it was too late. In the Michigan waters of that lake, 892 thousand pounds of trout had been taken in 1941. At the end of the war in 1945, the figure was 173 thousand. By the time serious research began in 1948, it was four thousand. The decline took longer in the Canadian waters, particularly in Georgian Bay, but when it came it was just as devastating. In 1940, 2.7 million pounds had come from provincial waters. In 1950 the figure was 416 thousand. Lakewide, trout production fell from 3.7 *million* in 1940 to 1 *thousand* in 1960.

In the period 1936-39 lake trout had constituted 24.1 percent of the dollar value of the commercial catch. In the years 1945-49 it was 2.2 percent of the dollar value. There were 1,118 fishermen in the U.S. waters of Huron in 1930. In 1950 there were 513. In the same period the number of vessels declined from 60 to 48, and the number of boats from 363 to 184.

Looking back it is easy to criticize federal and state fisheries officials. The most significant thing that can be said in their defense is that they were not psychologically set up to react to the first alarm from Huron. True, catches in Lake Ontario had been declining for some years, but the actual collapse of stocks would be simultaneous with those of Huron. Closer to home, the lamprey had been in Erie for a decade and made little impact. State officials had cooperated in setting up the first weir during World War II.

Nevertheless, a great opportunity had been lost. It is difficult not to sympathize with the bitter assessment that appeared in the November, 1948 issue of the *Fisherman:*

"The lampreys have spread throughout such a large area that spawning runs were observed in almost 70 streams in Michigan. Similar runs have been observed in Wisconsin and a number of Canadian streams and rivers. The possibility of controlling the lamprey by trapping them during their spawning migration, which appeared possible in 1938 and 1939 when their runs were confined to one or two streams, is now impractical and impossible. The assistance was *too little and too late.*" (4)

The plague spread into Lake Michigan. There is a report of a lamprey being sighted off Milwaukee as early as 1936 but real abundance was a few years away. If the disappearance of trout in Huron was swift, it was mind boggling in Michigan. The best trout catches in a decade began in 1940. Over 6 million pounds per year were taken in the five years from 1940 to 1944, peaking at 6.8 million in 1943. Ten years later they were gone. Watch the process:

Year	Pounds of Fish
1943	6,860,000
1944	6,498,000
1945	5,437,000
1946	3,974,000
1947	2,425,000
1948	1,197,000
1949	342,000
1950	54,000
1951	11,000
1952	4,000

In the fall of 1951 the Wisconsin Conservation Department's patrol boat, *Barney Devine* set out to check the results of an experiment set up by the Department to determine the status of trout in Lake Michigan. The results of the experiment were described in a 1951 article entitled "The Trout Are Gone."

"Lake Michigan fishermen might just as well begin to strip their trout nets if the results obtained in a recent experiment by the Wisconsin Conservation Department is any criterion on which the balance of the lake can be judged...."

"A gang of eight boxes of good cotton trout nets with mesh sizes ranging from 4-3/4 to 5-1/2 inches were set about 30 miles east of Milwaukee by Leland Lafond. The nets were set on October 29 and lifted three days later. The total catch consisted of one adult trout weighing just 2 pounds, 1 immature trout, 126 pounds of lawyers, and 190 pounds of bloaters. This same gang of nets, set on the same reef for a three-day period would have produced a minimum of 4,000 pounds in 1944.

"When the first gang was lifted on November 1 a second dry gang of the same length was set on another reef some 41 miles east of Milwaukee that was always noted for its abundance of trout during the fall season. This second gang was lifted two days later and not a single trout was taken. There were 125 pounds of lawyers and 60 pounds of bloaters in the nets. Milwaukee fishermen who set on this reef before 1945 always planned on approximately 5,000 pounds to lift immediately prior to the closed season and also after the season opened."

"Thomas Wirth of the Sturgeon Bay research station made the two trips on the lake when the nets were lifted so that he could take biological notes on the catch. Lester Sharon of Delafield went along to take any spawn available, but didn't have to work...." (5)

Peshtigo Harbor, Wis.

With trout gone, the lamprey turned on other fish. The species attacked depended on the season. As soon as the larval-parasitic transformation is completed, the lamprey moves to deep water where it remains during the summer. There it attacks trout, lawyer, or chub. In Lakes Huron and Michigan the trout were destroyed and the lawyer brought to the brink of extinction. In fall the lamprey moved shoreward and attacked whitefish, lake herring, walleye, suckers, and perch. These fall attacks were likely the most deadly because of the size of the lamprey. One such movement into shallow water occurred in the fall of 1953 when the lamprey were near peak abundance in Lake Michigan.

"Lampreys in such vast numbers that the water literally teemed with them invaded Green Bay early this fall bringing fishing operations practically to a standstill. All important commercial species were attacked, and so great was the destruction that dead and dying fish littered the surface of the water. Fishermen of northern Green Bay, discouraged by dwindling catches, by the presence of large numbers of lampreys in their nets, and by the necessity of discarding the high percentage of mutilated fish in the catches they did make, removed most of their gear from the water by the end of September.

Both trap-netters and gill-netters suffered. Trap-net fishermen reported as high as 60 to 70 percent of their catch scarred and many dead fish when the nets were lifted. Gill-netters fared even worse. One of the last fishermen to remove his large mesh gill nets from Big Bay De Noc took between 4,000 and 5,000 pounds of dead fish from each of two gangs.

Fishermen captured large numbers of lampreys in addition to those taken in their nets. Some removed daily as many as twenty that had attached themselves to their boats. Others added to their take of hitch-hiking parasites by towing a white box astern. Although the fishermen are to be commended greatly for their efforts in destroying as many lamprey as possible, there is small chance that they made any important inroads in such a tremendous population." (6)

lamprey scarred whitefish

58

Peshtigo Harbor, Wis.

During the early period of research much of the work was done in an atmosphere of public optimism that was in direct contradiction to the private pessimism of public officials and administrators. Obviously the problem had to be investigated, political pressure alone necessitated that much, but the idea of actually finding a solution was felt to be a public relations imperative rather than a real possibility.

On the research level a significant change came when new federal legislation was approved and funded in late 1949. In January, 1950, a greatly expanded federal program was launched. The new U.S. Fish and Wildlife organization brought with them an enthusiasm and a positive approach about getting something done. The various experimental structures built by the Michigan Conservation Department were turned over to the federal staff to operate and use in their work. Thereafter the main thrust of research was conducted by the federal government with some assistance from Michigan and Wisconsin.

The scope of the lamprey threat made it clear that any repeat of the immediate post-war procrastinations would be disastrous. The valuable life cycle study was completed. Lamprey spawning areas had been located and the dimensions of the problem were clear:

> "The presence of spawning runs of the sea lamprey has now been demonstrated in every major Michigan watershed in the Lake Michigan basin and in every major watershed north of the Saginaw River in the Lake Huron basin. . . ." (7)

Lamprey Spawning

Now followed an intense period of experimentation. The line of attack was based on the weak point in the lamprey cycle, residence in, departure from, or return to the spawning-larval streams.

1. There was a period when it was hoped that electrical shocking devices would be the answer. Tests showed that "although effective for making scientific collections of larval lampreys, their utility as a control device for destroying the larvae in their beds was negligible and highly impractical." (8)

2. Another attempt to intercept the downstream migrations showed that the primitive creatures were remarkably insensitive to electricity at this stage of their lives. "Application of enough electricity to kill them was far beyond sensible economics." (9)

3. Construction of a fine meshed screen built on an inclined plane through which the entire stream flow was to be diverted and strained was designed to catch newly hatched adults as they entered the lakes but "maintenance of this structure during spring when migration was at its height was almost impossible." (10)

4. Anticipating the psychedelic period, there were experiments with sound and light. Unsuccessful.

5. An organic poison, rotenone, was used for killing larvae while they were burrowed into silt beds. Unsuccessful.

6. Mass poisoning of spawning populations was apparently considered but, with relief, we read that it was rejected "as it would be necessary to make a stream lethal to all fish life for a four-month period at the expense of the spawning activities of many food and game fish." (11)

7. Turning out the stream bed onto the banks with a bulldozer, thereby destroying the lamprey habitat, was considered. Again with relief, we find that this suggestion was rejected possibly because the destructive potential of the cure approached that of the disease.

8. Some variation of the weir or trap concept first tried in the mid-1940's near Rogers City seemed to be the only feasible plan but the prognosis was not encouraging:

> ". . . Weirs and traps if properly constructed and given continual attendance and maintenance will capture entire spawning runs. In some cases, these traps may be utilized for taking the young lampreys migrating downstream. However, the cost of construction and of operation over a seven-year period is excessively high. It remains to be demonstrated if the cost of a program of weir and trap construction and operation for the destruction of spawning runs is justified in view of the value of the fisheries involved." (12)

The last was a grim note, but it reflected the growing feeling among the researchers that the weir was seriously limited. It was necessary to constantly maintain these structures and experience had shown them to be vulnerable to human error and the vagaries of nature, notably spring floods. Destruction of the weir for even one day during the lamprey spawning season was sufficient to allow repopulation of the stream bed.

9. A selective poison, which would destroy larval lampreys but would not affect other aquatic life in the streams, was considered. The obvious limitations and cost of the weirs led to an active search in 1951 for such a chemical.

In the meantime the lamprey was moving into Lake Superior. It had been briefly slowed by the St. Mary's River. Populations established themselves in the eastern part of the lake and began moving westward. The war years had seen steady, high trout yields that ranged from approximately four to five million pounds. In fact, 1944 produced the largest lake trout harvest since the early years of the century. This high productivity continued through 1952. That fall there was disturbing news:

> ". . . Spawn-taking crews of the Wisconsin Conservation Department that operated on Lake Superior in October to secure lake trout spawn for the Bayfield hatchery reported a big increase in the number of lamprey scarred fish over those that were noted a year ago. The crew caught 470 pounds of trout—averaging 7.4 pounds in weight. About one out of every ten fish was scarred by lampreys." (13)

The seemingly irreversible process of collapse began the following year, and for the first time since 1940 less than four million pounds were taken from the lake.

The situation in Lake Superior put researchers under the gun. The limitations of weirs reinforced the need to search for a selective toxin. Why not attempt to destroy the lampreys when they were sedentary in the larval stage, burrowed in the stream beds? Why not accomplish this by avoiding mass poisoning and searching for the chemical substance with a selective toxic effect? It seemed imperative, however, that if even a remnant of the trout in Lake Superior were to survive, that an electrical barrier weir program on that lake's streams be expanded and intensified. The decision was made to split the efforts of the lamprey control group. One segment would continue the search for the toxin. Another would attempt to utilize the weirs as a stop-gap to preserve a Superior trout stock until the day when,

hopefully, the chemical research produced a successful result.

That research was centered at Hammond Bay, Michigan where an inactive Coast Guard Station was turned over to the researchers. Here laboratory facilities were constructed and the exhaustive search for a specific toxin began. Tests had to be conducted so as to simultaneously explore the effects of each chemical on the sea lamprey and a desirable species. Thus the lamprey and, usually, rainbow trout were placed in ten liter test jars which were maintained at a constant temperature of 55 degrees. Laboratory facilities were maximized to the point where 100 to 104 simultaneous jar tests were run each day. Each testing group was geared to a twenty-four hour cycle. Every day the old group was torn down and another set up. The routine was repeated day after day, month after month, in a grinding, monotonous exploration of thousands of compounds.

In 1955 a great organizational advance came with the creation of the Great Lakes Fishery Commission. The passage of the treaty creating this commission followed the withdrawal of a much stronger and more comprehensive treaty which would have placed control of the Great Lakes fisheries under a Canadian-U.S. control group. This earlier treaty had been strenuously opposed by various groups, notably commercial fishermen, ostensibly on the grounds of state's rights. The 1955 treaty was limited to lamprey control activities. An equal number of members from each country were appointed to the advisory board. Their task was to eliminate all overlap between U.S. and Canadian agencies in the search for a solution to the lamprey question.

Meanwhile weir construction continued. In February, 1957, an article stated that the weir program could possibly cover all the Great Lakes tributaries infested with lampreys by 1960. Significant control would take another ten years. In 1957 the Superior trout catch was nearly a million pounds less than that of the previous year. The end of the Superior population seemed only a few years away and this was the *last* lake trout stock. Hope for any solution was diminishing rapidly. The weirs had proven only partialy effective and were susceptible to floods and power failures. My uncle lived in the Keweenaw Peninsula along the upper Michigan Lake Superior shore and on one of his visits in 1956 brought us a magnificent lake trout. After he solemnly announced that the fish would soon be extinct, it was cooked with great ceremony. The meal had some of the aspects of a religious cermony, particularly as someone could not resist mentioning the last supper.

It was beginning to look as though the lamprey was too versatile in its choice of prey, too numerous, too widespread, and control attempts too late. The lake trout seemed destined for a museum spot next to the Lake Ontario salmon and the passenger pigeon. It didn't happen, as there was to be a last minute rescue worthy of Hollywood. It was a supreme irony, in view of what would happen in the next decade, that salvation would come in a chemical form.

A part of the search involved a chemical mystery. The research at Hammond Bay was, in itself, controversial. At the time, the opinions of biochemists were split roughly in half over the question of a selective poison. Approximately half of this scientific community believed that selective toxicity was simply an accident unique to an occasional single compound. The other segment believed that biological activity might be unique to a *family* of closely related compounds. Since the research at Hammond Bay was based on this latter premise, it came under severe attack from those that held the former view. At one point Director James Moffett and the head of the chemical research program, Dr. Vernon Applegate, were informed that they were perpetrating the greatest biological boondoggle of the age on an unsuspecting public.

Photo by Woodrow Jarvis   Vernon Applegate holds trout with attached lamprey.

63

Adding a dissolved chemical to a test jar

At Hammond Bay the tests continued through the mid-fifties. Then one day something happened with one of the myriad chemicals being tested:

"The fellow who was working with me came upstairs and said, 'You better come down here and take a look at something that is happening in one of the test jars.' I looked and said, 'What the hell chemical is that?' because they were all code numbered. We went into the records and found the name of it and we thought, 'It must be a mistake. We'll run it again.' We ran it and re-ran it and kept getting the same results." (14)

It was an obscure chemical known as 3-Bromo-4-nitrophenol and it was specifically toxic to larval lampreys.

This was only a clue towards unravelling the mystery. The substance was basically a laboratory chemical and there were perhaps two ounces available in the United States at the time, scattered across the country on various research chemists shelves. For early research purposes a single, custom made, pound of the substance cost $1,600.

The search also focused on closely related compounds. Here the researchers were extremely fortunate because they were dealing with a family of compounds known as halogenated mononitrophenols, of which there were a limited number, less than forty. Again, the problem was availability of these compounds. Research chemists assigned to the project synthesized some substances and contacts were made with chemical companies as the search zeroed in on the near relatives of 3-Bromo-4-nitrophenol.

It was discovered that less than half of the mononitrophenols containing halogens were selectively toxic to lampreys. Further tests centered around the fifteen closely related compounds that

Photo by Woodrow Jarvis

displayed this characteristic. Staff chemists and interested chemical companies worked to produce sufficient quantities for research and manufacture. It was one thing to have a laboratory answer and quite another thing to have a usable, workable chemical. It had all been a research exercise if favorable answers could not be found to the following questions:

1. Could a chemical be manufactured with sufficient purity? A negative answer to this question ruled out the original 'clue' chemical, 3-Bromo-4-nitorphenol because it was discovered that from a practical standpoint the substance couldn't be manufactured with consistent quality. Any contaminants spoiled its selective toxicity. A usable chemical had to have only one nitrogen group on the benzine ring; it had to be a *mono*nitrophenol. With two nitrogen groups on the benzine ring, a *di*nitrophenol, you had a general poison. There was, in short, need for a very fine and precise product.

2. Assuming consistent purity, could such a chemical be manufactured economically?

3. Could a substance be concentrated to the point where it could be packed into remote areas to treat less accessible streams?

4. Could proper proportioning pumps be developed that would feed the compound into the stream in such a way that all larval lampreys would be killed without destroying significant numbers of fish?

5. Could a desired substance be batch processed or continuously processed by the chemical industry?

6. What would be the eventual price per pound?

7. What would be the cost of treating a typical stream?

8. Would the substance actually work in a stream?

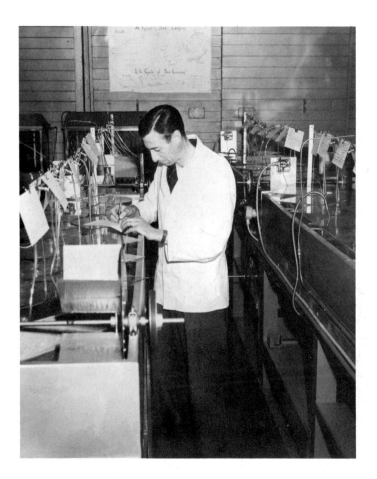

Photo by Woodrow Jarvis   Test facilities at Hammond Bay

"... Over what ranges of temperature and concentration would these chemicals work? Would their potency hold up over long distances down a stream course? Was there a means available to measure the concentration in streams? How many miles would have to be treated? The particular chemicals were not manufactured by anyone. Methods of production and problems of formulation had to be worked out...." (15)

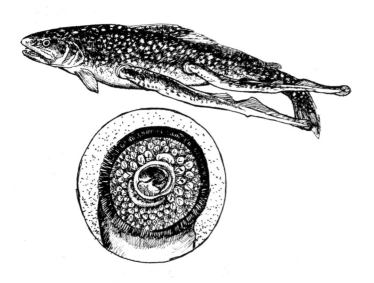

Two chemicals became targets for possible use, one developed by Dow Chemical and another by a German chemical firm. These two substances reached the point where they could be engineered, processed, and delivered in sufficient quantity to enable simulated stream tests.

Experiments in this phase were conducted in a running water raceway so as to approach natural stream conditions more closely than was possible in the laboratory. The raceways were concrete troughs, sixty-five feet long, six feet wide, and thirty inches deep. An artificial stream bed was constructed on the floor of the raceway with materials taken from the beds of local rivers. The troughs were also constructed so as to simulate the variety of stream conditions found naturally. There was a small mixing pool at the head of the stream, followed by a shallow gravel riffle, and a number of other pools and shallows with sand and silt bottom materials. Test animals were placed in the raceway sufficiently in advance of the tests to allow them to adjust to the environment. Approximately fifteen different species were used in each test and generally included a number of lampreys at various stages of their life cycle, trout species, panfish, rough fish, forage minnows, turtles, crayfish, and aquatic insects. (16)

Each experimental treatment lasted for twenty-four hours with the chemical metered into the water by a pump that mixed chemical and water to a perforated pipe at the head of the raceway. It was the same procedure planned for natural streams. Results were encouraging.

Now came the time to try the substance in a real stream. The Dow chemical was the first available in sufficient quantities to make this possible. The test was held at Little Billie's Creek in Cheboygan County, Michigan, in October 1957. A concentration of thirty parts per million was applied to the stream.

Ninety-six percent of the larvae were killed and there was very little effect on other fish. A second test of this same substance at nearby Carp Creek produced similar results. The test had been a success. There was surprise in some administrative and scientific quarters. The lakeside public was thunderstruck.

The second chemical under consideration also needed testing and time was of the essence. This chemical, 3-trifluormethyl-4-nitrophenol (called TFM), was rushed to Lake Superior in the spring of 1958 where the Mosquito and Silver Rivers were treated. As close as could be determined by the large staff of assembled American and Canadian biologists and visiting state and federal administrators, it was observed that both tests had been one hundred percent effective in killing all lamprey larvae in both streams in a more efficient manner than the first chemical tested. An answer had been found.

There were now so few trout in Lake Superior that it was thought essential that their numbers be supplemented by hatchery fish. The superintendent of the Marquette, Michigan, fish hatchery, Russ Robertson, had been gathering fish eggs from various parts of Superior since the 40's. He was told that no one had raised lake trout in a hatchery and that they were a doomed species in any case. Sportsmen complained that hatchery space was being wasted, a feeling shared by some of his superiors in the Department of Conservation. Nonetheless, techniques were developed for raising and holding the fish, and in 1958 they were to prove valuable indeed. It was decided to plant that year because trout are not generally subject to lamprey attack until their third year. Schedules were pushed to provide all fifty-five lamprey infested Superior streams with larvacide treatment in the three years provided. The schedule was met and the lamprey reduced to from ten to twenty percent of its former abundance. Lamprey control and trout restocking shifted to Lake Michigan in the mid-60's and to Huron in the latter part of the decade. In Huron the lamprey was at ten percent of its peak abundance before the treatment of tributary streams with larvacide. The reduction of favored species had apparently led to either a decline or movement of the lamprey population.

The achievement of the larvacide is a truly impressive piece of scientific work. Dr. Vernon Applegate had put six years into the investigation of some six thousand chemicals and development of a workable compound. In the course of investigation and developement of the successful chemicals, it was estimated that close to *sixty thousand* individual tests were run. In the last year and a half of the project, from 1957 to 1959, the lab at Hammond Bay operated twenty-four hours a day, seven days a week, and many of the personnel put in continuous seven-day weeks during that period. It has to be understood that this work involved a leap from an incompletely tested chemical theory to a practical application in the space of seven years:

> "These compounds for controlling the sea lamprey represent the first known selective toxicants discovered and used to destroy a particular vertebrate without harming other vertebrate or invertebrate animals occupying the same habitat." (17)

Foresight by Russ Robertson provided stocks, and swift, coordinated work by several governments and agencies helped to preserve remaining native trout in Lake Superior. For those who are used to dealing with government agencies, it is stunning to think that within three years of the first stream trial test of the chemical all the lamprey streams of Superior had been treated and restocking begun. There is much to be criticized in the management of Great Lakes Resources but the breakthrough at Little Billie's Creek was a masterpiece of dedication, skill, and coordination.

Smelt

Chapter 3:
Aftershock— The Colonizing Species

The secondary effect of the destruction of major predator species was a wild upsurge in abundance of prey species, notably alewife. The tertiary effect may have been a decline in native fish, although these declines are probably the result of a number of factors.

Smelt

The spread of the smelt was outward from its base in Lake Michigan. Most of the year the fish is found in waters 60 to 120 feet in depth. In spring the fish move inshore into rivers to spawn. By far the largest population of smelt in Lake Michigan is centered in Green Bay. In recent years that bay has provided in excess of three-fourths of the total lake catch. During the thirties amazed residents discovered that the spawning runs were so intense that great quantities of the fish could be taken with small nets from shorelines and bridges as the smelt crowded into the rivers.

One of the chief spawning runs was into the Menominee River, which forms the boundary between Wisconsin and upper Michigan. The annual event early acquired the air of a festival, aided by the fact that the runs are primarily nocturnal. As a child I remember the lights lining the shore as hundreds of people stood along the river, often dipnetting bushels of fish in just a few hours. It was often necessary, and certainly tradition, to sip on a pocketed bottle of brandy, beer or whiskey to ward off the spring chill. In the early years a concessionaire set up in the river area about the time the run was expected and became the nucleus of what became the "Smelt Carnival."

A resident of the area recalls that while being stationed in Florida during the 1940's he was amazed to see a former classmate appear larger than life in a Movietone Newsreel. This classmate was engaged in a wrestling match that had become an annual feature of the carnival. What made this wrestling match newsworthy was that it was conducted in a foot of dead smelt. A large number of the spectators tended to cluster to the up-wind side of the ring.

The commercial catch of smelt was 4.8 million pounds in 1941 and 3.4 million in 1942. In latter years it is estimated that the dip net catch of the sport fishermen was 5.5 million pounds in Michigan alone, with near amounts taken by Wisconsin residents. That means that individuals with dip nets harvested close to *10 million* pounds of fish.

The smelt then proceeded to go through the greatest recorded population gyration in Great Lakes history. In the winter of 1942-43 an infectious disease roared through the Huron-Michigan stocks. A number of fish were taken through the ice in the winter before stocks had been wiped out, and the commercial catch for 1943 was 2.2 million pounds. In all of 1944 only *5 thousand* pounds were taken. The next year the figure had increased to a hundred thousand, by 1948 it had climbed to over a million, and ten years later the figure went over 9 million. Later figures are somewhat inaccurate indicators of abundance because of fluctuating market prices. Catches declined sharply from the 9 million of 1958. Since 1961 they have moved from slightly under one million to two and one-half million. Market conditions played a part, but it is believed that the drastic drop of the early 60's reflected reduced abundance perhaps brought about by competition from the alewife.

Smelt were first sighted in Lake Huron in 1925. Their abundance was never reflected in the commercial fish statistics, but according to all accounts the fish exploded in Huron during the 30's much the way they did in Michigan. This rise paralleled the collapse of the trout, whitefish, and chubs. Then came the great die-off of 1942-43:

"... The following spring saw the emergence of the greatest year class of whitefish ever recorded for Lake Huron. Ciscoes reversed their precipitous decline and from the mid-1940's until the early 1950's, annual production of this species was relatively stable. ... It is obvious that the larger smelt populations prior to 1942 were utilizing vast quantities of food organisms near the base of the production pyramid. We suspect that in the virtual absence of the smelt population following the die-off 1942-43, populations of whitefish and ciscoes (chub-ed) may have capitalized on this large reservoir of available energy." (18)

Smelt were first recorded in Lake Superior waters in 1930. The first significant catches were recorded in 1952 and the pattern of rapid increase was repeated, resulting in harvests of over a million pounds in 1961. Amounts have remained high, with a record 4 million taken in 1976.

Smelt arrived in Lake Erie by 1932. They apparently became significant in the early 1950's. The impact of smelt on Erie may have been more intense and significant than on any of the other lakes. The fishery exists almost exclusively in Canadian waters, with trap nets and trawls primarily used in the harvest. Just over a million pounds were harvested in provincial waters in 1952. In 1960 the figure was 11.5 million, and in 1962 an awesome 19.1 million. Since that year production has been over 10 million in all but a single year, and was a considerable 17.2 million in 1976.

The first Lake Ontario specimen was taken in 1929, three years prior to the first sighting on Erie. This has led to some interesting speculation as to its origin. One view holds that the fish was part of a population left from the post-glacial days of the Champlain Sea. Such relict populations exist in the Ottawa Valley. It is thought that the smelt were not detected for many years because of their low density.

Others feel that it is unlikely that the fish would have escaped notice for such a long period of time and that it was likely unofficially introduced by an amateur or accidental planting. A third possibility is that the fish came from the upper lakes by way of the Niagara River or the Welland Canal. The fourth and most accepted explanation is that the smelt were successfully introduced in the Finger Lakes of New York and moved to Lake Ontario in the same way that stocks moved from Crystal Lake into Lake Michigan. Whatever the origin, their ascendancy coincided with the decline of chubs and lake herring and the possibility is raised that the overlapping habitat, particularly of the herring, was overwhelmed by the rapidly increasing numbers of smelt.

The smelt fishery of the lake is almost exclusively concentrated in Canadian waters of the eastern area. The first catch figures show over 200 thousand pounds in 1953. Since that time the figure has varied between 100 and 300 thousand pounds. The rise of the smelt may have been aided by the final passing of the trout and burbot. We have seen, however, that a period of high smelt abundance coincided with near record trout production in Lake Michigan. Nonetheless the Lake Ontario increase of smelt was abrupt in the early and mid-40's. The Ontario SCOL Report suggests another possibility. Both smelt and walleye are spring spawners. Both increased at the same time and the post-war springs of the lake area were extremely mild. (19)

It is clear that the smelt have established themselves as a major factor in all of the lakes. Their rise somewhat coincides with lakewide declines in trout and burbot stocks, but they have not in turn declined significantly as some of these predators were restored to greater abundance. There may well be a more significant connection with the decline of chub and herring stocks. It is obvious that a population explosion, the magnitude of that experienced by the smelt, must have had some impact. The problem is that this effect has been muted and confused by the near simultaneous explosions of the lamprey and alewife. Unlike the other invaders it has a redeeming feature; it is delicious.

Alewife

The exact role of the alewife in subsequent declines of other species is a topic of debate among fish management personnel. In Lake Ontario a long period of coexistence, as with the lamprey, preceded the final decline of other valued species.

The argument over their impact centers around the extent to which they usurp the food of other species. The alewife has been most often implicated in the decline of the chub and herring populations. In Lake Ontario there is a problem with this. The great recovery of major species in the 1920's occurred a full fifty years after their introduction. However, they occupy the shallower areas of the lake during the warmer months where they would compete with young chubs. Large chubs are in deep waters at this time, making summer food competition an unlikely factor with these adult fish. There is also the possibility the alewives feed on chub eggs. The shortnose chub spawn in deep water in late April or May at which time alewives are already out of the deep water areas but the alewife could feed on chub fry which rise to the surface. There is a possibility of interaction during the fall spawning time of the bloater and kiyi chubs and it is also a fact that chubs and alewives live at the same depth in winter, and food competition at that time might become important.

It appears that in the upper lakes the large chubs declined with the onslaught of the lampreys while the smaller chubs, perhaps relieved of interspecies competition, increased. These smaller fish then declined in the face of rapidly growing numbers of alewives.

The alewives might become a serious factor only after the decline of their major predators. The resulting population explosions might then seriously inhibit the reestablishment or introduction of other species because of their mass effect on food supplies. These questions are still open.

As previously mentioned, the alewife had little effect in Lake Erie. It arrived in Huron in 1933 at the same time as the lamprey. Here they found a deep water environment much to their liking. Most important, they were able to take advantage of the destructive effects of the lamprey. As predator stocks were reduced, populations exploded on a grand scale and increased rapidly in the late 40's until numbers surpassed those of all other species combined.

Even more swiftly, the fish came to dominate Lake Michigan. The first specimen was observed in 1949. By the winter of 1956-57 fishermen in the southern part of the lake were complaining of the numbers infesting their chub gill nets. Extremely large concentrations moved into Green Bay waters. Commercial catch figures, reported in 1956, began to reflect the explosion. In 1957, 220 thousand pounds were taken. In 1960, 2.4 million, 1966, 29 million, and in 1973 a staggering 45 million. These figures are even more impressive when it is realized that the alewife is generally regarded as a highly undesirable junk fish and subject to pet food market fluctuations. The fish reached Lake Superior but has not as yet reached epidemic numbers.

Two views sum up the impact of the alewife and the rapidity with which perception of the invader changed. From 1963:

"Three new types of fish have come without invitation to Michigan waters in recent years and while not too troublesome, none is really very welcome. . . ."

"The alewife as a matter of fact may be a blessing in disguise . . . it is known that the lake trout will eat large numbers of alewife, so that if the sea lamprey can be controlled and the lake trout re-established, the alewife will provide a ready form of food for these big, delicious, and highly prized trout. One estimate indicates that if lake trout return to their former abundance in the Great Lakes, they could consume as much as 90 million pounds of alewife each year." (20)

From 1965:

"At first glance this small non-predatory fish might seem unimportant. But we are assured by those best informed that the alewife currently is a far more serious problem to the fish resources of the upper Great Lakes than the sea lamprey ever was. While this fish normally feeds on extremely small food particles, *it is so numerous that it now poses a threat to the survival of all species spawning within the Great Lakes. . . .*"

"This species is still increasing in the Great Lakes. Just when it will reach its peak we don't know. Nor can anyone be sure when its population will stabilize. We can't predict for sure its future abundance. *But the alewife presently makes up over 90 percent of the weight of all fish present in the Great Lakes;* and from past experience in Lake Ontario where alewives are well known, we can expect it to stabilize somewhere near this high level." (21)

Basically the question surrounding the alewife was whether it caused the decline of the other species, accelerated their decline, or just took advantage of an extraordinary opportunity. The question was somewhat moot by 1965. The unmistakable fact was that it was *there*. To fish management officials this presented both the danger and the opportunity described by the two commentators.

In the spring of 1967 the alewives in Lake Michigan were temporarily checked by an experience similar to that of the great smelt collapse of the early 40's. It is estimated that perhaps 70 percent of the alewife population died that year. U.S. fish and wildlife personnel pegged the figure at several billion fish, and corpses heaped on the beaches and clogging water intakes made the spring particularly memorable. Commercial catches dropped sharply the following year but had recovered by the mid-70's. Recovery from a nearly three-quarter drop is an indication of how powerful alewife dominance has become. (22)

White Perch

It isn't really a perch at all. The fish, related to the white bass, reaches an average size of eight to ten inches. It apparently arrived in Lake Ontario about 1950, coming from coastal areas by way of the now classic invasion route, the Erie Barge Canal. Stocks built up and spread out so that by 1960 there was a large population in the Bay of Quinte. Commercial catches began in 1961 with 20 thousand pounds, reached 602 thousand in 1965, and 774 thousand in 1976.

This population explosion occurred at the same time as a substantial drop in walleyes, white suckers, and smallmouth bass. The Ontario SCOL report points out that all major predators except walleye had greatly declined before the appearance of the white perch, and their absence might have aided the quick expansion. It further appears to have a higher pollution tolerance than other fish and is flourishing in the badly polluted Bay of Quinte.

As yet, this fish is confined to the waters of Lake Ontario but this fact should not offer any great consolation. Their expansion is certainly modest when compared to that of the smelt or the alewife, but this must be measured against the historically small fishery and fish populations of this lake. Previous experience should point to the likelihood that sooner or later an adventurous couple is likely to take the scenic trip through the Welland Canal.

White Perch

SECTION 3:
FISH POLITICS

"With reorganization of the Department of Natural Resources in 1966, the entire Great Lakes Fisheries situation came under close scrutiny. Nearly every important fish stock had been depleted and the commercial fishing industry was accelerating its own downhill course. In 1966 a basic policy change was struck which recognized, first and foremost, the vast potential and economic benefits of a Great Lakes recreational fishery. It also recognized that the commercial fishery was only one interest in the management of the resource, rather than the dominant interest. With this policy change established, the entire rehabilitation effort shifted into high gear. Pacific salmon were introduced, use of gill nets was controlled, sea lamprey control enabled steelhead runs to rebound spectacularly, and the legislature amended the basic commercial fishing statutes to provide direct, rather than indirect controls, on the fisheries. . . ." (1)

". . . Unfortunately, some aspects of the very restrictive measures aimed at the commercial fishery in order to protect these introduced fish, particularly in Lake Michigan, seem to be based on political expediency rather than sound biological considerations. These restrictions will very likely bankrupt the remnants of an already moribund commercial fishery rather than achieve a sorely needed regulatory framework based on the productive capacity of different parts of the lake community. It is clear from long experience, however, that an appropriate form of effective control on the commercial fishery is long overdue." (2)

"If you call something 'conservation' nobody wants to be opposed to it and so they rarely analyze it to see if it is conservation. Our legislature is very reluctant to interfere with anything the DNR does in the name of 'conservation' but the fact that a government agency is called a Department of Conservation or a Department of Natural Resources doesn't necessarily mean that what it does serves the interests of conservation or sound management of a natural resource. The problem is that nobody, not even the legislature, is eager to do much more than read the label by way of analysis." (3)

Chapter 1: A New Policy

The destruction of the commercial fishing industry that was wrought by the lamprey and the invading species was significant. All across the upper lakes, marginal operations folded and for those families to whom fishing had become a way of life, it was a time of getting along as well as one could. Members took other jobs or attempted to struggle along with either lower value species or reduced incomes. By the mid-sixties, however, the fishermen looked with great hope to the increasingly successful lamprey control programs and the subsequent restocking of Lake Superior with trout. This program was soon scheduled for Lakes Michigan and Huron. Fish management officials had generally turned a sympathetic ear to the needs of the commercial fisherman. Fishing was a valuable source of food, an important factor in the economy of numerous lakeside communities, an honored way of life, and the prime source of what little knowledge management personnel possessed on the nature of the ecosystem and the environment of the Great Lakes. The tradition was particularly strong in the state of Michigan and a 1955 *Michigan Conservation* article summed up the prevailing attitude in the darkest days of the lamprey plague:

". . . Whatever reasons may be given, the fact is that Michigan today still has the core of a commerical fishing industry, and fortunate it is that we can say this. Commercial fishing is good conservation, it's 'wise use' of a renewable natural resource and it's important to Michigan that the industry continue to live. Without it, a colorful chapter in Michigan history would be lost and the 27,000,000 pounds of fish taken annually from Michigan waters would be largely wasted. In the years to come,

the struggle for survival of the industry may wax or it may wane but right now we know it can use, it needs, and it deserves whatever support the public can give.'' (3a)

During this same period great changes had taken place in lifestyles. The post-World War II era provided a great increase in the monetary standard of living in most areas. Some areas of the northern lakes, however, suffered continuing economic depression, and the population of many northern counties of Minnesota, Michigan, and Wisconsin stagnated or declined in the period 1945–65. Mass population movement to the major lakeshore cities combined with the baby boom and the decay of U.S. city cores to make these urban areas less and less desirable. More leisure along with better highways increased the weekend exodus of city dwellers to the relatively unspoiled northern areas. It became extremely fashionable for the suburban middle and upper class to have summer homes. It was even more fashionable to have a home on the shore. The great recreation boom was on.

These people demanded, and increasingly received, facilities designed to enhance enjoyment of their increasing free time. One of the most popular recreational activities was fishing. In the early years most of this activity was confined to inland lakes, rivers, or the immediate shoreline areas of the Great Lakes. Gradually, however, affluence and technology combined to produce a growing fleet of boats that ventured into deeper and more exposed lake water. Unfortunately, this happened just as the really desirable angling fish were in pitiful post-lamprey shape. It is a rare angler who is happy with a day on the open lake and only a nibble. A successful weekend fisherman, however, is likely to return to the scene of his success while an

Sturgeon Bay, Wis.

unhappy angler is likely to try his luck elsewhere and with him goes that marvelous green harvest of tourist dollars, a cash crop increasingly important to many northern cities. The pressures grew to make sure the visitor went away smiling. A new theme was, therefore, gradually introduced into Great Lake fish management and it centered around the rational goal of maintaining an adequate stock of desired sport fish.

"... Since fisheries' research funds derive solely from license sales, it has been considered improper to spend the inland angler's money on Great Lakes fisheries research. This is unfortunate, though necessary, since it seems obvious that the Great Lakes provide our last frontier for sport fishing, and the potential needs to be explored if our growing army of recreation seekers is to be served." (3b)

As the middle sixties approached, it became apparent that there might be some opportunities in the seemingly depressed state of the fisheries. The entire predator-prey sequence had been disrupted. There was a great mass of alewives being incompletely utilized. The food chain was lacking a key link. The obvious answer was restoration of the trout through planting, but would that provide an adequate balance? How long would such a restoration take? Was there another solution? Would another predator species speed the restoration of balance? What were the dangers of such an introduction? The idea was considered for a number of years and the following negative reaction appeared in a 1957 issue of *Michigan Conservation:*

"True or false: The sea bass, or some other predator, would be a good fish to introduce into the Great Lakes to check the lamprey's depredations.

False. When such a predator ran out of lampreys to eat he would have to turn to some other fish. More than likely, any predator with a strong enough stomach for eels would probably eat most other fish as well. We would be very liable to lose a lot more ground than we would gain. In addition, there are a number of biological reasons why introducing a predator might be very dangerous." (4)

These issues were the subject of debate among management people. They had a golden opportunity to create a balanced commercial/recreational use of fish resources. There seemed to be no particular reason why a commercial and sports fishery could not exist side by side in relative harmony, for the goals were not inherently incompatible. With a bit of imagination, seasonal and regional divisions could set a standard that would ensure maximum recreational use and optimal food production. It would be a standard readily accepted in region where arguments for ecologically sound management had not come from the universities, but from the savagely applied object lessons of the preceding century.

By the summer of 1965 the first results of the trout stocking program were appearing. Commerical fishermen were used to make the assessment. It was an optimistic time.

"... The story, you see, lies in experimental fishing now under way, and for that tale we must shift to the shoreline of Lake Superior. There, amid the rotting fish docks and tangles of unused nets, commercial fishermen who held on through thin times are beginning to look forward to better days. Those who have been able to qualify for the work are now carrying on experimental lake trout fishing under government contracts. Biologists, working from a wide-ranging research plan, tell the commercial anglers where to fish, when to fish, and how to fish. Commercial fishermen are a notoriously independent lot and seldom take orders from anyone, but in this case the arrangement is working out extremely well. Last year, Michigan fishermen took 20,927 lake trout, amazingly close to the pre-season allotment of 22,000. Often these fishermen must fish in one spot when better judgment tells them that more fish will be found elsewhere. They accept this, set nets, and note results. Details of each fish are recorded, scale samples taken, length and sex noted. Fishermen can then sell the fish to offset labor, boat operation, and other costs." (5)

Any hope for a balanced utilization of reconstructed fish stocks was shattered that same year. In a sweeping policy statement, Howard Tanner of the Michigan Department of Natural Resources laid out the future of the state's fishery. Michigan's direction was of vital importance because of its dominant position on the Great Lakes. Tanner began his statement by stressing just how important that position was:

"... While not now the greatest fishery, these Great Lakes of ours represent the greatest single fresh water resource in the world. Of this resource, 41 percent belongs to the State of Michigan. ... We share this enormous Great Lakes responsibility with the province of Ontario and seven other states. Of the total area of the Great Lakes, Ontario has 36 percent, and the other seven states share the remaining 23 percent. These figures are important. They should indicate clearly Michigan's role in leadership in all Great Lakes matters. The major responsibility for whatever happens to the Great Lakes fishery must be ours." (6)

From this opening statement, the article goes on to recount the current sad state of the fisheries. A passing appraisal of commercial fishing minimizes its importance:

"... The commercial fishery, while providing livelihood for several hundred people, was never a major fishery by marine standards. Being small, it suffered numerous problems ranging from marketing difficulties to overharvesting, and through the last several decades, it has suffered a long gradual decline." (7)

Tanner is apparently referring to state fishermen. In the year the article was written, 1965, there were 51 fishermen engaged in harvesting in the U.S. waters of Lake Ontario, 523 in Erie, 353 in Huron, 867 in Michigan, and 542 in Superior. In 1936, during the depression, 5,388 fishermen were working the U.S. waters of the Great Lakes. It is important to note that not all of the fishermen in either year were exclusively engaged in fishing.

The article further recounts the struggle against the lamprey and the increasing domination of the alewife. Tanner then expresses doubt that the planted lake trout will be able to spawn in the face of the enormous number of alewives. The important immediate consideration is to control somehow the immense number of alewives and to support the need for sport fishing. Then came the statement that reversed the previous ninety years of Great Lakes fish management objectives:

"Faced with the obvious growing need for sport fishing opportunities on these lakes, how do we proceed to solve our problems? First, I think a policy needs to be laid down that recognizes recreational fishing as yielding the most good to the most people; and that the fisheries of the Great Lakes will be managed first for the benefit of the recreational fishermen. In those instances where recreational fishermen are either not interested or incapable of achieving what is judged to be an appropriate maximum harvest, then those fish resources will be made available to commercial fishermen . . ." (8)

It is important to note what is *not* discussed. The whole question of "yielding the most good to the most people" is discussed without mention of the food contribution of the commercial species. In 1965 close to a hundred million pounds of high protein fish were removed from the Great Lakes. For years commercial species had provided a valuable low-cost supplement to the diet of lakeside residents. The importance of this might have seemed dim in the 1960's, but it was vital during the depression and World War II.

There was more, however, to this landmark statement. The question of reconstructing the balance between predator and prey could not be left to the dubious future of the trout. Therefore:

" . . . It is our considered judgment that the best chance for achieving success is through introduction of so-called anadromous predators. The term is used for fish that live in lakes, but enter streams to spawn. A species that spawns in streams where alewives are not found protects the eggs and young to some extent. Then the young of these predators can descend to the Great Lakes and enjoy the enormous abundance of the alewife as food supply. This is the reasoning that has led to the program calling for new species to be planted in the Great Lakes."

" . . . One fish we want to introduce there is the coho salmon. We have examined all facets relating to this fish, and now believe it an excellent choice for introduction to the Great Lakes . . ." (9)

A curious thing was done in this article. Two separate decisions were juxtaposed as though they were mutually dependent. With considerable political skill, a popular move was merged with a potentially troublesome one. Actually there is no reason at all why the decision to stock the salmon had to lead to the subordination of commercial to sport fishing. There was no middle ground explored and no discussion of seeking a way to divide resources on an equitable basis between the two interests.

On a purely economic level it was a shrewd move. The overwhelming alewife populations would be controlled by highly desirable sport fish which would generate tourist dollars. The commercial fishermen would not be allowed to touch this valuable addition to the lake. It was also a fairly gutsy program for there were no assurances that the salmon would establish themselves or, if they did, that they would not so dominate the food chain as to endanger other native species. A calculated, if popular, risk had been taken.

Chapter 2: The Salmon

It was a spectacular success. In the spring of 1966, 850,000 coho salmon were planted in a single stream of Lake Superior and in two Lake Michigan streams. That autumn Howard Tanner reported that the first fish were being caught:

"... On the Manistee River and its tributary, Bear Creek, hundreds of anglers were concentrated in October, fishing Michigan's first historic salmon run. The catch is estimated to run to one or two thousand or more fish averaging about three pounds in weight. The current record at this writing is a hefty two-foot fish that weighed slightly over seven pounds! Despite the evidence, it's still difficult for some Michigan fishermen to conceive a growth rate from one ounce to seven pounds in four months. Yet in this respect, the coho promises to be Michigan's most outstanding fish." (10)

But this was nothing. By the next autumn coho madness had spread throughout the area.* Gone was all discussion of the seven-pound fish. Now they were being caught at averages of sixteen pounds. Charter fleets developed quickly and some of the quiet northern towns that had shuttered up after Labor Day experienced a second tourist season. Plans were laid out to develop a whole program behind the new sports fishery. Hatcheries were suggested, the removal of dams and natural barriers was urged to provide more spawning areas, and expanded research facilities were to evaluate and monitor the results of the great experiment.

The height of the enthusiasm was reserved for the monstrous chinook salmon. The first plantings of this fish were made in the spring of 1967. In the fall of 1968 first spawners were being caught in the range of five to twelve pounds. In the spring of 1970 a four-foot chinook weighing fifty pounds washed up on a beach. Residents of the area had never seen anything like that and visions of fifty-pound fish made other angling seem tame by comparison. The thought was enough to send the entire recreational fishing business into overtime. *Michigan Conservation* described the experience in a very unbureaucratic burst of ecstacy:

"... There is no bigger letdown in sports than when a trophy fish slips out of the net and only the lure remains enmeshed. However, when the opportunity to net him presents itself, seize it with firm resolve. This is no time for fishy-washiness. Net him headfirst with a clean decisive sweep—get all of him deep in the net. Once he's in the net, whisper a brief prayer that the twine not be rotten and that the netman ate his Wheaties and KERSPLASH-KATHUMP* GOT HIM* YA HOOO!!" (11)

It is no surprise that anadramous planting spread to other jurisdictions quickly in the wake of all this. By 1970, 4.1 million chinook fingerlings had been released. The dominant position of Michigan in the salmon program is illustrated by the fact that through 1970 the state planted 94 percent of the coho and 93 percent of the chinook.

It is not widely known that the coho was preceded by another successful salmon introduction. The story of the arrival of the pink salmon is one of the more bizarre events in the history of the fisheries. The pink salmon was designated to be planted in areas of Hudson and James Bays in northern Ontario. The Ontario Department of Lands and Forests designated a hatchery at

80   (For an account of Salmon fever, see article at the end of this chapter.)

Port Arthur (now incorporated with Fort William as Thunder Bay) to develop the eggs into fingerlings.

By the spring of 1955 the project was completed and the fingerlings were ready to be transferred to their northern destination. Then came a series of events out of science fiction:

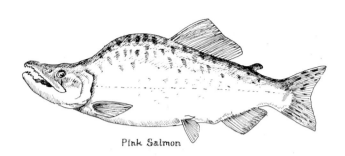
Pink Salmon

"While hatchery personnel loaded the four seaplanes for the trip to Hudson Bay, approximately 100 pink salmon were spilled from a tank and escaped down a ditch into Lake Superior. Then about 300 were accidentally mixed with lake trout scheduled for a later planting in Lake Superior. Finally, as the last aircraft flew north, it was discovered that three troughs of pink salmon had been left behind. Each trough contained 7,000 fish, so what do you do with 21,000 surplus pink salmon? Well, the hatchery manager decided to just dump them down a nearby sewer. The sewer led to the Current River, a tributary which flows into Lake Superior. The manager thought that the pink salmon, being properly disposed of, would never be heard from again. After all, he knew that naturally occurring populations of pink salmon in fresh water had never been found.

End of story? Not quite. Mother Nature fooled us once again. The pink salmon not only survived their ride down the sewer, they began to reproduce, so that today we have a self-sustaining population of saltwater pink salmon in the freshwater Great Lakes, the only such population in the world." (12)

The preceding is one of the more detailed versions of what happened, but there may have been an additional item. According to an authoritative source, after one plane was airborne someone voluntarily dumped a can of these salmon into the lake, thereby providing those of a mystical cast of mind with an irresistible symbol. All in all, it was an interesting day in the history of Great Lakes management.

At this point, it may be useful to recall the dedicated efforts to plant salmon since the 1880's. These attempts, using the best scientific methods available at the time, were unsuccessful in producing self-sustaining stocks until the massive plantings of the late sixties and early seventies. Imagine, then, the skeptical attitude that must have greeted the first fish presented for identification. No one, at that time, was aware of the events at Thunder Bay.

The first spawning run, which had to have occurred in 1957, went unobserved. The salmon were seen for the first time in Minnesota waters:

"In 1959 we picked up the first three specimens and identified them as pink salmon. We sent scales and pictures to labs around North America. The lab at Nanaimo, British Columbia, had to agree they were pink salmon, the species voted least likely to succeed in fresh water because of their low stream dependence. Almost their complete life cycle was spent in salt water." (13)

By 1969, Ontario was reporting fairly large spawning runs. In the early 1970's the fish increased rapidly in both abundance and distribution. Spawning was soon reported throughout Lake Superior and then, abruptly, in Lakes Michigan and Huron. In 1977 there were streams in Ontario, on the eastern end of Superior, reporting tremendous runs; one was estimated to have seen 180,000 fish. Some people were beginning to express a bit of concern:

"... The pinks have persisted in small numbers by natural reproduction and recently have noticeably increased in abundance. If their numbers continue to increase, the lake herring . . . may be faced with significant competition for food." (14)

At first glance you might infer that this fish would provide a tasty addition to the sport fishery. A number of fish managers have stated that its potential in this regard may be limited. The fish appears at the streams in an advanced state of sexual maturity, generally not feeding, and stream life is extremely brief. There is another factor of interest to be weighed in speculating on the future of the fish.

"Think of what a small gene pool these fish come from. This would tend to cause the fish to be attenuated or reduced in size and vigor after a certain period of time. In fact, this may have happened. The first ones we saw were about 22 inches long and weighed a couple of pounds. Now some are as small as 14 inches and weigh only a pound." (15)

Further, the habits and impact of this fish on other stocks has not been fully explored. Where do Superior populations spend their adult years?

"We know nothing of their pelagic life. No one has picked them up out there and they are not sampled by any agency. They don't show up in the incidental catch taken by commercial fishermen in the assessment netting work. It's a mystery." (16)

This amazing tale, which may just be beginning, is all the illustration needed of the totally unpredictable ability of marine species to survive in fresh water. It is also a jarring comment on precautions surrounding the state of the stocking art as late as the 1950's. The pinks have remained persistently unaware of their limited fresh water potential.

The kokanee salmon was introduced in 1964 to the Canadian waters of Lake Huron. It was reported in 1976 that 5 million eggs, fry, and fingerlings had been planted. In spite of some natural reproduction, there has been uncertainty as to the ability of the population to become self-sustaining.

One of the main reasons the lake trout was so vulnerable to the lamprey was that males reached sexual maturity no sooner than age five and females no sooner than age six. This meant that they reached a size where they were prey for the lamprey long before they were reproducing. This led to a search in the fifties and sixties for a hybrid that would mature early enough to spawn before being subject to the remaining lamprey populations. There were various experimental plantings of a hybrid brook and lake trout that could meet these requirements. A strain of this new fish, called the splake, was found to be sexually mature as early as age two, a year before size would make it vulnerable to the lamprey. It also had the advantage of being a deep swimmer, and in 1969 the hybrid was released. The main focus of planting activity was in the Canadian waters of Lake Huron. There has been some natural reproduction of the fish, but it is too early to discover whether it has the potential for widespread introduction.

Another fish deliberately introduced was the first native fish to have disappeared from the Great Lakes. In 1972, some eighty years after it had become extinct in Lake Ontario, the Atlantic salmon returned to that Lake and was planted for the first time in Huron. The motive for the planting was, ironically, a desire to extend the range of the fish to the Great Lakes because of danger to the species in its Atlantic habitat. Apparently overfishing and damming of streams have greatly reduced the once plentiful fish. Michigan Department of Natural Resources trucks hauled some 20,000 two-year-old fish from Quebec's Gaspé Peninsula to two rivers in the state. It is too early to tell whether this once native fish will be able to survive in modern Lake Ontario or flourish in the upper lakes.

The coho and chinook stocking programs spread to all of the Great Lakes in the late sixties. The result in Superior was not as fantastic as in Lakes Michigan and Huron, as the colder water produced slower growth. An attempt in Erie was made to reestablish a climax predator. Between 1958 and 1973, 54 million lake trout, 28.4 million coho, 19.5 million chinook, and 19.1 million kokanee were planted. Smaller amounts of the other species discussed were introduced. Michigan was the leader in this experiment with a total of 66.6 million introductions. Ontario provided 29.7 million, about half of the Michigan effort, and Wisconsin came in with 16.2 million. The other jurisdictions were minor partners with totals of less than 4 million each.

A massive and concentrated attempt had been made to reconstitute viable fish populations in the Great Lakes. The initial success was considerable. There was reason to believe that an answer had been found to the effects of the lamprey crisis and its aftermath.

The following account of the first days of salmon fever on the Great Lakes appeared in the November-December, 1967 issue of *Michigan Conservation*. There is no better description available and we have reprinted the bulk of the article.

Fish Story

by Russell McKee

What could be so unusual as to drive a tight-fisted penny pincher to a cheerful squandering of $2,000 of hard-earned cash? What could cause dozens of peace-loving citizens to assault each other bodily with fists and poles to the extent of considerable personal injury? What could cause scores of automobile owners to park illegally and then to cheerfully accept the consequences of their actions—a plague of costly summons? What could cause a man of modest means to spend $3,500 for a piece of fast-moving equipment without a) having ever operated it personally or b) without ever having been on it when it was operating or c) without even knowing how to place it in operation? What could cause hundreds of men to go away on a treacherous sea —against all advice—in rubber rafts, bicycle boats, floating cars and trucks, canoes, and a host of other illogical craft? What could cause a man of usually normal habits to spend a night attempting to sleep on the bony frame of a boat trailer wrapped in a single blanket? What, indeed could cause such domestic upheaval, threats of divorce, loss of sleep by thousands, clashes, running, shouts in the night?

The answer to all these questions, in case you have any lingering doubts, is quite simply the prospect many men have of catching many big fish. In this case the fish is the coho, spell it in capitals—COHO. Ask any housewife in Michigan, or man on the street, or man-child over ten what it means, and he'll tell

you it means salmon fishing has come to Michigan.

We have seen it all here in the Wolverine State in the last couple of months, and there seems to be no concern on the part of anyone that the whole spectacular uproar may well continue for as long as any of us lives.

Some have expressed uncertainty over which end of the line the fish is on, but there can be no uncertainty over the fact that many thousands of lines have been stretched, yanked, torn, or busted by the struggle between fish and fisherman this fall. The struggle has not been confined to fish and fishermen. It started about the end of August near Manistee and Frankfort on the colorful northwest coast of the Lower Peninsula. Later, it broke out at one spot, the mouth of the Big Huron River west of Marquette. It never left these two locations, though shock waves of the event were felt by anglers all over the northeastern United States. During the two months that the fever lasted, the merchants of those two areas of the state were swamped with business, particularly in the Manistee-Frankfort area. Simply swamped. Picture the weary gas station owner filling gas tanks in cars and boats at four A.M. on a Tuesday morning, his eyes droopy from lack of sleep, smiling through yawns to tell you his business is up 600 percent. Picture bait shops out of bait and tackle bins empty. Picture one angler paying another angler $10 for one much-used, silver-colored fishing plug, simply because it or anything like it was unavailable anywhere within fifty miles. Picture bait and tackle manufacturers—of which Michigan has many—working around the clock to solve the sudden need for massive quantities of equipment. Picture a man with a downstate license driving up to a Lake Michigan launching ramp near Frankfort. On his car is a 18-foot boat on a trailer, with a 40 horse outboard attached, all right off the showroom floor at a total cost of around $2,500. Picture a commercial fisherman making three times his normal income, without ever setting a net, simply by selling ice and smoking chubs for fishermen. He even made money *cleaning* salmon, that for anglers too tired or so new to the game that they didn't know how. Restaurants opened earlier and closed later. Bars were jammed. Additional parking lots and launching ramps were hurriedly bulldozed into use. A full-fledged charter boat industry popped into existance, almost overnight. One town got mad at another town for claiming the title "Coho Capital". Motels and hotels in the area, normally dull stuff after Labor Day, kept "No Vacancy" signs blazing.

The fish, meanwhile, often seemed unaware and uninterested in all these frantic attempts to draw their attention. They would suddenly appear 50 feet offshore in lake Michigan, idling in bunches of 50 or 100, causing waves of apoplexy among on-lookers. They were sometimes seen splashing along the surface of the lake like bands of porpoises. At other times they struck every plug, lure, spoon, and spinner in sight. There were often times, however, when they either weren't present or weren't interested. Manistee anglers then explained that the school was at Frankfort while Frankfort anglers said it was at Manistee. There was in those fishless days a lot of learning taking place.

But for every day without fish, two exciting days might be counted, when the take was often phenomenal. Most of the cohos weighed from 12 to 20 pounds with an average of about 16 pounds. They were spectacular on the line, making long runs, jumping, tail dancing on the surface. When they first began to hit, back around Labor Day, some anglers mistakenly used smallish lures. These came back from underwater assault with all their hooks straightened—if they came back at all. Anglers content at the time with 100 yards of line often found themselves with empty reels, burned thumbs, and broken drage—and the fish gone. As the season advanced, eight-pound test line was changed for 12, and 12 fo 20. There was a scramble for stiffer poles and heavy-duty reels.

Anglers, as might be expected, were ecstatic. Photos of them wreathed in smiles, hoisting huge silvery fish, appeared in newspapers all over the Great Lakes region. A fairly typical scene of family joy occurred at twilight one evening when a small boat buzzed right up on the sandy beach at Manistee. A man in the stern jumped out, reached back into the boat, and lifted one of the huge fish as high as he could. Down the beach came his pretty young wife, running pellmell. At water's edge, she leaped into her husband's arms and fish, wife, and fisherman all went reeling happily backward into the surf. He had come all the way from Pennsylvania and said he had been thinking about that fish for six months. Was it worth it? "You bet it was worth it," he grinned. In another case, a man and his wife and two young children were out in a small boat. Suddenly the wife—obviously newly converted to fishing—found herself attached to eighteen pounds of furious salmon. She shrieked and yelled. Her husband hovered over her, pouring out advice. Others boats drew close and shouted encouragement. The two children cheered as she gained line, moaned as she lost. The battle see-sawed back and forth for fifteen minutes before the husband finally scooped the fish into the boat with one mighty swoosh of the net. Cheers went up all around as husband gave wife a bear hug that nearly tipped over the boat.

Not all was domestic harmony, however. At one crowded boat launching ramp, a man and his wife arrived to launch their boat. They were in violent argument when they arrived, and the argument continued in loud tones all the time they were launching the boat, parking the car, stowing the gear, and until they had gone right out of earshot down the river. "There was never any doubt that they were both going fishing," one observer noted later, "but we weren't sure they'd come back together."

As it turned out they did return later that day still arguing loudly. Again the argument continued as the boat was hoisted onto the trailer, the tackle stowed in the car, and the car driven off.

The excitement was too much for some, however. Several persons died of heart attacks. Over-anxious fishermen clashed at boat launching sites, or when trolling lines tangled, or they fought for places to park cars and trailers. Out on the lake many small boats were swamped and occupants were fished from the water by other boats nearby—a grim warning of events to come.

Sadly, when the storm came on September 23, hundreds of boats were caught offshore and scores were wrecked in six-foot waves that piled up under 30-40 mile winds. At least seven fishermen drowned and that tragedy brought inquests and public hearings and demands that "fishermen not be allowed on the big lake in unsafe boats." Despite the deep and justifiable concern, many cooler heads have noted that safety at sea will never be absolute and will always remain a matter of degree. A year ago, a lone sailor named Robert Manry crossed the North Atlantic Ocean in a 13-foot sailboat, the same ocean that has buried countless large ocean-going vessels. Similarly, in the storm that claimed those seven fishermen off Frankfort, there were dozens of others who were nearly lost but somehow came through. Many rather large fishing boats were wrecked, while many small ones came through unscathed. Who's to judge between safe and unsafe boats? Nonetheless the tragedy of that storm predicted in numerous public warnings by Coast Guard, sheriff's offices, Conservation Department, and other agencies—will not soon be forgotten, and hopefully will not be repeated. Many safety measures can be publicized and some can be enforced. Perhaps as the salmon fever abates with experience, better sense will emerge among fishermen.

If there was tragedy, there was also comedy. When a man arrived at a boat launching ramp with an unusually large boat and trailer—all obviously brand new—others stood aside while he attempted to back the monster into the water. Five times he jack-knifed car into trailer before asking an onlooker if he'd help. The onlooker took over and eased the boat into the water. When the owner stood aside, puzzled by the problem, others freed the boat from the trailer and tied it to the dock. The owner climbed aboard his new boat and someone cast him adrift. For five minutes he floated freely in the channel before calling to shore from under the canopy.

"Hey," he yelled, "does anyone know how to start this thing?"

Another onlooker rowed out, showed him gear shift, throttle, and starter button. That was a mistake. As soon as he got it started, he ran it ashore, throttle wide open.

Another fisherman, with a big coho on his line, stumbled about in the Platte River trying desperately to coax the fish within range of landing net. Intent on this, he failed to notice that a news photographer in a small helicopter was easing down on top of him. When helicopter and angler were separated by only a few dozen feet, the angler suddenly looked up, dumb with shock at seeing the plane so close. The fish pole went in one direction as the angler dived for shore, which he missed. When the helicopter circled for another set of photos, the drenched fisherman scrambled to retrieve his pole, caught on a log. The fish was gone. He was so mad that when the helicopter angled down a second time, he threw his landing net at it.

Chapter 3: The Restriction of the U.S. Fisheries

The chief of the Michigan Fish Division wrote in 1967 of his vision of the 1975 sport fishery. It was a scene of year-round angling, ample fish of many varieties, summer charter boats, and prospering lakeside communities. There was going to be a price tag and commercial fishermen should have been left with no illusions as to who was going to pay that price and what it was going to be:

". . . As the sport fishery builds in the Great Lakes, we can expect that conflicts of interest will require solution. Two problems loom on the horizon: namely, the extensive use of gill nets and the rapidly increasing fishery for the industrial production of fish meal.

Gill nets are used to fish whitefish, herring, chubs, and other valuable species. Unfortunately, they also take the game fish. To avoid a serious mortality of trout and salmon, additional controls on gill net fishing appear to be essential." (17)

". . . Our policy will be to rationally settle conflicts, but to generally encourage the growth of the sports fishery. At the same time, the commercial fishery must become more selective by taking fish which are not of value to the sport fishery. Too, the industry can be assisted by necessary controls to maximize profits for those few dedicated men now involved." (18)

These concepts were not restricted to Michigan but, as majority stockholder on the U.S. side of the Great Lakes, its influence was considerable. Other states were equally enthusiastic and notice was served on the fishermen that their role in harvesting was to be regarded as secondary to the recreational interests. Restrictions were viewed with enthusiasm by sports groups and growing alarm by commercial fishermen. Various state agencies tended to reveal their programs on a step by step basis. The methods fell into several categories:

1. Closure of fisheries by species.
2. Limited entry.
3. Restriction of maximum fish length.
4. Restriction of net mesh sizes.
5. Restriction of net types.
6. Geographic restriction.
7. Fish quotas.

Michigan

Michigan's efforts to control commercial fishing came in four general stages. The first step was the movement for limited entry. Basically, it required that a man have fished 50 days in two of the preceding three years in order to retain a license. The stated purpose was the elimination of part time fishermen, but there were charges of inequity from fishermen who claimed that for various sound reasons they had been prevented from meeting this requirement. One of the bitterest complaints came over the issue of whether catch records, submitted by the fishermen during the years being used to determine eligibility, formed a sound basis for judging the number of fishing days. Some fishermen had adopted the habit of combining up to a week's effort in a single report. In all cases where diputes arose over this issue, the Department is reported to have relented. (19) The Department denies arbitrary enforcement of the limited entry requirements and, in fact, states that efforts were made to evaluate each disputed case fairly. Passions ran so high on either side of this issue that it is difficult to come to any conclusion other than the statistical fact that licenses were reduced.

The Department maintains that the part-time fisheries were a detriment to the economic health of the industry. One estimate states that in 1967, three to four hundred fishermen were grossing an average of ten to twelve thousand dollars apiece annually, while by 1977 approximately 140 licensees were grossing around seventy thousand dollars apiece. (It is important to note that we are here speaking of *gross* income. The fisherman has the considerable cost of maintaining boats, crews, and equipment). The Department feels that limited entry greatly increased the stability of the industry.

Others dispute that limited entry has solved any problems:

"I don't think that any legislature has the right to put a man out of business because it doesn't think that man is making enough money. If he is overfishing, then it is the prerogative of the legislature to take action. They are charged with protecting the resources of the state.

"When they were trying to put some of the little fishermen out of business I told them, 'This doesn't make sense. First of all, you're worried about this guy because he's only making $4,000 a year. He lives in the upper peninsula, his truck is his only means of transportation and he drives it to church or wherever he goes. He lives in a small house and probably heats it with wood he cuts from his own lot. He eats a lot of fish and trades some of it for groceries. He may own one good suit but, hell, he's happy. You're going to put him out of business because he's not making enough money, but he's not on welfare and that is where you are going to put him.'

"So you take fifteen fishermen who are making

Naubinway, Mich.

$5,000 a year and put them out of business, leaving one fisherman who has the equipment to catch $75,000 worth of fish. You deprive fifteen people of a livelihood and turn it over to one who is probably already making enough to go to Florida in the winter and send all his kids to college. Limited entry is not the answer." (20)

The second phase of control came with the establishment of zone management. Areas of Michigan-controlled waters were divided into sport, recreational, commercial, and rehabilitation zones. The sport zones were to be reserved for sport fishermen except for selective harvesting of food and rough fish. The rehabilitation zone was to remain open to impounding gear but largely closed to gill nets. In the commercial zones all conventional gear was to be allowed. The vast majority of Michigan's lake water areas were placed in the rehabilitation or sport zones. Nonetheless, the commercial zones contained

Manistique, Mich.

many of the traditional areas of high production commercial fishing and, ''Their establishment will allow commercial fishing to continue without a greatly reduced catch.'' (21)

Commercial fishermen again protested and felt they were being forced into narrowly confined areas to (a) deliberately increase harvest pressures so that stocks would be depleted and (b) create conflicts among fishermen. Again, the Department felt the move was a rational attempt to allocate areas among user groups to *prevent* conflicts.

The third phase of control was spread over the entire period we are discussing and was aimed at controlling the catch of individual species. The perch was banned from the commercial catch in 1970, and incidental catch of coho also ended that year. In 1973 the walleye was given 'sport' status and in 1975 the chub fishery in Lake Michigan was closed because of declining stocks. In the same year quotas were placed on chub harvests in Lake Superior.

The fourth, and most controversial, phase involved various efforts to abolish the gill net. In 1971 small mesh gill nets were banned from Lake Huron except in Saginaw Bay. In 1972 the Department appeared to have banned all gill nets. A four-year period was allowed for conversion to impoundment gear. This directive was applied to all of the productive shallow water fisheries under Michigan jurisdiction.

The fury generated by the use of the gill net deserves closer examination. It has become an issue of considerable passion with a number of sport fishermen who claim:

1. The net is unselective; it catches a great variety of species and sizes prohibited to the commercial fisherman.
2. The net is a killer; fish are caught by the gills and die before the net is lifted.
3. The net interferes with sport fishing and recreational boating by limiting access to bay and harbor areas.
4. The use of modern materials has made the net far too effective and increased the likelihood of overfishing.

These arguments generally conclude with the demand that the dangerous gill net be banned and fishermen be required to use other gear.

Commercial fishermen believe that this line of reasoning is sustained only by a total ignorance of the gill net and how it works. Their arguments:

1. In certain seasons and sections of the lakes the net is extremely selective.
2. It is the only net that can be used in the vast majority of Great Lakes waters.
3. It is the gear of choice of biologists and researchers investigating the status of fish stocks. Extensively used by these groups, fish are caught, tagged, and released. These

scientists are generally interested in studying the biology and behavior of *living* fish and some fish have been captured as many as five times.

4. The net is six to eight feet high and rests on the bottom of the lake. It is limited by mesh size and location to catch a certain size of fish. Smaller fish swim through it and larger fish swim around or over it. There are often several hundred feet of water over the net.

5. The amount of cotton and linen netting was virtually unrestricted while the amount of synthetic netting is controlled in many places. Would not control of the amount of netting, placement of nets, quotas, or seasonal restrictions more selectively accomplish the goals of fish management?

I have tried to present a summarized version of the rational arguments presented on either side. In fact, the argument generated little rational discussion. Fish politics are largely the politics of emotion. When Wisconsin was pressured to follow the Michigan lead, the State investigated the whole gill net matter. University of Wisconsin biologist Ross Horrall reached some conclusions similar to those of the commercial fishermen:

" 'For one thing 95 percent of Lake Michigan cannot be fished with pound nets. . . . Both practically and legally, they can't be used in water deeper than 80 feet, and this restricts their use to just six or eight weeks of the year, when species like the whitefish are in shallow water.''

Furthermore, Horrall points out, the gill nets can be very selective. The mesh size of the net and where it is placed can generally dictate what is caught.

"A few tenths of an inch difference in mesh size can eliminate a whole species or size of fish,'' Horrall explains.'' (22)

This view was seconded by Ron Poff of the Wisconsin DNR. He stated that the sportsmen might not have considered the practicality or cost of their proposals. Horrall and Poff both felt that the sportsmen would be better off concentrating their energies on problems common to all fishermen, notably the growing chemical menace:

" 'Unless PCB discharges into the lakes are stopped, it could spell disaster for all the fishery,' says Horrall.

In their newspaper, the Northeastern Wisconsin Great Lakes Sport Fishermen ask: Is Lake Michigan to become a wasteland?

'Perhaps,' says Horrall, 'they should give a little more thought to that question.' '' (23)

Ironically, Minnesota allows *sport* fishermen to use gill nets to catch whitefish and tullibees (lake herring) in inland lakes during a restricted season. Anyone holding a Minnesota resident license is permitted to use two of the one-hundred-foot gill nets upon payment of a dollar fee for each net. The nets must be set in water less than six feet deep and picked daily to guarantee freshness and allow for release of any game fish that may have been caught. The nets must not be tended between sundown and sunrise but there are no limits on the number of fish that may be taken. It is stated that few walleyes enter a legally set net. An obviously ardent practitioner of this late fall netting comments on the nature of the sport:

"Those who worry about the 'sport' in whitefish and tullibee netting might wonder about the sport in pursuing a walleye with a laboratory consisting of contour maps, electronic depth indicators, temperature meters, thousands of dollars worth of boat and motor equipment, and an arsenal of advice and 'secrets' from the pros on how to murder 'em. Perhaps the harvest of bountiful rough fish for a few cold days before freeze-up, by a handful of dedicated fishermen, is more sporty than those scientific angling ventures which in many waters have cut the average size of walleyes in half and have made it necessary for some guides, even the so-called pros, to travel across three counties to find a fish.'' (24)

It must be stressed that Michigan shouldered some of the economic consequences of its decision to eliminate the gill net. In 1974 the Michigan Legislature voted $1.5 million to compensate fishermen affected by the state's policy. Governor William Milliken cut the appropriation in an attempt to balance the 1974–75 budget, and instructed the DNR not to implement the gill net ban until such time as funds were available. In addition, those who were converting to impoundment gear were given until June 30, 1975, at which time their progress was to be evaluated. Milliken stated that his office would personally review each case of an individual denied an extension. The Department was clearly instructed on this point: ''. . . The Department is to act with reasonableness and leniency regarding these cases.'' (25)

The DNR estimated that 86 gill net licenses would eventually be affected by the compensation. The appropriated money was paid to fishermen operating in three categories: large mesh, small mesh, and those combining the two methods. A further delay was caused by a ruling of the Attorney General which stated that the legislature should pass a bill stating exactly the terms under which the money would be paid. Since that might have taken another year to work through the legislature, a method was found that released the funds through a ''stipulation and consent'' order. The actual formula for compensation was based on the total value of fish caught in gill nets during the license periods of 1971, 1972, and 1973. An individual's cash portion was based on a pro-rata share of the

Fish Creek, Wis.

total value of the reported catch, estimated to be 83 percent of his average for the three-year period. Under this formula payments ranged from $200 to over $70,000. The impact of these payments varied:

''In some cases it was sufficiently adequate to permit a person who wanted to stay in business to convert his boat and buy new gear—in very few cases. In other cases it was a substantial help toward doing that. In the case of people who were getting up in years, it was a pretty good retirement.

''But we then get into a group of people who had not been fishing too hard in those few years on which the payment was based. It was certainly not enough for them to convert or retire. These were the people caught in the squeeze.'' (26)

Illinois

Illinois ended commercial fishing of planted salmon and trout by prohibiting, "all commercial salmonid catch." This ended the policy of allowing an incidental catch which had permitted fishermen to take salmonids as a percentage of their unregulated catch of other species. Trout and salmon were being reserved to sport fishermen throughout the Great Lakes either as a matter of policy or because the fish showed increasing signs of being dangerously contaminated.

The entire matter of commercial fishing was solved swiftly by Illinois. The state DOC (Department of Conservation) was motivated by a number of factors. There was a serious concern about the future of chub stocks. Sex ratio changes, similar to those that accompanied the collapse of the fish in Lake Ontario, were occurring in Lake Michigan. There was also a great deal of pressure from surrounding jurisdictions to put controls on commercial fishing. Finally, the legislature was being pressured by an extremely powerful sport lobby. The DOC studied the situation and concluded that only a very limited number of fish could be safely harvested. Based on these studies, the Department determined that there were to be three active full time fishery crews selected through a lottery procedure. In order to be eligible for the lottery, the individual fisherman had to meet eight requirements. Among them, he was to have fished full time in at least one of the three preceding years, own a vessel of at least five tons, possess at least 6,000 feet of legal gill nets, generally retain all necessary licenses, and, if selected, permit fishery biologists to obtain data from his catches.

Fourteen of the 48 licensed fishermen met the criteria. The three selected fishermen (with their crews) were to be allowed an assessment/rehabilitation quota of 10,000 pounds of chubs, and 137,000 pounds of yellow perch per year. The limited Illinois coastline is almost completely contained within the Chicago urban area. The vast numbers of sportsmen in this region were an overwhelming political force. The allocation struggle was a close contest in other places but in Illinois the commercial fishermen were brushed aside. The 34 part time operators were simply eliminated without a chance to participate in the lottery. (27) There was no suggestion of compensation from the legislature in Springfield for the eleven full-time fishermen who were to be eliminated by the drawing.

This policy was naturally challenged in the courts and, after the lottery, two of the fishermen and a trade association sought a temporary restraining order pending a full hearing on the constitutionality of the administrative order. The DOC modified its position prior to the hearing and stated that all previously licensed fishermen could retain their licenses and were free to fish for any species except chub, perch, or trout, which were the species of commercial value. Significantly, one of the parties to the suit was one of the lottery winners. He stated that it would be impossible for him to operate on his third of the chub and perch quotas. Pointing out that perch involved seasonal operation and that he could not maintain a crew on a seasonal basis, he concluded ". . . that unless more liberal rules were enacted, his investment of more than $100,000 wouldn't be worth twenty-five cents on the dollar." (28) The other fishermen party to the suit stated that it was impossible to simply continue fishing operations for smelt, alewives, suckers, and carp. This contention was backed by the trade association member who stated there was a very limited market for such rough fish.

The Department called Ed Brown of the U.S. Fish and Wildlife Service to testify on the current condition of the chub stocks: "In cross examination, Mr. Brown admitted that there were a number of factors that had brought chub stocks to the present low level and that it was possible that the chubs would continue to decline even if commercial fishing was discontinued.'' (29) The Department felt that this possibility made it even more important to give the chub stocks a chance to recover by eliminating the bulk of the fishing pressure.

Throughout the case, the fishermen pleaded for a share of the planted lake trout in order to provide them with an opportunity to remain in business. The DOC pointed out that commercial harvests of trout couldn't be sold because of contamination and that a commercial trout harvest was inconsistent with rehabilitation goals. In addition, the state was able to counter that lake trout were off limits to commercial *and* sport fishermen, a position then unique to any lake jurisdiction. The injunction was denied and, by the end of September 1975, appeals had been exhausted and both the quota and three-man limited entry fishery were being enforced. Early the following year, the Illinois Department of Conservation reiterated its position regarding the commercial fishery. There was a small change in the attitude toward the sport fishermen, however, and money changed hands in ports around the Great Lakes.

"Last year the Illinois Department of Conservation banned the taking of lake trout from Lake Michigan by both sport and commercial fishermen. When the regulation was announced, several fishermen and dealers took bets that this regulation would not stand up under the pressure of the sportsmen and that the ban on sport fishing would be lifted within a year. The ban has been lifted and sportsmen may now take three trout per day. It's time to pay off the bets.'' (30)

Ohio

"Less than 30 years ago the U.S. catch represented about three-fourths of the lakewide landings; today the fraction has decreased to one-fourth and continues to decline. This decrease may be pleasing to some American sportsmen who fail to recognize the potential and importance of the U.S. commercial fishery; yet it is not only unfortunate, but also unnecessary, that the U.S. fishing industry of Lake Erie does not now produce an equitable share of the basic food resource available to it.'' (31)

Nowhere is the contrast in jurisdictional attitudes more apparent than in Lake Erie. The U.S. commercial fishery continues to decline while on the north shore the Ontario fisheries prosper. One government limits and the other encourages commercial fishing.

The key to understanding this situation lies in an examination of the population densities along the two shores. The massively developed Ohio coast includes the urban areas of Cleveland and Toledo and a population hungry for sport opportunities, a hunger not likely to be satisfied by the 223,000 acres of inland state waters. As a result, the state's 2.25 million acres of Erie waters have provided a vastly expanded outlet for these recreational desires. It is estimated that 32 percent of all licensed sport fishermen have utilized Lake Erie at one point.

The relatively lightly populated northern shore, by contrast, is dominated by the most intensive of the Canadian Great Lake fisheries. Here, an extremely profitable industry has moved beyond the traditionally limited operations of the single fishermen to trawl and processing procedures which supply an increasingly profitable export market—the United States.

In 1974, Ohio moved to restrict the approximately 300 commercial licenses then held. All persons who held licenses at the time were included in the new fishery. Criteria for retaining a license under limited entry included condition of boat and equipment, years of experience, ports of entry utilized, posting of a $1,000 bond, previous harvest records, residency of at least six months, and history of fishing regulation violation. Under this system, licenses were reduced to slightly more than 130 in 1975 and have stabilized around that figure. State DNR spokesmen have pointed out that many of these licenses were not even held by part-time fishermen, and in fact were only utilized occasionally. Increased fees drove additional people from the fishery.

Remaining commercial licenses have been recognized as a valuable property to a greater extent that in most other lakeside jurisdictions:

"An interesting point on licensing commercial fishermen was made at the recent meeting of the Ohio Commercial Fishermen's Association when it was announced that a license could be held in escrow up to two years. Fishermen who might find it impossible to operate because of illness, low production making it impractical, or a number of like reasons would have their licenses protected. Licenses can also be passed from father to son without any difficulty. This is a system that could well be considered in other states where a fisherman can only be licensed if he has had an active license in the preceding year." (32)

The state has also imposed a wide variety of geographic restrictions. Some are designed to prevent conflicts with nearshore sport fishermen. Certain other zones of high spawning concentration have been closed to commercial fishing. Walleye, sauger, and the endangered blue pike, chub, sturgeon, and whitefish are prohibited to the commercial harvest. In addition, individual operators pay a fourteen cent per pound royalty on the amount of their catch of catfish, white bass, walleye, and yellow perch that exceeds one half their previous year's catch for that species. There are also the many mesh size restrictions aimed at increasing the selectivity of the gear used.

In 1974 the Lake Erie jurisdictions created a quota management system under the auspices of the Great Lakes Fisheries Commission. A portion of the lakewide quota set for certain species is divided among the political units based on the area of the lake under the control of each of these units. The arrangement is voluntary and the quota may be accepted or rejected as the jurisdiction sees fit. The allocation of the quota between user groups within each jurisdiction is the sole decision of the individual province or state. Ontario allocates some of its quota to commercial fishermen. Ohio and Michigan made no allocation. This is the hottest item dividing state resource managers and commercial fishermen. A 1977 GAO Report stated, ". . . Michigan and Ohio had comprehensive data on walleye in western Lake Erie that showed the recreational catch would probably be considerably less than the allowable harvest. However, the two states did not allocate any walleye to commercial fishermen because they did not wish to risk damage to the recreational fishery." (33) Ohio DNR spokesmen report that the recreational fishermen took 91 percent of the state's quota in 1977. This is not "considerably less" than the suggested allowable harvest.

As in some other states, the rule making procedure of the Division of Wildlife is essentially removed from the legislature. Proposed regulations, generally based on field data, are presented to the Chief of the Division of Wildlife. If he recommends the regulation to the Wildlife Council, a public hearing is held where anyone wishing to testify for or against the proposal may do so. Later on the eight-member Council considers the public testimony, plus the technical data, and acts on the proposal. The Council must approve the regulation in order for it to become law.

There is also a Commercial Fishermen's Advisory Committee composed of five commercial fishermen and three employees from the Division of Wildlife. This Committee is responsible for developing a method of apportioning quotas within the commercial fishery and although possessing no official powers, allows the industry a direct line of communication with the management agency. As with appointees to the Wildlife Council, there are provisions to prevent the domination of the Committee by any one political party.

One of the strongest criticisms leveled at state fish management is the inadequacy of the data based on sport fishing. How much is caught? Where is it caught? What is the overall impact of sport fishing on individual species? It is notable then that Ohio has received high praise from other jurisdictions for its recent efforts to answer these questions.

The state has completed what is likely the most extensive creel census ever attempted on the Great Lakes:

> "A direct contact sport angler survey was conducted along the 240 mile Ohio shoreline of Lake Erie and on two major tributary rivers. Fourteen clerks surveyed eight hours per day, five days per week, on randomly selected hours and days. Nearly 60,000 anglers were interviewed between the dates of 1 January and 31 October, 1977." (33b)

The lake was divided into various districts, and winter, spring, and summer sport efforts were examined. Computers helped to evaluate and process the results of the surveys. Areas of greatest sport pressure were identified along with composition of the catch in each season. The overwhelmingly desired species were walleye and perch. One of the most dramatic findings illustrated the recovery and popularity of the walleye on Erie. The charter catch of walleye increased 273 percent by weight in 1977, while angler hours spent fishing for walleye increased from 14,660 in 1975 to 90,640 in 1977.

The number of hours fished by each angler and his success were calculated, and it was found that 1.57 fish were caught per angler hour. The figure for charter boats was a surprising 2.09. Most fishermen, naturally, were hoping to catch certain fish in certain seasons. A good portion didn't care what they caught. The survey of summer anglers revealed that while 49 percent were after yellow perch, the next largest group, 23 percent, were fishing for "anything that bites."

Ohio's major position in the Lake Erie commercial fishery of the south shore is underscored by the fact that the state accounted for close to 90 percent of the U.S. catch. The dominant Canadian position is highlighted by the fact that the Ohio catch was only 20 percent of the *lakewide* harvest. Thus we have seen a complete reversal of the situation that prevailed in the early years of the fishery.

Interview with Dr. Wayne Tody

Deputy Director, Michigan Department of Natural Resources

"Our position is, and will be for a long time to come, that depletion is the primary issue and that it is the primary duty of resource managers to prevent depletion. Whoever uses the resource is going to do so under controls so that stocks are not threatened as in the past. That is *not* negotiable. If we err, it will be on the tough side.

The allocation question is just the opposite. Once the matter of depletion is settled, you can argue all you want to over who cuts the pie and for what share. That's fair game. Sport fishermen can contest with commercial fishermen. Within the commerical fishery, the Indians can contest with the non-Indians, but the bottom line of the conservation issue cannot be compromised. Whenever it is, there is trouble. We may be in error on what is required to meet the conservation ethic, but we will aim for it with the best of our understanding. Maybe, just maybe, somebody will realize the value of optimum yield, the greatest value to mankind."

"If you criticize the decision we made on the commerical fishery as having been so abrupt as to exclude consideration of other alternatives, you are not on solid ground.

The shift in the sport policy was tied to lamprey control and alewife abundance. The key species in early thinking was the steelhead, traditionally a sport fish in Michigan. The idea developed of putting greater emphasis on this fish as it came back in the wake of lamprey control. At the time policy was mainly directed at steelhead, and possibly lake trout.

Then came the realization that we had too small a basket. The steelhead is an anadromous species. The alewife was preventing reproduction of all species in the lake. We thought, 'Let's get a fish like the steelhead, perhaps striped bass or Pacific salmon, and aim them mainly at the sport fishery.' At that point there was no thinking to greatly restrict the commercial gill net fishery.

The decision to hold the lake trout back from the commercial fishery was a hard-fought decision, both within and without the Department. After the lake trout had been planted, some of the biologists told us we were going to have trouble re-establishing salmonids in Lake Michigan, or in any of the other Great Lakes, unless something was done to regulate the gill net fishery. The prediction was made that the stocked lake trout would be annihilated before they reached spawning age. At the extreme, the operators were running a hundred thousand feet of gill net a day for six days, and then going back and running the first gang. My God! I couldn't believe it. There were even nets set across each other. I began to listen.

The next year we ran a research fishery and asked for voluntary reports on the incidental catch. In addition, we had a field monitoring program. To make a long story short, there were sixty thousand lake trout involved in the samples, probably at least a hundred thousand by the time we eliminated the hanky-panky. At ten percent of the stocking rate, figuring any mortality at all, the biologists appeared correct. The fish would be annihilated before they were six or seven years old. That is when the gill net war started here. We decided they had to be restricted, and that led to the Zone Management Plan, where we designated the productive whitefish grounds for gill netting, and most of the remainder was placed in a rehabilitation category.

Our decision didn't come overnight. One event led to another and it wasn't all part of one grand plan."

"We had a number of options at the time of the salmon planting. The option favored by the commercial fishermen and federal officials was the industrial use of alewives. Remember, our objective was control of the alewife. Everybody knew what was happening. From the data before us, we could see that from 1962 to 1964 the alewife had increased from twenty to sixty percent of the biomass of Lake Michigan. We had that data, as did the federal government. We were absolutely convinced the alewives were going to dominate the lake. From my perspective, narrow-minded people just looked at the alewife as a fish, in terms of tonnage, fish protein concentrate, and oil. The commercial fishermen were after subsidies. The federal government was lining up massive skimming gear to get the surplus off the beaches so the industrial fishery could get on top of the situation. They tried to pressure us into that alternative.

Our thinking was just the opposite. If we were going to control the sea lamprey, stock lake trout and steelheads, why not use the forage base? Why not convert them into salmonids and game fish of large size? Why not convert them into predatory fish and give first crack at them to the sport fishermen.

So there were the two alternatives. We could have played it conservatively, just followed the program with lake trout and some combination with an industrial fishery. You could have cut it any way you wanted. We said, 'Hell, if they're going to push so strongly for an industrial fishery—and they were already planning processing plants—we'll go for the sport fishery.'

This brought us head to head with the federal government. It got pretty vulgar at times. Director McMullen fully understood the sport potential. At the same time the commercial
98

possibilities were being eyed by operators from as far away as the Gulf coast. We had all kinds of takers. It was the breaking point. We were threatened politically and the decision went to the Commission. They decided to back us up. In the end we didn't buy the industrial alewife option. If there was a surplus, yes, it could be utilized commercially. But there was no way we were going to allow industrial domination of a needed forage base."

"We had a very nerve-wracking period as we waited for the first planted salmon to return to the streams. We had no facilities designed particularly for the salmon project, and we had used slack trout hatchery space for the original planting. Before the first spawners reached the streams, we had raised a million dollars for piers and egg-taking facilities. We really had our necks on the line.

In addition, many biologists, excepting a few on the West coast, thought that the planting wouldn't take. I had researched the literature on the subject, however, and it all fit together. It was worth a gamble. I never understood those who claimed it was impossible. The physiology was there. The salmon was a fresh water fish and in Japan some of them never go to the sea. The real question was whether you could duplicate their spawning regime and get good, viable eggs."

"In order to get a handle on the situation, we broke it down into large and small mesh. Small mesh gill net fishing for chubs can be done rather selectively and has a limited effect on lake trout. With large mesh, however, you're going to have depletion of lake trout stocks. Our data supports this rather conclusively. Once again it relates to strategy. First we had limited entry, and then we forced conversion to trap nets.

This is a controversial issue in commercial ranks, and they make some good points. The fishermen know that it is an expensive gear and there is controversy in the commercial fishing community itself over it. Fishermen who use traps like them. Those who don't question whether, in an uncertain world, they should get into an expensive gear. There is also the question of available grounds for trap nets. As far as marketability, the trap produces a fresher product and has a better retail reception. The gill net fisherman doesn't want this pointed out. Thus there are many subtleties to this question.

Again, our strategy is to take conversion on the whitefish fishery to an end point, where all convert. We're willing to do some research on trawls and purse seines. But the large mesh gill net issue we'll take to an end point. We still feel that way and we will appeal or do whatever is necessary to take it to that ultimate resolution. I don't see how we can compromise. The gill net is the cheaper gear, easier to fish, and we'll be right back where we started.

As you narrow the number of gillnetters from six hundred to thirty, obviously you reduce impact. Indian fisheries start with Jondreau and has built up to the point where there are 155 cards issued and some fifty operations. Whitefish Bay is no longer adequate for their fishery. Keweenaw Bay is no longer adequate. They've been fished down. To support the Indian activity, their operators have to go elsewhere. Is that depletion or not?

Philosophically, you can come at all this from two points. You can spend your time proving the horse was stolen, but that doesn't do you a lot of good. Or, you can lock the barn door before it is stolen. In rational management you try to take the latter approach: argue depletion before it wipes you out. We've seen the results of the first approach for over a hundred years. With it, you write the obituaries and say the hell with it. Depletion, or the threat of it, is just as much a problem as it ever was. It is a very strong possibility.

We're still in the Dark Ages until we get to quotas or area management. This is where the Fishery Division's new Task Force comes in. I tried to get something like that started years ago, but could never succeed because I couldn't get the support of the commercial fishery. My rule was, 'I have a duty to control you—to prevent depletion—but also have a duty to help you build a bigger, better, and stronger fishery, but so do you. You recommend the regulatory regime and we'll sure as hell help you impliment it, but without your help, we're not going to do it. We'll wait for you.' That is the point we're at now. I think the responsible element of the commercial fishery sees the handwriting on the wall. They really want franchise type fishing in which we contract with each operator. With it, we can get down to some fine points.

You may not believe this, but we have at times considered allowing a take of game fish for local markets. Besides the profit involved, it would augment the tourist industry. Wouldn't it be nice to go into some restaurant and buy a brown trout? But it *has* to be a carefully controlled quota fishery which is no threat to the sport fishery. That is the final chapter in this story. We've gone through an era of horrible depletion in the lakes, similar to the depletion of forests in their watersheds. We've gone through an era of realization and crudeness. I admit we overkilled the commercial fishery. We had to in order to allow rehabilitation and recovery of fish stocks. Then we had a long search to find a common ground. Now we're entering a new era. In a few years we'll be there.''

(Michigan protested the planting of Lake Trout in Whitefish Bay by the federal government. This came about after Michigan had decided to suspend its planting activities when Indian fishing expanded into the Bay. Why such a protest against the planting of lake trout?)

''Whitefish Bay has been claimed by the Indians. We don't recognize that claim but to avoid violence three or four years ago we had a policy of non-enforcement up there and more or less agreed to a hands-off attitude in the area. The Indians proceeded to take over the Bay with their own laws. We don't think their conservation code is sound. It is not going to prevent depletion, but it is in place. The fish were rather quickly removed from Whitefish Bay. You can say the impact is minor but that is simply not true. They're capable of taking whatever is availalbe, and more than what is available. We're not stocking trout to maintain that type of commercial fishery.

To meet the goal of self-sustaining trout populations, we stock some offshore reefs. Under the protocol of the Great Lakes Fisheries Commission, fish from the federal Jordan River Hatchery are allocated among the jurisdictions, but *we* decide where they are to be planted. It is a state management, jurisdictional issue and we're sensitive on the point. When you get down to toying with our jurisdictional prerogatives, I guess we do get irrational. It is not so much the issue as the jurisdictional principle involved.

We have a lot of contact with the federal people, most of it very friendly and candid. I am familiar with the principle of supremacy. You have the question of allocation of resources whether it be in forestry, fisheries, minerals, or energy. The federal government has a jurisdictional urge in these matters. They don't think that we fifty states are responsible enough to allocate the resources. Off the record, some of the federal people will admit that.

In some areas, they may have the better argument. With Fish and Wildlife, we should have the jurisdiction, and we intend to fight for it. We'll be reasonable with them, but they aren't going to come in and take over management without a fight. Over the years many, many battles have been fought over a number of issues: national parks, national forests, and licensing to name a few. There is nothing new about this struggle.

Generally the federal government respects the state's rights in the area of Fish and Wildlife management. With other topics, their view is different and they don't have the respect built up over many years. We have to be on guard. It has a lot more to do with this issue than it does with the Indians.

The Indian dispute is an interesting and very complex one. We don't feel the Indians have treaty rights. They do and the Feds do. They say they have them, have been denied them, and are going to start exercising them now. It raises the issue of sovereignty and brings us to conflict. Sooner or later, someone was bound to go to the courts. The federal government has chosen to sue us.''

''The press likes to deal with things in a spectacular manner. They often goad the participants in a dispute to stupid moves, or try to pressure you to do things so they can write about them. Look at the matter of the PBB's here. Who was responsible for whipping up that hysteria? You get so angry at those people you could throttle every one of them. I am not very impressed with the objectivity of the press.''

''I wouldn't worry about the pink salmon. I don't expect them to be much of a sport fish. They may build up. In fact, I expect them to and if they do we'll turn them over to the commercial fishery. When they are in deep water they are still an excellent food fish.''

''In the past, the Department of Conservation was almost completely dependent on sportsmen's license fees for Fish and Wildlife programs. That speaks for itself. Michigan United Conservation Clubs does, basically, represent the state's sportsmen so they have a lot of influence. Times have changed and fish and game receipts amount to less than twenty percent of our budget.

Nonetheless, they are an important clientele group and we don't like to be at odds with them. People power is people power. We are more responsive to the general public than to one small user group. Yes, they have a lot of influence, but not as much as they used to have.''

''Our management approach, philosophy, and resource is different than Canada's. We don't have the hinterlands. We don't have the great northern areas to develop. Our priorities will continue to differ. Our hatchery attitudes on natural reproduction will differ. I'd say those are the normal differences between two jurisdictions with different basic makeups. I see us, however, coming closer and closer. Canada has acquired a large population in southern Ontario. They're much closer in attitude than when I started in this business thirty years ago.''

''The biggest obstacle to our management goals is the Indian fishing dispute. It is a major disruption. Without that, I think we could get on to this optimal yield management. You've got to get to that level before you can straighten out these remaining problems and get back to another age of normalcy. We've got the capability to manage. The understanding level is a lot higher than it was ten years ago.''

Naubinway, Mich.

Cedar River, Mich.

101

The Battle Lines

At this point a question must occur. How did the commercial fishermen allow themselves to be maneuvered into this situation? They had, after all, maintained a significant position in the lakeshore communities and held a relatively high reputation because of their courage and independence. Collectively, they could have exercised considerable political influence. This, however, was the heart of the problem. Their very independence was their downfall. Anyone who has tried to work with them has told a similar tale. Commercial fishermen are some of the most difficult people in the world to gather for collective action. Organizations would spring up in response to certain crisis situations. Efforts would continue for a period of time until the crisis passed, at which time the organization tended to dissolve over regional divisions, or squabbles among those fishing different gear types, or representation, or a combination of all these reasons. Further, fishermen were scattered over a thousand miles and eight state jurisdictions. Power was fragmented when there was sufficient organization.

Nonetheless, it was the lack of collective political strength or even political common sense that left them at a total disadvantage when dealing with state agencies, sport fishing groups, and gear manufacturers who understood the value of lobbying their point of view and had both organization and the funds necessary to pursue this course of action.

The battle between conservation groups and the commercial fishermen had begun as far back as the late 1800's. The history of this discussion is one of progressive disintegration of rational debate. In the early years it was conducted on a relatively high level among fish management officials and academics. There was no clear consensus and it was possible to see disagreement among scientists and managers. The raging squabble among commercial fishermen over the deep water trap net demon-

off the Door Peninsula

strated that these concerns penetrated deeply into the industry itself. Conservationists debated among themselves as to whether commercial fishing performed a service in balancing stocks or whether it placed certain species in peril. The intensity of the debate fluctuated with the rise and fall of valued fish stocks.

After World War II the lines began to solidify. Conservation clubs became more and more closely identified with sport groups and the cry for restriction on fishing grew. Nonetheless, the status quo was maintained until the lamprey had seriously reduced the economic power of the commercial fisherman at the same time that the crowded cities and improved transportation were stimulating the tourist industry in lakeside villages and towns.

The planting of salmon and trout, as we have seen, greatly accelerated this change and gave birth to tourist-oriented groups of great power. One facet of this tourist industry is the charter boats that offer hassle-free access to the open water for the casual fisherman. These relatively recent additions to the tourist industry perceived the commercial fisherman as a direct competitor and threat to their continued operation. They added a strong voice to sport groups and further hardened attitudes. When the sport view was taken up by state resource agencies, commercial fishing was confronted with a coalition that could have been countered only with skill and organization. Instead there was division and indecision.

Michigan fishermen had hesitated in the late sixties to declare war on the policy decision of the DNR to give primacy to sport fishermen and adopted a wait-and-see attitude. Many of their advocates regard this as a tremendous tactical error, for it put them permanently on the defensive, constantly fighting a rear guard action on individual moves of the Department. Even then, as we shall see, it was a very close battle where organization might have made the difference. The fishermen were to discover the immense cost of political naivete.

The sport-oriented policy triumphed throughout the various U.S. jurisdictions until the mid-seventies. Great pressures, of the kind we have examined in Illinois, were exerted on other states to follow the Michigan lead. Gradually, however, questions and oppositions began to develop.

Charter boat

Gillnet tug

103

Wisconsin

By the middle 1970's the only U.S. jurisdiction in the Great Lakes basin with a significant commercial fishery that had not passed to strict control was that of Wisconsin. We have already seen the stand the state had taken on the gill net. Nonetheless, pressures were mounting for a common Lake Michigan policy and the drive for restrictions was backed by regional and local sport groups. Wisconsin commercial fishermen had, however, the examples of Michigan, Ohio, and Illinois to follow and began to organize in opposition. The resistance group was supplemented by citizens of the lakeside communities and, even more importantly, by some politicians and scientists. During the period 1974-77, these forces and issues converged on the legislature and the Department of Natural Resources. (33a)

In 1974, then-Lieutenant-Governor Martin Schreiber struck a policy note in sharp contrast to that of the neighboring states. Noting the increasing world population and need for protein, he stressed the importance of Great Lakes food production. He then addressed the current issue: the proposed ban on chub fishing and its effect on commercial fishermen. He emphatically rejected the idea of allowing the chub fishery to pass out of existence because of the ban. He drew a comparison between fishermen and other food producers:

"When farmers are threatened with financial hardship because of natural disaster, we provide funds and assistance to keep them going. We realize the overriding need to keep them in business and producing food. Similarly, we must provide interim assistance to these commercial fishermen who are threatened with disaster, as a means of maximizing food production.

"This assistance should be two-pronged. First, there must be an immediate means of cushioning the impact of the dwindling chub population. And second, there must be an intensified effort to develop additional species in the lake which can support a sustained commercial harvest." (33c)

Schreiber commented favorably on the concept of a "put-and-take" fishery for lake trout, whereby they would be planted and harvested on a strictly controlled basis with the commercial industry bearing the bulk of the cost for the planting. Another series of programs would concentrate on the utilization of rough fish. The extent of his departure from the dominant theory is revealed in the following statements:

"It will take time to get these programs into full operation. That is why a quota of lake trout should be considered immediately as a means of sustaining the commercial fishing industry and making more food available immediately.

"Another deterrent to commercial fishing has been the procedure by which they have been regulated. The sense of powerlessness and buffeting which commercial fishermen often feel in their relationship with the DNR prompted fishermen to get out of the business, an unfortunate result.

"Commercial fishermen should have the right of due process in all aspects of DNR regulation . . .'" (33) d

The Lieutenant-Governor then proposed the creation of a task force composed of all interested user groups with the aim of formulating steps to be taken by the DNR for lake management. The long term plan should balance, not only commercial and sport needs, but also "world food needs."

All of this was a far cry from the 1968 policy statement of the Wisconsin DNR which flatly followed the Michigan lead: "Precedence shall be given to sport fishing, since this provides the greatest returns to society." Schreiber's policy attitudes were never fully implemented even though, or perhaps, because, he became Governor in 1977. Still, some of his proposals were adopted and Wisconsin moved in a somewhat different direction, and a substantially different manner, than other lakeside states. The task force met in early 1975 and was charged with designing a plan for allocation of the fishery resources. The group came up with a far broader policy than that of 1968 and disavowed preferential treatment for any one group. The new policy emphasized that biological principles should be utilized to "attain optimum sustainable utilization." (34) The new policy also endorsed a wide variety of commercial controls, including the limited entry approach.

One of the most interesting studies that came out of the task force deliberations was a report on the comparative economic worth of the commercial and sport fisheries to the State. Figures estimating the value of either fishery had traditionally involved a comparison of basic dollar outlays by sport fishermen and dockside values for landed commercial fish. In considering farm production, however, there had always been a multiplier used to represent the increase in production value from wholesale to retail. No multiplier had been applied to commercial dockside prices even though such an increase in value obviously took place. It was estimated, according to one source, to range from 2.44 to 2.70 times the dockside price. The application of such a multiplier brought the worth of the 1977 commercial catch into the $4.8 to $5.3 million area and ". . . These figures are of the same order of magnitude as those of the sport fishery provided by the Wisconsin DNR." (35) Sport fishing values on the other hand, were always based on the *retail* impact of fisherman expenditures.

The report, compiled by personnel of the Wisconsin Sea Grant program, also noted that government expenditures for lamprey control and lake trout planting were not reflected in the comparative figures. The sport figures generally depend heavily on angler outlays for transportation, food, lodging, and equipment. The most obvious benefits came from out-of-state anglers whose visits to the state, presumably inspired by the superior fishing, bring dollars into the economy that would not otherwise be there. It was estimated that 15 percent of the 700,000 sport trips were made by non-residents. The report questioned, however, whether the food and travel expenditures of state residents might have occurred even in the absence of lake fishing. In other words, it makes little difference whether Harry Jones goes to a lake port to fish trout rather than to an inland lodge to fish a trout stream. The main point of the study was that an adequate comparison of the economic value of the two fisheries could not be made without a much deeper investigation of relative benefits and costs.

The tendency to underestimate the value of commercial fishing was emphasized when the National Marine Fisheries Service released a study prepared for them by Centaur Management Consultants, a private firm. The study was focused mainly on ocean fisheries and found that the $907 million catch of 1973 translated into associated commercial activity estimated at $6.7 billion. This amounted to a stunning multiplier effect of *seven* times the dockside value. In an editorial *The Fisherman* commented that several additional salt water processes made this multiplier a bit high for the lakes. It suggested the use of a multiplier of five times dockside value. This translated the 1974 $4.1 million catch into a $20.8 million operation. (36)

So what difference does it make? The difference is crucial, for these figures are presented to legislators in order to persuade them to enact certain laws or support policies proposed by various user groups or state agencies. These decisions affect people's ability to make a living whether they are involved in the commercial fishing or tourist industry. Whether the mulitplier is 2.4, 5, or 7, it is apparent that commercial fishing has been undervalued. The most disturbing question is why such a basic value in policy formulation should have been raised *after* major decisions were made in many states and raises some strong questions about the independence of groups charged with investigating these matters.

The struggle over Wisconsin's fishery allocation produced a series of legal battles. Perhaps the most significant was a civil action filed in October, 1975. The suit alleged that the State DNR employed discrimination in favor of sport fishing and against harvest of fish for food purposes. The allegation continued by pointing out that lake trout are raised and stocked with funds from federal tax revenues and that because of the discrimination policy, citizens, other than recreational fishermen, were barred from enjoying the resource. The relief requested of the court was either that the state be stopped from interfering with the commercial harvest or that federal officials be barred from raising and planting lake trout and controlling lampreys. There are those who say that the latter request, particularly that applying to the ending of the lamprey control efforts, was an unwise move. The judge dismissed the case, however, on the broad grounds that the states had the authority to regulate the fishery:

"The plaintiffs argue that the program for the propagation of lake trout was designed for the benefit of commercial fishermen and, therefore, the latter are entitled to enforce such right by legal action. I believe it

to be clear that regulation of fisheries is within the police power of the individual states, and the State of Wisconsin has the exclusive power and authority to regulate fishing within its territorial waters . . ." (37)

In Wisconsin the recommendations of the task force, and the desires of state agencies, crystallized into Senate Bill 409. The battle over this bill brought the DNR, as well as commercial and sports interests into a head-to-head confrontation. There had been a number of skirmishes prior to 409 which had taken place mainly in the courts. In the most notable, an attempt to establish what amounted to a zone system had been successfully challenged by commercial groups. With 409, the Department sought to have its powers over fishing clearly and broadly defined. Bill 409 establishes limited entry, permits the DNR to close areas of Lake Michigan to commercial fishing, and imposes stiffer penalties for both sport and commercial violations. Specifically, there is a $1,000 maximum fine for anyone using illegal gill nets or selling game fish. There is also the possibility

Bayfield, Wis.

of a nine-month jail sentence, fine, or a combination of the penalties. More to the point, fishing equipment and catches may be seized and licenses revoked.

Reaction among the sport fishermen ran the gamut from those who passionately believed that commercial fishermen were to blame for virtually every decline in fish stocks to those who emphasized the role of pollution and the need for its control. It was an article of faith with some speakers that a number of commercial fishermen were taking and selling illegal fish and that the existing penalties were totally inadequate. One cited a case where fishermen involved in selling an enormous quantity of illegal fish were fined $100:

> ". . . Why rob a bank for $10,000 and risk a jail term? Why not catch and ship illegal fish, make your $10,000 and then maybe, if you are caught, pay a $100 fine? (38)

Other sport fishermen stressed the need for stronger search authority and noted what they regarded as the dangerous efficiency of commercial gear. There was also considerable support for the salmon and trout stocking programs.

The commercial fishermen attacked the continuation of what they regard as the double standard which, for health reasons, disallows harvest for public sale. They pointed out that public tax money is being used to plant trout while harvesting of the fish is confined to one group. It is interesting that although Bill 409 had nothing to say about trout, the topic was raised by all groups. In general, the commercial interests regarded the bill as too restrictive and pointed to the Wisconsin waters of Lake Superior for evidence of inept management programs. A spokesman noted the effects of the introduction of smelt, carp, and salmon on the decline of native species:

> "You call this management?" Johnson asked bitterly. "This is preservation of our natural resources? If Lake Superior's experience is typical of DNR management, God help all of us. There won't be a native fish left in the Great Lakes if they continue the way they're going." (39)

DNR representatives stated the main purpose of the bill was to provide the Department with a sound legal basis for its regulatory activities. They pointed out that the bill put controls on charter, sport, and commercial fishermen. The limited entry provisions were basically designed to remove part-time participants from the commercial ranks. Limited entry had already reduced the number of commercial licenses on Wisconsin Lake Superior waters from 50 to 20 and it was felt that this action could only aid the serious, full-time commercial operators as would the increased licensing fees. Department representatives repeatedly stressed that the application of limited entry would be flexible and that commercial ice fishing, an activity almost exclusively confined to Green Bay, might be continued under crew cards which allow each license holder a four-man crew.

It is notable that a considerable portion of the opposition to Bill 409 was the result of policies of other lakeside states. To an extent, the Wisconsin DNR has harvested ten years of bitterness from other jurisdictions. Spokesmen went to some length to differentiate state policies. It was pointed out that Wisconsin raised chub quotas against the advice of the three other Lake Michigan jurisdictions. Fish manager James Moore articulated this point:

> "The commercial fishermen think we're trying to put them out of business," Moore said ruefully. "They point to what happened in Michigan where commercial fishing is just about wiped out and say this is what is going to happen here. I don't blame them sometimes for feeling that way, but there is a world of difference between the DNR philosophy in the two states. Wisconsin's policy is not dictated by the Michigan DNR and our view of the commercial fisheries is vastly different." (40)

In the end, the fight waged by the commercial fishermen produced two amendments which substantially altered the original bill. The first provided that five of the seven members of the commercial fishing regulatory commission set up under the bill would be commercial fishermen. This gave the industry a strong voice in policy formulation and, more importantly, political access. The second provided for prior legislative consideration and approval of any administrative rule set up by the DNR to implement 409.

This was far from the Michigan approach which had originally provided neither protection. Both houses of the state legislature adopted the bill by wide margins and, in May of 1978, Governor Martin Schreiber signed the measure in substantially the form passed by the legislature. It seemed that a compromise solution had been found.

Interview with Jim Addis

Director of Fish Management, Wisconsin Department of Natural Resources and

Ron Poff

Boundary Waters and Great Lakes Specialist,
Wisconsin Department of Natural Resources

(On S.B. 409)

Poff: We didn't have a policy prior to 1968. Also, at the time, we had no formal commitment to the Great Lakes for money or manpower. We didn't even have a sport fishing license. We had to begin somewhere and it was with a simple one page policy statement that indicated we would give preference to the sport fishery because of the greater economic value to the public as a whole. There was nothing but problems with the policy, so we got rid of it.

Addis: "With 409, we sought to obtain a clear enunciation of the authority necessary to run a resource agency. Prior to passage of the Bill, we had been operating under a broad omnibus power under which we could supposedly do anything. It simply stated that the state should regulate the fisheries.

With the more specific requirements of language in the last ten years, particularly in the last seven, the agency initiated modifications in the statutes. In doing so, we were given some specific powers. After that the court said, in effect, 'If you have omnibus authority, you shouldn't have specific powers, and we find you don't have power beyond those specific rights.'

The general thinking behind the legislation is that the fisheries are a common resource. A common resource is not effectively managed under an open market, laissez-faire system. If the resource is depleted and the individual user can still increase effort, he will benefit more from further exploiting the resource than from conserving it. The idea being, quite simply, that if he doesn't, somebody else will. The answer to that has been limited entry, designed to control further capitalization so that it doesn't exceed ability to manage the resource.

Limited entry seemed to generate strong opposition to the bill. The other thing that was feared was that, with ability to open and close certain areas and controls on gear types, we would take the same approach as Michigan. They feared we would zone out the fishery and license by zone.

The basic reason, however, for the opposition to 409 was the matter of trust. The fishermen didn't trust the administrators, the state, or the state's purposes. They have recognized that most of us, by our training and inclination, come into an agency like this as sport fishery managers. There is very little inland training in the United States for commercial fisheries management. They've seen the continuing trend of declining commercial fisheries. They know that, by and large, we feel that dollar for dollar sport fishing generates more than commercial fishing.''

Poff: "The real point was the Michigan example and that was brought up at every hearing we had on any administrative rule. The serious people in the industry usually came to our support and noted the differences in position between the two agencies.

The zone management system was a real bastard as far as the industry was concerned. They could not stomach the program, especially the way it was put to the Michigan fishermen, as an after the fact issue, rather than as something to which they could adjust.

Addis: We felt that in Wisconsin's social and political setting, that was not a feasible alternative. At an American Fisheries Society meeting in Vancouver, I had an opportunity to talk with an international authority on commercial fishing. We talked about limited entry experiences around the world. He felt that the key to any successful system was a participatory role for the industry so that it felt a part, rather than a tool, of management.

Our approach, therefore, has been to establish Commercial Fishing Boards almost completely dominated by the industry. The single exception is the appointment of a citizen at large to the board, a position we perceive to be one of consumer advocacy.

The Commercial Board's role is to deal with industry decisions such as relicensing and allocation of any harvestable surpluses that may be determined. It is almost a rule making authority. The main management policies will be set by the Natural Resources Board. Given the way the bill is written, if the Commercial Board comes up with a feasible way of achieving management objectives, I don't see anyone in the agency turning them back for minor reasons. The fishermen, through the Board, now have enormous power in terms of controlling their destiny as an industry. In addition, the Board will be used as a sounding board and focal point.

Our objective is to get hold of the resource so that it can be managed to produce a viable and continuous commercial fishery, and to try and make commercial and sport activities as compatible as possible. The Secretary has stated publicly and privately, that, as a Department, we feel the commercial industry has rights equal to those of the sport industry. In fact, he

and I spoke recently to that effect at sport fishing banquets in Milwaukee and Manitowoc.

As a result of trying to protect themselves, I think the commercial interests introduced something tragic into the legislation. One of the things the Council of State Governments emphasizes is that once a management agency has a decent institutional structure, it ought to be able to react quickly to both the needs of the industry and the resource. By installing increased legislative review, commercial fishermen have tangled us up in what easily may be eight or nine months, and possibly a year, of internal review processes.

Poff: For example, one of the things we'd like to do is open the chub fishery. It has to be opened by April to do any good for the industry. To do that and go through the full procedure, I'd have to take it to the Natural Resources Board this month. We just got back the preliminary drafts of a chub assessment report and there are a couple of things that require comment from the industry. Our first position was that we would get permission for hearings from the Natural Resources Board and, in the meantime, go to the industry for comment and thereby utilize the thirty to forty day waiting period before the hearings would be scheduled.

Well, in talking with several individuals, they feel the industry should have the input before the draft. Trying to block in these meetings when the fishermen are still fishing and the Board hasn't begun to operate, puts us in a real tight bind. If we could get a good deal of consensus so the legislative committee could sign off on it, then we could make the deadline within six months. If we get into a hassle, we could end up not being able to take care of the chub fishery.

Addis: Our objective now is to get this thing operating to where we can get a trust relationship established. It can't be trust

110

dependent on Poff or myself, because we could die or be gone at any moment. A system has to be developed that has both equity and credibility. That is what we are going to try to pull out of all this. I don't know whether we can or not.

Poff: It is going to require a shift in the Department in terms of our methodology for commercial fisheries. We never did a great deal of work in administering them, other than by traditional methods. Now we're into limited entry, quota control, and amount of gear. It is much more intensive management so we're going to have to change the theories by which we administer the fisheries. It involves modeling populations, making allowable harvest estimates, and looking more intensively at mortality and recruitment rates than we ever have before. This means training our people and the citizen advisors that we have. There is a great deal of new public information that we've got to generate so that our advisors know what is going on.

Addis: One of the problems is that we've got to interface with the economists. We've got to have better economic information on this system. The other problem is that the industry cannot support the added management costs of its own administration. Most state funds are coming from the sport fishery. Even the funds available from increased commercial license fees, will constitute a small amount of the total cost. That will have to be resolved somewhere in the future. The sport fishermen are going to expect more and more of a voice if they are the ones paying the bills.

Poff: We will get about $44,000 in license revenues from commercial fishing.

Addis: And we are talking about a $700,000 program on the Great Lakes.

Poff: Of course the $44,000 is five or six times what we used to get from commercial operations, so we still gained appreciably. I don't think anyone is saying that commercial operators should bear the full cost of managing the fishery because none of these costs are that well isolated. Advantages to one user group are not that completely separated from advantages to other user groups.

(On the role of Overfishing in the Depletion of Stocks)

Addis: I am more familiar with the historical background of Lake Erie than with that of Lake Michigan. There was enormously high production as modern gear came into use. There were very high levels of exploitation. In Lake Erie we had among the most significant whitefish fisheries in the world. Production was over seven-million pounds in 1949. But what happened to the whitefish wasn't a result of overfishing, it was the result of a total loss of habitat.

The thing that surprised me is that when they closed Lake Erie to commercial walleye fishing because of mercury contamination, the stocks recovered enormously. At the same time I think you could also detect a significant water quality improvement in the lake. Thus it was a confounded experiment, but I think it is now a source of enormous support for the overfishing argument.

I think the closure allowed for a little more structure in the population. Now there is a dominant year class, but some of the weaker year classes are still going. The reason I think there has been some environmental improvement, is the increasing success of the sauger. Thus, I still have to conclude that earlier declines were due to a combination of factors.

Poff: If you look at Lakes Superior and Michigan, the most effective management measures we've had so far have been

111

ones directed at both commercial and sport fisheries in a rather drastic way, such as refuges and total closures. Nothing is black and white out there, but there is a considerable impact on the stocks from the sport fishery. A lot of people will tell you that with some of these critical species fisheries, such as lake trout, sport fishing has as much, or more, impact than a limited commercial fishery. We try to avoid reference to exploitation as the one and only cause of our problems. Yet, by controlling exploitation, as with chubs and lake trout, you may achieve some recovery by removing one of the group of stresses. Once you have achieved recovery and the fishery is reopened, you can do a lot by regulating the exploitation level.

Addis: Take the Gull Island Shoal area in Lake Superior where we were having a significant recovery of Lake Trout. Exploitation increased, and we saw that process turn around. We then put in a refuge and we've seen a substantial improvement in the population in the refuge area. Outside that area we see the population leveling off. This is pretty damn direct evidence that exploitation can have an impact. We have closed the area to both sport and commercial fishing to protect the spawners.

Poff: We had a strong case for doing that because of the number of fish tagged. We were able to determine that sport exploitation was responsible for about 13 percent mortality, over a two year period, in the spawning population. We were able to conclude that sport fishing was a significant factor, as was Indian fishing, and as was our own sampling effort. We were responsible for two percent of our total mortality rate. The total mortality was 46 percent.

(On measuring the relative value of
sport and commercial fishing)

Addis: I think that as expenses for sport fishing programs were justified—legislatures like cost/benefit data—economic measurement by use of the multiplier was encouraged. There has not been an equal interest, except locally, in enhancing commercial fisheries.

Poff: The University of Wisconsin did a marketing study and found virtually no effect from the Great Lakes, in terms of fish in the marketplace, once you get thirty miles from the lakeshore. Most of the fish produced in the whole Great Lakes system ends up in the major markets, such as Chicago and Detroit.

One thing about this, when the fish go out of state, the returning money is new dollars. It is not a transfer of funds. The fish sold locally, where a guy might otherwise buy hamburger, represent a transfer of funds. One thing you can say about Wisconsin is that a dollar produced in the commercial fishery has more of a chance of being a new dollar than one produced in the sport fishery. There is much more translocation of funds in the sport fishery.

Addis: Some of the economists argue that the money generated in the sport fisheries is essentially transferred disposable income from one form of spending to another. If there were no Lake Michigan fishery, they would probably spend that money on an inland fishery, horseback riding, or whatever. Economists who look at it this way, say you can't qualify such expenditures as production and that it simply represents transfers within the system and that the only part of the sport fishery that accrues economic benefit, is that which brings in new money.

I think it is an argument the economists will be at for years for, on the other hand, we hear the Great Lakes sport fishery is worth $350 million. Somebody will have to nail down some numbers on the situation.

(On the Indian fishing rights issue)

Addis: What we've done that Michigan hasn't done is to accept a court decision to the effect that there are treaty rights. Michigan hasn't been able to go that far. They are still arguing about whether there are treaty rights. That is why they have such a totally different approach to things. We've allocated a forty thousand pound quota to the Indians. The Indians have allocated sixty thousand pounds and we are now in the process of evaluating the stocks. We feel that that level of exploitation is excessive and we have a case in court where we are trying to document this fact. We hope the case will be a basis for forcing the Department of Interior and the Indians to develop a management program that can be worked with.

Our process has been kind of orderly. We accepted the Supreme Court decision. Now we're trying to establish some pattern for enforcing it and working with the Indians. The next step has been to document the over-exploitation. A further stage will be to sit down with the Indians and show them what we think is harvestable. We'll try to gain acceptance of that allocation in the Department of Interior and come up with a plan that will be acceptable to everyone.

Indians are presently trying to rewrite their tribal rules. They do have their own wardens and they have had trouble with enforcement and administration. I'm not surprised. Since the 1800's we've been administering the commercial fisheries and we have trouble. They are having the same kinds of problems we have.

Our feeling is that we need better data from them so we can construct a management plan. We hope we can get that through negotiation rather than court battles. Our problem is that we haven't seen court settlements as at all successful. Michigan hasn't gotten anything. As far as I can see, they've lost everything. They don't agree with us, they feel it is the only way to go and they get quite defensive with this comment. The basic thing is that we have a court decision and they don't.

We start from the position that the Indians have treaty rights. While details of these rights may not be fully understood, we should nonetheless work together to protect stocks. They have exactly the same interest in protecting these stocks as the white commercial fishermen. If they fail, the fishermen are hurt as a result. I think they understand this and it is the important thing. If a man sees that it is in his interest to work with you, he will. If he doesn't, I don't care how articulate you are, you're not going to get him to cooperate.

(The Major Present Management Problem)

Poff: As far as I'm concerned, our biggest problem is our inability to react in a timely fashion to changes in the stocks, and to changes in the industry. Sport or commercial, it doesn't make any difference. This thing of having to wait eight months to do anything is always hanging over our head. It works both ways, either opening or closing a fishery. To modify a simple regulation could take eight months. That is unheard of; you can't expect to manage intensively when you are saddled with something like that.

If you're serious about managing a resource you have to be able to respond. If you see something going wrong, you want to be able to stop it. When you see an ability to harvest a year class at an acceptable level, you want to be able to do that, and you want to be able to do that before the year class has gone by without any exploitation.

Addis: The problem that causes me the most concern for the long run is contaminants. It appears to me we've just seen the tip of the iceberg. There is no doubt in my mind that the trend is going to be toward lower contaminant tolerance levels. If we don't see it this year, we will see it eventually.

The data is growing on the negative effects of PCB's. There are whole species of contaminants we don't know about. It is a dark cloud over the whole of the Great Lakes.

I think the sport-commercial conflicts are all things that can be dealt with. They are people problems. Contaminants are something quite different. You've still got about 4.8 million pounds of PCB's sitting around. Unless the sources can be identified, and the material properly disposed of, it will enter the system over a period of twenty to thirty years. Medical research is beginning to show that there are substantial health hazards. You can argue that most of the tests are with highly sensitive laboratory animals, but some of these same symptoms are showing up in people exposed to similar compounds.

Softball Game
Fishermen vs. D.N.R. Wis., 1978

Algoma, Wis.

Suamico, Wis.

Algoma, Wis.

Minnesota

"There are certain decisions that can and should be made by the state regulatory agency which pertain to the management of the resource. There are others that are political and that should be made by elected officials. If sport fishermen wish to eliminate commercial fishing, they have access to the state legislature. It is not our proper function to make such a decision." (41)

Minnesota was one of the last jurisdictions to move to limited entry and commercial fishery controls. The small Lake Superior fishery was historically centered around trout and herring. The steep shorelines and lack of suitable bottom meant that the gear of choice was almost exclusively gill nets. Sport fishing, until recent years virtually nonexistent, has developed to the point where it is estimated that the 100,000 man hours recorded for 1976 was exceeded by a full 50 percent in 1977.

In developing its limited entry formula, Minnesota was able to observe the neighboring jurisdictions and has absorbed certain lessons from their experiences. Legally, the state Department of Natural Resources is exempted from the state Administrative Procedures Act. The commissioner has the authority to promulgate orders by publishing legal notices in certain official publications.

In practice, the Department has not developed regulations in this manner. The construction of the limited entry bill was accomplished with major input from sport *and* commercial fishermen. The major argument for any resource agency having powers outside of administrative procedures controlling other departments, is to give it sufficient flexibility to react to rapidly changing conditions as information becomes available. Without this power, the setting of fish, game, and bird seasons would be extremely difficult. As a political reality, however, retention of this power requires that it be used with discretion:

"We have a lot of discussion with affected user groups before we put forth a regulation. We don't want to promulgate regulations that are going to be extremely controversial and end up having ourselves in court fighting injunctions. If we operated in that manner it would only be a short time before we were back with all the other departments under the Administrative Procedures Act. While we have the power to set regulations outside that procedure, we have advance publicity and discussion of the propositions before they become regulations. We have, in short, tried to be prudent in the exercise of this power." (42)

The criteria that emerged from this process has required potential license holders to own 5,000 feet of gill net, and have fished 50 days per year to produce a $1,500 catch in two of the three preceding years. There are about 40 licenses now outstanding and the DNR envisions an eventual reduction to near 20 although there is no specified goal.

The general purpose of the regulations is to produce a full-time commercial fishery and the Department feels that full-time operators will be protected from those who may fish only those years in which successful year classes produce abundance. In order to protect long-time fishermen, a ''grandfather'' clause gives special considerations to those who have held licenses since 1947. Minnesota has bypassed quotas in favor of licensing the amount of net used. Imposition of quotas would require personnel to monitor records and this is simply too expensive considering the size of the fishery. It is felt that the relationship between catch and the amount of net used is well enough known to permit flexibility in response to changing conditions. The total amount of net permitted on the lake is limited as is the amount allowed each fisherman. Presently the allotted quantity is considerably less than the legal limit and thus can be adjusted in response to changes in abundance.

As yet there have been no court challenges to the law, but this may be a reflection of the Department's liberal attitude in the first year of its operation. In succeeding years, fishermen will be required to demonstrate that they are, in fact, fishermen. There is, however, a definite place for commercial activity in management plans:

"We think that commercial fishing is as legitimate an outlet for these species as sport fishing. We haven't adopted any policy for eliminating commercial fishing administratively." (43)

Minnesota has planted lake trout and there is optimism that the fish is gaining strength in the lake. There may be a larger population now than existed in pre-lamprey days. A good brood stock and egg deposition has led to real hopes for natural reproduction. The state has sought to expand sport opportunities by stocking the kamloops strain of rainbow trout. These fish mature in January, thus providing an extended sport season by moving into streams ahead of native rainbow. Streams on Minnesota shores are so short and steep that 56 streams provide a mere 75 miles open to steelhead spawning. There is a lot more growing room in the lake than these streams can supply by natural reproduction. Brook trout are planted in local areas.

After the Michigan salmon success, the resource agency was forced by political pressure to stock coho salmon. The fish were never terribly successful, as they reached spawning areas in the late autumn when streams were colder than the lake. The fish were not interested in spawning under these conditions and passion for fishing was considerably reduced in this traditional deer hunting period. The DNR has turned to experimental stocking of spring run chinook which become available to anglers as they move shoreward in mid-summer. It is not expected that these fish will be able to reproduce as their mid-July spawning runs come at a time of low water.

The stocking of herring is a far more controversial matter. The state has stocked forty million fry each year for the last four years. The manner in which the effort was launched is also indicative of the different management climate in Minnesota. The drastic decline in herring had led the agency to demand a three-month closed season in 1973. The Minnesota Fish Producer's Association (MFPA) sought, and was denied, an injunction against the closure. Instead of parting in mutual hostility, both sides worked to find another solution:

"The resultant program was a two-month closed season coupled with the restocking effort. Three MFPA board members . . . volunteered to conduct the fishing operations during November on Brule and Greenwood Lakes with DNR crews handling the spawn collection. The relatively untouched stocks in these lakes are descendants of Lake Superior herring planted in the 1930's. The new program merely reversed the procedure." (44)

This approach, using inland fish originally taken from the Great Lakes, is one of the most interesting changes in planting techniques. There is a growing recognition of the fact that a species may have a number of subtle genetic differences developed over long residence in a lake. Thus restocking with strains descended from fish originally taken from that lake may be a major advance over more random methods. In any case, the cooperative effort produced one of the rarest tributes in the recent history of U.S. Great Lakes management: "(Minnesota Fish Producer's Association) president Stuart Sivertson commended the DNR for the constructive course set by the stocking program." (45)

Lake herring stand on the brink of extinction. There has been no observed natural reproduction of the fish in the last 12 years and although fish of the stocked age groups are being noticed, there are no representatives of earlier year classes. A certain amount of courage and a good deal of vision is required to stock fish that appear doomed. Criticism of this program recalls that directed at the lake trout program of the forties and fifties at the Marquette fish hatchery:

"On a big lake like Superior you don't have the resources to effect the major changes. What can you do for chubs? What can you do for herring? We stock herring. I know a lot of people snicker and regard this as a pretty naive proposition. I think, since we are stocking in a void, that we might be successful. If a can full of pink salmon can go forth and populate the earth, we just might have a chance." (46)

The future of the sport fishery is bright while commercial efforts face the continuing crisis of the chub and herring stocks. As elsewhere, lake trout are the main source of controversy between the two user groups. Since 1962 lake trout have been, except for the usual assessment fishery, off-limits to commercial harvest. If the relatively uncontaminated stocks of superior trout show substantial natural reproduction and the population expands, this controversy could become a major issue. Commercial sport trolling is presently limited to three boats, but it is expected that this activity will increase with development of marinas. Presently, the most hopeful spot in the commercial picture is the growing market for smelt. One trawler is now operating and permits are issued to allow stream entrapment of the fish.

Indiana

The short Indiana coastline stretches for forty-five miles along the southern shore of Lake Michigan. It might seem that such a small area would be insignificant in its effect on the lake, but anyone who has seen the region knows better. On a clear day the multi-colored hue of the sky can be seen for miles. This is the center of one of the great industrial concentrations of North America. Steel, petroleum, and chemicals are manufactured within a short distance of one another in the Illinois and Indiana watersheds. Great Lakes vessels bring the ores of Ontario and Minnesota to the mills where they are transformed into steel.

This shoreline is also one of the most densely populated sections of the United States, and people have demanded use of the lake for recreational purposes. It is the Indiana Department of Natural Resources that must attempt to meet this need. It might seem an impossible task but it is here, interestingly, that some of the more significant progress in improving water quality has been made, something discussed in greater detail in the next section. It is sufficient to note that two preconceptions of the state coast are incorrect. First, it is not by and large visually offensive. The algae, stench, and floating secretions found along the southern shore of Lake Erie are largely absent. Second, it is not so much the industries as the cities that continue to be the main problem:

"Certainly there have been improvements along the shoreline, but we still have a long way to go. The quality of discharges coming from industry has improved markedly. I think the biggest problem is the time that it is taking the municipalities to get their act together in upgrading the quality of the effluent coming from the municipal treatment plants. It isn't completely the fault of the municipalities, as they have considerable difficulty in getting the funding for improving and upgrading their sewage facilities. Still, much greater progress has been made with industries than with municipalities. Cities that aren't able to bring their secondary or tertiary treatment up to par are still one of our major sources of poor water quality." (47)

The Environmental Protection Agency recently prevailed over United States Steel on pollution deadlines and the corporation was fined four million dollars. Air pollution is increasingly understood as a prime source of water pollution and, as the steel mills gradually change from open hearth to blast furnaces, air quality is slowly improving.

The water quality of streams along the Indiana shore has improved noticeably in the upper reaches, but downstream they continue to be badly polluted and the scene of occasional fish mortalities. This poor water quality, and the fact that streams and spawning areas are extremely limited, means that it is unlikely that planted fish will become self sustaining. The straightforward goal of the Department is to sustain the stocking mix that will provide the best blend of variety and seasonal availability.

Indiana stocks about 600,000 fish a year to meet the desires of sport fishermen. Steelhead, lake and brown trout, and coho and chinook salmon are the fish of choice. The brown came close to being discontinued because of fishermen complaints over their scarcity. It was designed to be the backbone of the warm water discharge fishery, essentially a winter angling venture. In the past year, however, it has been appearing in increasing numbers. Current projections aim at increasing steelhead plantings to 200,000, while maintaining brown and coho at 100,000 each.

Indiana is the only Lake Michigan jurisdiction that has not gone to limited entry. There are only two full-time fishermen among the 35 to 45 commercial licensees. In recent years the fishery has concentrated almost exclusively on the yellow perch, with total catches ranging from 200,000 to 300,000 pounds. There is the traditional antagonism between sport and commercial fishermen. Many trolling sport fishermen have never learned that when they move between the flags marking a gill net that they should lift hook and line ten to fifteen feet off the bottom. The failure to do so results in a tangle that produces everything from resignation to rage, which sometimes finds its outlet on the commercial net.

The Department has the general power to regulate the limits and conditions of both sport and commercial fishing. Other matters, such as license fees, remain with the legislature. Gill nets are currently the only gear used in state waters and regulations have been designed to put commercial operators far enough off shore so that conflicts are avoided. Nets may be set no closer to the shore than the twenty-five foot depth contour and must be a mile from stocked creeks and a half mile from public fishing areas.

Some Indiana fishermen are still allowed a small number of salmonids. Until 1974 they had been allowed a ten percent incidental catch of these fish. This was replaced in 1975 with a tagging system based on the size and number of fish caught in the 1972 and 1973 seasons. This privilege applies only to men who were fishing at that time and is not being extended to those now entering the fishery. It is also no longer applied to lake trout because of excessive contaminant levels.

Management officials hope to maintain some balance between the two user groups:

"The whole program here is being paid for by the sale of trout and salmon stamps and fishing licenses. Our objective is to develop the best possible sport fishery we can. At the same time it is not our objective to destroy

Michigan City, Indiana

something which may be antagonizing some people that are participating in that fishery. We feel that there are enough fish out there to sustain both groups.

Frankly, we don't know where the happy medium lies at present. There are the usual complaints you have when the same fishery is going on in the same area at the same time. If we possibly can, we'd like to continue a commercial fishery in these waters. The perch is the backbone of that fishery and it is a popular menu item around here. I know there would be a lot of unhappy people if there were no longer a source of yellow perch." (48)

Monthly reports are required of the commercial fishermen even when not fishing, and licenses have occasionally been revoked for failure to comply with this provision. Currently the state has a program to verify these statistics and a Department employee is scheduled on a random basis to accompany commercial operators to their nets.

119

This project is funded by federal Coastal Zone Management money, as is a corresponding project to develop a year round creel census. Many state management agencies face similar problems of trying to find out what sportsmen are catching, where and when they are catching it, and what they would *like* to catch. An attempt will be made to create an all-season profile of sport fishermen. Another temporary Coastal Zone project is a survey of public access points. There is a large demand for such points and there are presently none under state control. The survey is not simply aimed at potential boat launching sights, as many people have expressed a desire to simply fish from the shore. Michigan is a cooperative partner in another venture. The St. Joseph River meanders through both states and a proposed program would involve construction of fish ladders and the stocking of the upper reaches of the river by Indiana. Because of excellent access, it is expected that this project would vastly expand fishing opportunities for state residents.

Cooperation is not always the order of the day between the two states, however. The northern boundary of Indiana runs across the narrow crescent of southern Lake Michigan. At the extreme eastern and western end of this crescent, Michigan and Illinois waters lie only a few feet offshore. As a practical matter, the problem is noticeable in areas such as Michigan City where the border is roughly two miles from the shore. In the summer as the larger species move into deeper waters, they move without knowing, or for that matter caring, that they are moving into Michigan. Michigan DNR personnel reportedly do not hover exactly on the invisible boundary, but they are certainly likely to be more familiar with it than the average boat fisherman who may be pursuing the large, deep swimming species. The result may be a fine.

This bit of craziness works both ways. If you hold a Michigan license, catch a fish in Michigan waters, and naively or

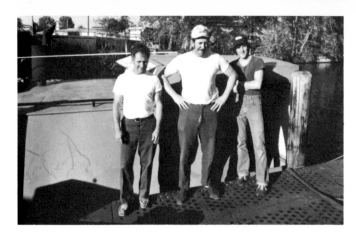

Michigan City, Indiana

mistakenly stray into Indiana waters, you are also liable as state enforcement officials have no way of knowing where the fish was caught. One wonders what happens if a huge, hooked, and very excited salmon drags a small boat across the border. Is this a mitigating circumstance? Is the salmon liable?

A few commercial fishermen have paid for their jurisdictional uncertainty by having their boats confiscated. In this region geographic ignorance can be a very expensive matter. Logic would dictate some form of reciprocity, but historically logic has not played a noticeable role in these matters. This is no exception. It is really a simple matter of barter. What can Indiana offer Michigan that would make reciprocity worthwhile to the latter state? Indiana, after all, controls only one percent of Lake Michigan's waters. The upshot is that the state advises sport fishermen planning to venture any distance into the lake to carry both state licenses. Further, the DNR people follow their own advice.

Michigan and the Indians

The Secretary of War, Lewis Cass, was concerned that the policy of the United States be understood by his negotiator. It was 1836, white settlement was moving west and northward, and the federal government was desirous of keeping the Indians beyond the white frontier. As part of this policy the government was negotiating treaties with a number of tribes offering new lands to the west in return for Indian promises to vacate ancestral homelands when they should be desired for white settlement. It was the interim period that provided the problem. Henry Schoolcraft had been sent to negotiate with the Ottawa and Chippewa residing in the northern areas of the upper lakes. Cass instructed his negotiator:

"You will allow no individual reservations. It is desirable, as far as practicable to extinguish the Indian title as our settlements advance so as to keep the Indians beyond our borders. But if it should be found necessary to allow particular bands to remain upon reservations, those reservations must be held upon the same tenure as the Indians now hold their country, that is, to allow them to retain possession of it till it shall be ceded to the United States." (49)

Schoolcraft negotiated the treaty and, while disallowing the individual reservation, created permanent tribal reservations. In addition, the Indians were promised money and services for a twenty-year period and mention was made of a resettlement area. The U.S. Senate, however, was having nothing to do with a permanent reservation and amended the treaty to limit the reservation status to five years. Thus was created an internally inconsistent document, establishing a permanent reservation, yet superimposing a five-year limitation.

Even the policy for removing the Indians to other areas was unusual. Other "removal" treaties which stated Indians must move by a certain date, sometimes contained provisions for the relocation of the tribe. This treaty contained language that encouraged removal but did not demand it. The Indians could move when they desired to do so. Even by the varied standards of Indian treaties this was a strange document. One of the articles stipulated for the retention of hunting, "with the other usual privileges of occupancy until the land is required for settlement." (50)

In 1855 negotiators returned to the area, in part because the Indians were not going to move west. Some of the bands had examined the land along the Osage River in Kansas and rejected it, while others had simply not bothered to look. The other matters to be settled were "legal and equitable claims" stemming from the 1836 treaty, notably money and blacksmith services. Blacksmiths provided hunting and fishing tools much valued by the Indians and demands for blacksmith services not uncommonly found their way into early treaties. Apparently some of the complexities stemming from the earlier treaty's ambiguity were already sufficiently difficult to cause the government to want to settle the entire matter. The Indians claimed that the Kansas resettlement lands belonged to them, and naturally the government pointed out that the lands would have belonged to the Indians only if they had been settled. The result was a general agreement whose provisions were to be "in lieu and satisfaction of all claims, legal and equitable on the part of said Indians jointly and severally against the United States, for land, money or other things guaranteed to said tribes or either of them by the stipulations of any former treaty or treaties . . ." (51)

The basic question is whether the settlement of "legal and equitable claims" has anything to do with hunting and fishing rights. If the 1855 treaty dissolved the tribal concept of the

the Indian Reorganization Act of 1934 and created an additional reservation at Whitefish Bay in 1936, both of which are located in the eastern part of the Upper Peninsula. In 1924 Indians had been declared citizens of the United States and in the thirties Michigan courts held that since Indians were now citizens, treaty rights no longer applied. Later, the U.S. Supreme Court stated that the granting of citizenship did not affect treaty privileges.

This set the stage for four major case lines which erupted during the 1970's. The question of a treaty right to fish came to a head with the major moves of the Michigan DNR to control commercial fishing. Suddenly these rights acquired great economic and political significance and there was a gathering realization of what was at stake.

Indians involved and ended their identity, then it is in the nature of a final liquidation of all claims. If, however, it was simply an attempt to clean up details of the 1836 treaty, it was something quite different. Under this latter interpretation, Indians were simply being recognized as a settled entity beyond the ambiguity of the ''removal'' concept. If this were so, traditional hunting and fishing privileges moved with them, for such activities were an integral part of Indian life and the right to them had been recognized as such by the 1836 treaty. In other words: Did the 1855 treaty liquidate the hunting and fishing privileges of the 1836 treaty?

It was an issue that did not require an answer for a century. The main currents of white settlement moved in other directions and Indians in the Upper Peninsula of Michigan enjoyed relative tranquility. Fishing rights were not really an issue until the first state controls were applied in the 1930's. The government established the Bay Mills Reservation under

1. The *Jondreau* line—In 1971 the Michigan Supreme Court moved in *Michigan vs Jondreau* to overrule the thirties' attitude that the granting of citizenship had ended treaty rights. The state DNR apparently believed initially that the case had broad application and stated as much. This led to an expansion of Indian fishing activities. Actually, the case had a very particular application and, shortly, the Department began insisting on this interpretation. The period of confusion, however, led to a rising recognition in the Indian community of potential rights. *Status:* completed.

2. The *LeBlanc* line—In a test case, the Bay Mills Indians sought to establish their right to fish in Lake Superior waters adjacent to their reservation. The Michigan District and Circuit Courts held there was no such treaty right. The lower courts were reversed by the State Court of Appeals, a reversal narrowly upheld (4-3) by the State Supreme Court. *Status:* completed.

3. The *Anthony* line—In the summer of 1971 the Michigan United Conservation Clubs sought a permanent injunction to prevent Indians from fishing contrary to state law in waters adjacent to lands ceded in the 1836 treaty. A Michigan Circuit Court granted the injunction. When the LeBlanc line seemed to demand a modified decision, the same Circuit Court amended the injunction to recognize treaty rights but continued the prohibition. This position was appealed and the appeal was to be decided in late 1978. *Status:* pending.

4. The *Federal* line—All previous court decisions had been those of Michigan courts. On April 9, 1973, the U.S. Justice Department moved for a broader-based determination of Indian fishing rights on Great Lakes waters by filing suit against the State of Michigan. The question was simply whether or not Indians have special rights to hunt and fish on the Great Lakes. Michigan initially moved to have all potential Indian claimants joined in the suit but later withdrew the motion. This extremely important case was divided into two phases.

a. The first phase will determine whether or not treaty rights exist. This is the point at which interpretation of the 1836 treaty will be all important. The trial on this phase began in February, 1978, but was postponed after four days because of the illness of the judge.

b. If it is determined that the Indians do have treaty rights, the second phase will determine the state's rights of regulation.

Status: phase 1 in progress.

To say that passions have been aroused by the issue of Indian treaty claims is an understatement. All sides recognize the stakes, for, if Michigan cannot regulate the Indians, it will be hard to continue current commercial fishing policies. The uproar was so great that it produced cries for congressional action. The recent debate over the Panama Canal Treaty may easily lead one to believe that Indian treaties have constitutional significance of the same level as international treaties. Such is not the case for the Congress may simply vote to terminate an Indian treaty. In 1977 the Michigan Natural Resources Commission fired off a resolution addressed to President Carter, the Michigan Congressional delegation, and the State Legislature which stated in part:

> ''WHEREAS, the Department of Natural Resources and the Michigan United Conservation Clubs are extensively involved in protracted litigation involving Indian treaty rights in State and Federal courts to try and control Indian fishing and;

> ''WHEREAS, a final resolution of the litigation is not likely to occur for many years and the Great Lakes fisheries restoration program could be greatly jeopardized or destroyed pending the outcome of such litigation.

> ''BE IT FURTHER RESOLVED, that the Department of Natural Resources bring this matter to the attention of the President, the Michigan Legislature and the Michigan Congressional delegation in Washington, asking them to immediately take action which will resolve this problem and restore control of the commercial fisheries to the State of Michigan and assure equal protection of the law to all citizens.'' (52)

The fury attracted a two-man congressional delegation to Petosky, Michigan on January 13, 1978. There, at a marathon ten-hour hearing, opposing parties presented their views. The undercurrent was obviously the question of whether congressional action should be taken to circumvent the upcoming court struggle. Arthur LeBlanc, Tribal Chairman of the Bay Mills Community, was one of the main speakers for the

Indian cause. He reiterated the Indian claim that fishing rights were federally derived and not subject to state control and documented the importance of fishing to the community. He then turned to the question of congressional action:

> "It is the assumption of the Bay Mills Indian Community that the phrase 'appropriate action by Congress' is a euphemism for abrogation of the treaty right to fish. We are well aware that the Congress has the power to abrogate any provision of a treaty with an Indian tribe, but that fact does not make such action just or wise. In this case, such action could only be attributed to a desire to accommodate the interests of Whites and a wish to punish members of the Bay Mills Indian Community for daring to assert a federally guaranteed right. It appears as though a treaty right is acceptable if no one exercises it, but once it is exercised, it will be taken away. Such action would also be discriminatory, for never, to my knowledge, has the Congress acted affirmatively to abrogate the provisions of a treaty with an Indian tribe. That such action is being seriously contemplated here can only be due to the fact that fishing by Indian people disturbs some very powerful people." (53)

The Department felt that their entire investment in planting and restoration of fisheries was in jeopardy. Speakers noted cases of stock depletions, the utilization of non-Indian boats and equipment and other encouragement from white commercial fishermen and wholesalers. The expansion of fishing effort was felt to imperil trout stocks in particular. John Scott, Chief of the Fisheries Division of the DNR, discussed what he thought to be the particularly dangerous aspects of the federal court case:

> "The major points of the U.S. Government's case need to be carefully reviewed. First, they are not seeking Indian rights on reservations or at usual and accustomed places off reservations; but, rather, Indian rights on all ceded lands covered by the Treaty of 1836. Second, the U.S. Government is not claiming that the Indians hold these rights in common with all other citizens; but that they hold them exclusively. Third, the U.S. Government is seeking to secure for the Indians hunting and all the usual privileges of occupancy including fishing and utilization of the natural environment in many ways (which we could assume to include farming, berry picking, mining, and practically any other common activity). Finally, the U.S. Government contends that these Indian treaty rights are not subject to monetary compensation." (54)

The last sentence indicates one of the potential settlements being explored by the state. The Indians are having none of it. How, they ask, can you place a value on hunting and fishing rights granted in perpetuity? These rights are regarded by the Indians as the foundation of their culture and economy.

The Congressmen were, however, interested in facts and figures. To what extent was the fishery being depleted by Indian activities? They were less than impressed when presented with figures that showed that 3.2 million pounds of lake trout had been taken by sportsmen, five hundred thousand pounds had been taken illegally, and three to six hundred thousand pounds had been taken by Indians. The DNR protested that accurate figures were almost impossible to obtain because of the secrecy and hostility of the Indians:

> "Many Indian fishing operations occur at night; 'in-and-out' type fishing makes monitoring difficult; and sales of fish occur at points of landing or fish are shipped directly out-of-state before a record or observation of the catch can be made.
>
> "Department personnel attempting to monitor the Indian fisheries are often met with obscenities and an-

tagonism. Consequently, there is an absence of solid information on catches and deriving therefore, an inability to determine the effects of this added exploitation on the fisheries resources." (55)

The Indians have moved toward self-regulation in an attempt to control the potential impact of their participation in the fisheries. One of the first steps was the identification of those who were, indeed, Indians and entitled to treaty rights. As part of the legal maneuvering prior to trial of the federal case, Michigan had filed a motion requesting that Indians be given identification cards. The Indians had long opposed such a measure but in view of the developing court battle, agreed to the idea. At this point Michigan, oddly, withdrew its own motion but the plan moved ahead and the "card-carrying Indian" is now a reality.

The Bay Mills Indian Reservation lies next to Whitefish Bay which the DNR had been stocking. In view of what they regarded as excessive Indian fishing in the area, the DNR decided that their efforts would be better expended in other areas. In short, the Indians were free to fish the Bay clean. The U.S. Fish and Wildlife Service, under the government's trust responsibility to Indians, established a fish processing plant and began stocking lake trout in Whitefish Bay. This action reportedly enraged the DNR and strong protests made their way to Washington. State officials protested that treaty rights had not been established and such facilities were premature. Yet, one would think, the assistance of the federal government would prevent the very collapse of trout stocks which Michigan had feared. The Department's anger in this matter is difficult to understand if one assumes that their main concern is restoration and maintenance of trout stocks in the area.

The Bay Mills and other Indian communities proceeded with self-regulation programs. They adopted conservation codes, set up conservation committees, and employed the services of a trained conservation officer. The Fish and Wildlife Service is providing biological data, and tribal fishing licenses are being issued. In fact, the Keweenaw group issues these licenses under a limited entry formula. In addition, attempts are being made by the Indians to voluntarily suspend their rights to fish in areas such as the Traverse Bays where there is a well-developed sport fishery and the possibility of conflict is very great.

The Department is not impressed by Indian self-regulation. The regulations are very similar to those existing in the state before the gill net ban. John Scott stated, "Upon close examination these 'codes' do not provide direct and meaningful controls because they are founded on historical regulations which did nothing more than accelerate the collapse of virtually every major fish stock in the Great Lakes." (56) The MUCC are even more emphatic, stating that the Indians have neither capacity nor experience sufficient for self-regulation. The Indians point out that these programs are only a few years old and such wide-ranging denunciation does not stem from any real evaluation of the impact of control measures.

Tom Washington of the MUCC feels that the time has come to settle the entire Indian question in the United States. He feels that the present situation has produced two classes of people, one of which possesses rights and privileges barred to the other. He advocates abrogation of treaties, the creation of a special court to handle liquidation of Indian claims, and abolition of reservations. He feels the Indians should be compensated, but once compensated, the question of superior rights and privileges should be ended. He then believes the survival of Indian culture will be the decision of individuals and groups, "If their culture survives, it will be because the Indians want it to survive, not because the government supports that culture." (57)

Interview with Jim Janetta

Upper Peninsula Legal Services: Research, Training, and Litigation Coordinator

"The very latest and best word on Indian fishing rights was a decision by a federal court in Washington state which was affirmed by the U.S. Court of Appeals and denied review by the Supreme Court. It held that if the tribes had effective self-regulation, then even if the state could regulate in terms of conservation, the state had to defer to the tribal regulations unless it could show that those regulations were not adequate to conserve the resource.

"There is good precedent, therefore, for believing that if the tribes can regulate themselves, the state can step in only at the point where such regulations prove to be ineffective or a sham. With that background in mind, both the Bay Mills and the Sault tribe have begun to take steps toward self-regulation. Bay Mills has a conservation code going back four to five years, and they have hired a conservation officer, equipped with a boat, who is being trained in the same program as U.S. Forest Service officers. There is a conservation committee issuing licenses, rules, and regulations which are remarkably similar to the DNR's rules and regulations prior to the gill net ban. They are highly regulatory but allow the use of gill nets, which is really the principal source of controversy with the DNR—that and the classification of trout as a sport fish. The Sault Tribe of Chippewa has similarly adopted a conservation ordinance in the last two years and similarly regulates the fishing of its members. The U.S. Fish and Wildlife Service has sent their biologists to consult with the tribes. In fact, a DNR man is on the Bay Mills advisory committee. Fish and Wildlife has mainly provided the biological expertise that goes with the regulations. They have done an assessment of Whitefish Bay and will be doing assessments of other areas as Indian fishing expands.

"The second main self-regulation item is the issuance of tribal fishing licenses. This is being done in conjunction with the BIA (Bureau of Indian Affairs) I.D. cards. The licenses are issued and those people with tribal licenses are then sent up to the BIA to get their identification cards. The BIA then checks to see if the persons are entitled to the tribal licenses. If they are, cards are numbered and expiration dates applied. A list of the identification card holders is then sent to the DNR so they have a list of Indian fishermen entitled to fish and thus assist them in their law enforcement efforts.

"The Keweenaw Bay Indian Community, which was the tribe involved in *Jondreau,* and not included in this treaty area, regulates mainly by limited entry. They issue only eleven or twelve commercial licenses a year and that is it. Anyone fishing without a commercial license is fishing illegally. They fish in Keweenaw Bay alone, and also have a conservation committee and rules and regulations.

"As the tribes and Fish and Wildlife learn to coordinate their efforts, I'm sure that the regulations will become more sophisticated and finely tuned to the biological realities. The tribes are new at this, and I think they have been remarkably responsible as, for instance, in closing Grand and Little Traverse Bay to Indian fishing generally, and Whitefish Bay to the taking of lake trout, all of this on the biologist's advice. To me, that severely undercuts the DNR-sportsmen complaints of completely unregulated fishing. I would be on their side if we were talking about completely unregulated fishing.

"The real battle is over the question of who is going to regulate. Ultimately the Federal Government could step in and this is something to which the state government is adamantly opposed. It doesn't look like that is going to happen, because the tribes are developing experience in self-regulation.''

"When LeBlanc was argued in the Michigan Supreme Court, Dr. Tanner came to hear the arguments and was interviewed afterwards. He said, in effect, 'If we don't put a lid on this now it is going to lead to violence.' Later a headline article dealing with the *LeBlanc* deliberations read, '*Tanner Predicts Violence.*' I thought Tanner's remarks were just inviting the violence to happen. It was a very irresponsible thing for him to do and seemed calculated to create a headline article. It may even have been an attempt to influence the decision. I thought it was an open invitation to violence. If the Indian fishing were going on in the southern part of the state, we might have a bigger problem in this regard. There is some friction between Indian and sport fishermen but nothing compared to the situation that would occur if the two groups were living and fishing in close proximity.''

(In June of 1977 G. M. Dahl, Chief of the DNR Law Enforcement Division sent a letter to all wholesale fish dealers in which he forbade sale of Indian-caught fish. *"However, this alleged treaty-secured right does not extend to a second party.* A wholesale fish dealer is, therefore, not authorized to sell Indian-caught fish of any species."* This directive was rescinded a short while later after legal action in the federal fishing rights case.) "A headline which followed was 'Judge Authorizes Sale of Tainted Fish.' The angle some of the media have peddled since then was that the levels of PCB were too high and the purpose of the letter was simply to try and keep these fish off the market. The letter says nothing about that. At the trial, the DNR never presented any testimony on that point, though the judge questioned them about it. We are not arguing that Indians can sell tainted fish. We are only arguing that it is discriminatory to say that you can buy from whites and not from Indians. If the Department has regulations to keep tainted fish off the market,

we're not going to argue that there is a treaty right to sell tainted fish. If the DNR wants to say you can't sell tainted fish, they ought to say that, not that you simply cannot sell fish. The whole thing was a gross distortion by the press of what actually transpired.''

"At the recent hearing in Petosky the sportsmen's groups testified all day about how terribly the resource was being depleted by the Indians, but none of them had any exact figures. They were waiting for the DNR. John Scott gave them the trout figures; 3.2 million pounds caught by the sportsmen. In addition illegal white commercial fishing amounted to a half million pounds while Indian fishing totaled two hundred thousand pounds. A congressional staffer was incredulous, 'You mean to tell me that illegal white commercial fishing constituted two and a half times what Indians are taking, and you're here to tell us you have to regulate the Indians?' If there is any group that is a threat to the lake trout it is the sportsmen who take sixteen or seventeen out of every twenty caught.''

"At the Petosky hearings several groups said that the Indians couldn't be allowed to fish because there couldn't be a body with regulations differing from those of the state. That is an interesting argument but it seems to point to international regulation because on four of the five lakes you have two countries involved, let alone several states. Lake Huron is as simple as the situation gets and even there you have a state, a province, and two nations. If you are going to pursue the argument of regulatory simplicity you had better be for strong, international, unitary regulation. Adding Indian tribes to the mass of regulatory agencies at hand, hardly matters at present.''

"It is clear that Congress has plenary authority to abolish provisions of Indian treaties. Although Congress could tomorrow pass a law doing away with the fishing right, the Supreme Court has also held that the fishing right is a property right and any such law would be a ''taking'' requiring ''just compensation.'' If there was such an abolition they would have to compensate the fishermen, and I cannot conceive of how you would figure the value of a perpetual fishing right in the Great Lakes. The amount of money would be astronomical and the chance of Congress doing such a thing is small. They never have abrogated such a major treaty right by statute. In addition it could ruin what is left of Indian culture, so it is a measure of cultural genocide to begin with.''

"I can understand sportsmen would be concerned about Indian fishing rights if they are consistently misled to believe that the right will mean the extermination of fish. Conservation clubs will stand on this principle, but what they are *really* concerned about is that the sportsmen may have to yield a share of the fish they are now taking if the Indians are successful. This has nothing to do with conservation whatsoever. It is simply the allocation of a given yield of fish between two user groups.''

"When you boil down the differences between the Indians and the sportsmen, it is a battle over who has the right to catch lake trout. That is it. It doesn't involve the major questions about the existence of fishing in the Great Lakes. There is no contest over coho because it hasn't been commercially exploited and probably will not be. One clear aspect of current law is that the state cannot allocate all the species to one user group in derogation of Indian treaty rights.''

"Because of the enhanced legal theories available to the Indians due to the special nature of their right, certain management motivations can be explored. We can probe the reasons for state regulations and expose them. This is not so easy if you are not dealing from a special right basis because the police powers of the state are pretty broad and you don't get to those questions. They are often raised on a political level, but we are in a position to raise them on a legal level. If the state is managing the Great Lakes for purposes other than conservation, strictly defined, they cannot impose their regulations on Indians. We know this is exactly what they are doing.''

"In Washington state, the DNR stated it had a wide management policy of allocation to the most economically advantageous user group. They were not allowed to impose these regulations on Indians. The state interest has to be strict species preservation and if the motivation is otherwise, it will not stand up.''

"If Indian treaty rights can be used as a lever to force the state into a different management position, which it clearly will, they will have to abandon the policy of favoring sport fishing to the extent that they presently do. There has to be a role for other commercial fishermen. The Great Lakes will cease to be a pond for sportsmen.''

"Commercial fishing, as a tradition, seems to run more deeply in the upper peninsula than in other parts of the State of Michigan. This is particularly true in relation to the preference of upper peninsula fishermen for, and their reliance upon, gill nets. Maybe it is because we are so far away from other employment that resistance to the DNR has been more vigorous here.

"Fishermen in the southern, more urban areas of the state can seek work in construction, auto or other industries. Fishermen in the upper peninsula, on the other hand, live in communities such as Fairport where commercial fishing is the only substantial economic activity other than farming. If the members of your family have been commercial fishermen for eight, nine or ten generations, you don't just put your nets in storage and take up farming. You certainly don't drag up and go to Detroit, some 450 miles away, to look for a job in the auto plants. The culture shock would be unbearable for most of these people. It would be just as severe if you were to take someone out of an auto factory, plunk him down in Fairport and put him to work on a gill net boat.

"Yes, the people of the upper peninsula have been more resistant to the policies of the Department of Natural Resources than people elsewhere in the state. I suspect that the upper peninsula is now the major producer of commercially harvested fish in the state. Unless drastic changes are imposed upon the DNR and the manner in which it operates, the upper peninsula may be remembered as the last Michigan source of fish for the consumer's table." (58)

Nowhere have the policies of a state resource agency been more fiercely resisted than in the Upper Peninsula of Michigan.

This statement stands as one of the few points of agreement between the Michigan DNR and opposition groups. Geographically remote from the centers of Michigan power and population, the Upper Peninsula has periodically produced home-grown separatists who dream of secession from Michigan and the establishment of an independent State of Superior. There is a widespread feeling that the Lower Peninsula takes Upper Michigan for granted, utilizing its resources and recreation potential when convenient, and ignoring the particular needs and lifestyles of its inhabitants. In recent years the main thrust of this regional antagonism has been directed at the Department of Natural Resources. Many conservation policies have been viewed as dictates imposed by distant city-dwellers to maintain private fish and game preserves for the residents of the crowded southern areas.

Such an attitude often exists in lightly populated areas of political units where residents feel themselves to be at the mercy of distant money and power. What is unusual in Upper Michigan is the extent and depth of this sentiment, crossing ideological and economic lines to embrace professionals, farmers, and factory workers as well as the factory owner. This is the land where cars and bars prominently display stickers which proclaim, "What God giveth, the DNR taketh away" and the even more emphatic, "Support the DNR—With a Rope." This feeling has even produced a motion picture, *Angry Joe Bass,* relating the struggle of Upper Michigan residents against the DNR.

It is not surprising, therefore, that this area has produced the strongest challenges, legally and illegally, to the controls placed on commercial fishing. By 1978 it would seem that if one thing had been established it was the fact that the DNR had banned large and small gill nets. But had they? In the case of the small mesh nets, they had simply banned the gear through a general rule. With the large mesh nets, however, they had amended the existing licenses to reflect the change. This technique proved to be a potentially vulnerable point.

In *Nylund vs Michigan Department of Natural Resources,* a Delta County Circuit Court considered that matter. In 1974 the DNR had proposed Rule 1074 which stated in part, ''It is unlawful to use gill nets, trap nets, pound nets, seines, and set hooks except in the manner, time, area and depths hereinafter prescribed by the director or in a research permit issued by a representative of the director.'' (Nylund p. 8) At that time Michigan administrative agencies had immense power in formulating administrative rules. Rules became effective unless both houses of the legislature voted *against* them. The legislative joint committee voted against 1074. It was overwhelmingly turned down by the Senate but the House supported it by a two-vote margin. Thus the rule was given the status of law against the vote of a majority of the legislature. The judge comments on this situation:

> ''Had the legislature desired to adopt Rule 1074 as a statute of the legislature, it could not have done so without a concurrence of the Senate. Since the legislature would not have the power to adopt a law in this manner, the Court seriously questions whether the legislature can authorize the DNR to do something which the legislature could not do itself.
>
> The Court would find the rule making procedure constitutionally infirm in this respect if that were necessary to the decision of the case; however, it is not.'' (58a)

It was not necessary because the approach was infirm in another respect. The amending procedure had been used, in effect, to adopt a rule of general application. Such a rule would normally give the parties affected the opportunity of a legislative hearing. Thus, the Court felt that the fishermen had been denied due process and on December 5, 1977 required that the temporary injunction remain in force pending agreement on a

Peshtigo Harbor, Wis.

Marinette, Wis.

permanent injunction.

It must be noted that the Court stressed that the large mesh gill net could be prohibited, as had the small mesh, by a general rule passed in the normal manner. In the meantime, however, this had become more difficult since the law on administrative rules had been changed to place the burden on the proposing agency. Now, the suggested rule required affirmative, rather than passive, action by the legislature, specifically by the legislative joint committee. There are various interpretations of why the procedure was changed. Some say that the legislature felt the old procedure gave the governor too much power while others felt the main motivation was a feeling that the DNR had acquired too much power.

There were other significant aspects of the Nylund case, however, most notably the figures produced by the DNR in support of the need for impoundment gear over gill nets. The Court refused to pass on this issue, stating such policy decisions were beyond its authority. The judge did, however, summarize the arguments of both sides. Fishermen objected to the cost of conversion and the seasonal nature of impoundment gear but utilized the figures of the DNR in one of their arguments:

> "The figures of the DNR reveal that the real threat to the lake trout and assorted game fish species is the sport fisherman who reeled in from 1,500,000 to 2,100,000 pounds of trout annually as compared to an approximate 300,000 pounds of commercial incidental catch." (59)

It is the first footnote to the preceding paragraph that is particularly interesting:

> "1. The DNR contests the figure of 300,000 which was a figure supplied by the commercial fish reports. The DNR monitoring of commercial catches in 1968 and after revealed inaccuracies in the reports.

The DNR arrived at the figure of 300,000 pounds by arbitrarily doubling the reported catch and testified that the catch was probably closer to 600,000 pounds. The fishermen claim that if the figures are inaccurate, the same inaccuracies exist in the sports fishermen's reports." (60)

What is going on? The Department has the same trouble quantifying the supposedly overwhelming threat to the trout stocks in this court case as it did in quantifying the danger from Indian fishing at the congressional hearings. The figures do not seem to support the concern. This same problem surfaces again in a footnote referring to the taking of 300,000 to 600,000 pounds of trout by the commercial fishermen. "This represents approximately 2 percent of the lake trout bio-mass in Lake Michigan according to DNR estimates." (61)

Others have noted that the Administrative Procedures Act, as constituted in 1974, had been upheld by the State Supreme Court. As to the footnoted asides, they point out that the bio-mass estimate was the judge's own extrapolation. They stress that general production statistics have nothing to do with the biology of the lake and that it is possible to simply fish a geographic hole in a fish stock, a situation which can hold back restoration efforts.

Nino Green, lawyer for the fishermen in this case, has another explanation for the seeming statistical contradiction: simple lack of knowledge on the part of the DNR.

"In a recent trial involving the right of Michigan's commercial fishermen to use large mesh gill nets, I had access to much, if not all, of the information available to the Michigan DNR when it adopted its policy to prohibit the use of such nets. Presenting themselves as experts, the DNR's own witnesses were unable to establish a rational connection between this policy and the data before them—data which, in large part, they themselves had gathered.

They could not establish the scientific validity of the methods used to gather this data. They could not explain the coincidence of the decline of harvestable species in direct proportion to the proliferation of exotic, predator species. They could not reconcile their claim that large mesh gill nets had obliterated their trout rehabilitation program with their own published claim, used for different purposes, that Lake Michigan, alone, supported a bio-mass of 11.5 million pounds of lake trout.

I don't know how they arrived at 11.5 million pounds. I'm not saying it was an accurate figure, nor am I saying that it was an inaccurate figure. But it was their figure." (62)

On September 6, 1978, the court issued a permanent injunction. It had been long delayed by a controversy over a provision proposed by the DNR, which would have required commercial operators to choose either gill nets or entrapment gear. The move was successfully opposed by lawyers for the fishermen who pointed out that information and testimony on this point had not been presented and the issue was improperly before the court. The fishermen covered by the decision are now theoretically free to fish both gear. As a practical matter, there is little inclination to take advantage of the windfall as it is simply too much trouble to fish two types of equipment at the same time.

By the late summer of 1978 there were signs that the entire question of commercial fishing was headed for a compromise solution. On August 11, John Scott, Chief of the Fisheries Division of the DNR, announced that a Task Force would be appointed to review the laws governing commercial operation. Pointing to problem areas and lack of flexibility in the current law, he stated that sport, commercial, and department representatives would begin deliberations on this matter.

Tom Washington of the MUCC, one of the members appointed to the Task Force, stated that the organization had never been in favor of eliminating commercial fishing. He feels that a fishery regulated by a combination of limited entry, zone, and gear restrictions should be utilizing that portion of the food resource that is now being wasted. He feels that a contract commercial fishery could even be allowed access to excess salmonid populations when contaminant problems are overcome.

A major effort to find a compromise solution on the question of Indian fishing rights appears to have failed. Following the Petoskey hearings, quoted above, Congressmen Philip Ruppe presented a bill in May, 1978 which included provisions for greatly expanded research on the matter of optimum sustainable yield, and a fifty million dollar hatchery program to increase fish stocks throughout the Great Lakes.

Other provisions proved more controversial. Ruppe proposed incorporating court decisions, which set aside the waters of Keweenaw and Whitefish Bays as reservation waters subject to Indian control, into the legislation. An amendment then called for a five year integration of Indian fishermen into the state system. It was proposed that the Indians eventually be allowed to hold fifty percent of the licenses issued by the state. A special program would train the tribal fishermen, and a loan program provide the boats and gear necessary for an economically successful fishing effort.

A second hearing in June, 1978, demonstrated that none of the parties affected were satisfied with this compromise approach and the effort was shelved. There were scattered reports during the summer of Indian-white confrontations and it appears the issue will be settled in the courts.

Unfortunately, not all battles were fought in the courtroom. In the past, DNR vessels have reportedly been the target of gunfire. Fishermen claim that DNR personnel have attempted to provoke violence and point to an instance where a commercial licensee was reportedly attacked by DNR agents when he attempted to take pictures of the seizure of his boat. The charges fly back and forth but, after the shooting incident, commercial spokesmen strongly condemned vigilante action. There is no doubt that the situation is tense and that tempers are running high on both sides.

Nonetheless, conditions are far from the open warfare that some accounts have suggested. The DNR and fishermen have behaved with restraint compared to some of the newspaper and other media representatives who have distorted and sensationalized events in the Upper Peninsula. Gross distortions of court, DNR, Indian, and fishermen actions have misrepresented the situation to a large number of people.

Regardless of the redneck behavior of a few individuals on both sides, the main issues are now in the courts. It is likely that they will either be decided by the courts or that a compromise will be worked out. All parties understand that the future allocation of resources is on the line. If the Indians or the commercial fishermen win a portion of those resources, the Michigan policy will have to be altered. When asked about the future of the fisheries, Asa Wright of the Michigan DNR responded, "It depends on the court decisions. If the state cannot regulate the fisheries, if the gill net is unregulated, there will be a drastic decline in many fish stocks." (63)

Fairport, Mich.

The other side just doesn't see it that way. The Indians believe that their right to cultural survival is at stake, and that a smokescreen of fear has been generated in an attempt to deny this right.

The commercial fishermen see their way of life and their right to make a living being denied in order to provide almost exclusive access to the fisheries to one user group. They argue that the public has a right to a share of this resource and they are, in effect, agents for the non-fishing public.

The debate discussed above is a struggle over allocation of a regional fisheries resource, but it is a preview of similar debates that will take place throughout the country as we begin the battle for control of limited resources. It is an opening hand of poker whose stakes will be raised as the century moves toward conclusion. Welcome to the game. Welcome to the politics of scarcity.

133

Interview with Nino Green

Attorney for Michigan's Commercial Fishermen

"I am convinced that the interest of the Michigan DNR in the Great Lakes fisheries has less to do with ecology than it has to do with the nature of bureaucracy, its irresistible urge to expand its power and influence, and its ever increasing need for more money to satisfy that urge.

"The Michigan Department of Natural Resources is funded in major part through monies received directly from the sale of licenses—monies apart from the general revenue of the state. In recent years, more than 60% of the Department's funding is paid directly to the Department through such sales rather than from legislative appropriations from the general treasury.

"To the extent that an administrative agency can secure to itself the funds with which it operates, without recourse to any legislative appropriation from the general treasury, it insulates itself from the legislative control contemplated by the establishment of three, separate branches of government. To the extent that the Department, or any state agency, is funded from sources outside the general treasury of the state, the balance of power established between the administrative, legislative and judicial branches of government is disrupted.

"Because the sale of commercial fishing licenses generates little revenue to the DNR, approximately $25,000 per year, while the sale of licenses to sport fishermen generates millions, the Department is compelled for political and economic reasons, rather than for ecological considerations, to favor sport fishing over commercial fishing, even at the risk of sacrificing commercial fishing altogether. The value of fish to the consumer, as food for the table, has no place whatsoever in the DNR's order of priorities. It profits by recreational use only.

"An alternative that has been considered by the Department is to put commercial fishing on a paying basis, that is on a basis that generates substantial revenues for the Department. They have considered the elimination of commercial fishing on the basis of licensing in favor of a contracting or franchising scheme. Thus, the Great Lakes would be divided into districts within each of which an exclusive privilege to harvest fish would be sold to the highest bidder. Additionally, the Departmen might assess the fishermen's catch on the basis of so much per pound. This would establish for the Department a direct, proprietary interest in the harvest of commercially valuable species. The Department would, in effect, engage in the business of selling the people's resource in order to generate revenues for the Department far in excess of what it now realizes through the licensing of commercial fishing."

"I am originally from the lower peninsula of Michigan. I left Detroit, where I was born and raised, some twelve years ago. At that time I was vaguely aware of a quarrel between Michigan's commercial fishermen and its Department of Natural Resources in relation to the harvesting of perch. I had acquired an image of a battle waged between huge corporate interests equipped with modern fleets and equipment with which they attempted to rape the lakes and game wardens likened to Mark Trail and his faithful dog Andy battling, alone, to save a resource on the verge of extinction.

"What I found in the upper peninsula were fishermen living in modest circumstances in small, usually isolated communities, mending by hand the nets they fish from weather and age-worn vessels. I have yet to meet Mark Trail. I don't think he operates in this neck of the woods. By and large, the game wardens I have encountered have been inadequately trained zealots imbued with the sensitivity and compassion of big city vice squad cops.

"Commercial fishing is as much a tradition as a way of earning a livelihood. It is an occupation handed down from generation to generation. These fishermen are hardworking individuals who earn a modest living when fishing is good and no living at all when fishing is bad. That they earn any living at all is attributable to the fact that they are intimately familiar with the nature and habits of fish populations that inhabit the waters of the Great Lakes. They share a knowledge and understanding that derives from the daily experience of their entire lifetimes as well as the lifetimes of ancestors going back for generations."

"Commercial fishermen have a more direct interest than sport fishermen or the DNR in preserving the fish populations that they harvest. They know that if they over-exploit the resource they will be out of business. The DNR has attempted to create a negative image of commercial fishermen. They would have people believe that these fishermen are opportunists who want to take all the fish they can, as quickly as they can, so that they can make a fortune and retire in luxury. This is nonsense. These fishermen, their fathers, grandfathers and great-grandfathers were all commercial fishermen. Fishing is a tradition to which families have clung, often in times of great adversity, for generations. Fishermen are the last people on earth who would want to damage the ecology of the Great Lakes. They want to preserve the resource for their children as it was preserved by their fathers before them.

"If commercial fishermen were so close to being driven out of business that any day of fishing might be the last, they might be tempted to grab while the grabbing is good. The DNR is pushing them in that direction, but we haven't reached that point yet, and hopefully we never will."

"Declines in commercial fish production are often attributed to overfishing by commercial fishermen. The DNR has made this a very popular complaint. But we have to recognize that this complaint is voiced by people who work for the government and are naturally embarrassed to acknowledge that government has been ineffective in its effort to control pollution. It is much easier to blame a handful of people in some remote, shoreline community than to confront a national or multinational corporate entity or the political machinery of a metropolitan agency that pollutes our waters with its wastes.

"Frankly, I don't buy the DNR's hysterical proclamation that overfishing is invariably the cause of any decline in production. I have studied the figures on almost every species of fish that has been commercially harvested in the Great Lakes and am totally unconvinced that after decades of consistent commercial fishing effort a sudden decline in a species can be attributable on any rational basis to commercial harvesting. Dramatic changes in the commercial production of fish have been incidental to one or the other of only two factors. First, the introduction of exotic species such as the lamprey, smelt and alewife, has invariably resulted in a decline of one or more harvestable, native species. Second, the fluctuations of our economy necessarily enhance or diminish the market for any product, including fish."

"They [the DNR] are always seeking ways to avoid legislative review of the policies they adopt and pursue. There is a legislatively established rule-making process applicable to all state agencies. There is also a legislatively established scheme to protect the rights of anyone who must be licensed by the state to engage in a particular business or occupation. The DNR employs various devices to avoid these limitations of its power.

"It issues 'research permits' rather than licenses so it can select the individuals it wants to favor. Privilege is conferred without licensing. Due process and equal protection guarantees are avoided.

"You can't change a license, restrict it, or suspend it without a hearing and without sound reason. But research permits are granted and withdrawn at the whim of the Department. They rarely have anything to do with research and are used to favor one individual over another. A fisherman will receive a research permit to take a marketable quantity of lake trout while other fishermen in his area are denied that privilege. If the privileged fisherman subsequently opposes the Department on any issue, the privilege may be withdrawn."

"The legislature has simply refused to look at the problem. I remember appearing before a legislative committee when the rule banning gill nets was first proposed by the DNR. One would expect that the members of that committee had a particular interest, if not some expertise, in the regulation of commercial fishing. However, they were amazed to discover that the authority to conserve and protect the natural resources of the state was vested in the legislature. They had been operating with the assumption that the DNR had powers of constitutional magnitude with which the legislature was powerless to interfere. In fact, the DNR is a creature of the legislature. The members of this committee didn't know that. How many other members of our legislature know it, even now?"

"The DNR is noted for its ability to pick a fight between two groups, one of which typically has power that vastly outweighs the power of the other. The Department invariably sides with the more powerful group in order to enlist its support for the Department's own other purposes.

"For example, the Department may issue a research permit allowing a certain fisherman to harvest a quota of a particular species of fish. The Department designates the waters and typically selects an area frequented by sport fishermen. The conflict between the two groups, which need not exist at all, is thereby intensified.

"The Michigan United Conservation Club, which purports to speak for sport fishermen, is large enough and powerful enough to call statewide attention to any situation in which it feels that its interests are threatened. The DNR invariably sides with the MUCC and, as an ally, enlists its support in other areas. Thus, the MUCC may lobby in support of the Department's request for increase in the fee for sport fishing licensing when it is convinced that rising law enforcement costs justify the increase. If it bothered to analyze the situation, it might discover that the Department itself created the problem to which its expanded law enforcement effort is addressed. I think the MUCC is being manipulated and used by the DNR."

"The Department has been trying for years to provoke antagonism between commercial fishermen and Indian fishermen. They have not succeeded and I doubt that they will. The Director (Tanner) has publicly professed his fear that competition between these two groups will lead to bloodshed. His remarks have been provocative and I think that they were intended to be provocative. However, the two groups, commercial fishermen and Indian fishermen, although they are competitive, are sympathetic toward one another. This sympathy arises, in large part, because of their shared animosity toward the DNR, the tactics that it uses, and the policies that it promotes."

"I have seen more restraint on the part of commercial fishermen than one would ordinarily expect from people subjected to the kind of harassment they have had to endure. For example, several years ago the DNR issued a blatantly illegal order directing all fishermen licensed in the northern part of Lake Michigan to remove their nets from waters within a five mile radius of St. Martin's Island. The order was issued on a Friday and delivered to the fishermen that night, after they had returned from setting, lifting and tending their nets. It directed them to remove their nets from the closed area by Monday morning and advised that any nets not removed, as ordered, would be seized.

"The purpose of the order was to create a private trout pond for a handful of sports enthusiasts who owned property on the island. The fishermen were upset—very upset. Nevertheless, after meeting on Saturday with their attorney, they went out on Sunday in the face of savage winds and, literally risking life and limb, they did remove their nets from the ''closed'' waters in order to avoid the threatened seizure or a possible confrontation with DNR officers.

"A suit was filed and the closure order was subsequently declared to be invalid. In the meantime, the fishermen had shown remarkable restraint. I cannot help but believe that the DNR had deliberately attempted to provoke an incident which could have resulted in violence so that it might generate publicity to further prejudice the image of commercial fishing in the eyes of the public and its legislative representatives.''

"Some DNR regulations affecting commercial fishing have been challenged in court. The Zone Management Plan was tested and was ultimately appealed to the Supreme Court of Michigan. The plan was upheld as a valid, regulatory scheme because the Court was reluctant to interfere with the exercise of power granted by the legislature to an administrative agency. The plan was never tested on its biological or ecological merits.

"Frankly, I think there is a very dangerous trend, not only in this state, but in other states and at the federal level. Courts are deferring to administrative agencies to the extent that the judicial check on administrative power, and the balance between the administrative and judicial branches of government is being severely impaired. The rationalization is that the power to check administrative abuse and to re-establish a proper balance can be exercised at any time. In the meantime, however, what has happened is uncontrolled bureaucratic expansion and a dangerous concentration of power in the administrative bureaucracy.''

Epoufette, Mich.

"Apparently, the DNR's program of stocking exotic species of sport fish has had considerable success in portions of the lower peninsula of Michigan. That may be fine, and perhaps the program should continue there. But it is not necessary to destroy commercial fishing throughout the Great Lakes on the theory that every drop of water is necessary to sport fishing and must be utilized by sport fishermen, to the exclusion of commercial fishermen. It simply isn't true. The sport fishermen don't utilize much of the water that is presently set aside for their exclusive use.

"Indeed, the commercial fishermen of this state have said to the DNR, 'Let us develop a hatchery capacity to stock the Great Lakes with lake trout, a species valued by both commercial and sport fishermen. We will reimburse you two to one or three to one the cost of raising these fish to harvestable maturity, and you can plant lake trout until you are assured that the population will satisfy both user groups.' I know the offer was made more than once because I was the one who communicated it. They [the DNR] wouldn't even consider it. 137

Epoufette, Mich.

"To sustain a viable commercial fishery, there must be both a gill net and an impoundment fishery. During certain times of the year fish will not lead, that is, they will attempt to swim over or through the lead mesh of a trap net. During other times of the year fish will not gill; and when they see a gill net they will avoid it rather than swim, or attempt to swim through it. When fish will not lead, they must be harvested with gill nets; and when they will not gill, they must be harvested with impoundment gear. Commercial fishing must be sustained on a year around basis. You can't expect to market your entire harvest during a single season. You can't expect a trucking company to provide transport during a part of the year only. Without gill nets, which can be fished under the ice, commercial fishing is virtually impossible in the upper peninsula from December through March. What happens to your market—to the buyers who have Canadian and other fisheries to look to for your product—while you lay up waiting for spring to arrive?

138

What happens to the trucker who hauls your fish to New York, Detroit or Chicago? If he finds other products to haul during the winter months, what inducement will you offer him to abandon these products and resume the transport of fish in the spring?

"The DNR's policies are not only ecologically unsound, they are economically blind."

"We did manage to obtain an injunction that allows commercial fishermen to continue using large mesh gill nets. The DNR, in its effort to prohibit large mesh gill nets, had authorized the same fishermen to use trap nets; and some of them now fish both gill and trap nets. This result was not intended by the DNR nor was it sought by the fishermen. It simply fell into their laps because of the ineptitude of the DNR, the efforts of which have made a hodgepodge of the entire scheme by which commercial fishing is regulated. At this point I suspect the only sensible approach would be to scrap the whole system and begin again."

Fairport, Mich.

Chapter 5:
The Eastern Jurisdictions

"I think resource agencies are in the middle and that they belong in the middle. It is our job to determine the size of the fish stock and determine what it can stand in terms of total allowable catch. It is our job to keep a finger on the pulse of the fishery and determine whether current regulations are adequate. We can say, 'Here are the options,' and I think it is our responsibility to recommend options. Beyond that, it is out of the bailiwick of the resource agency if their advice is not accepted. That is the point where you go from the biological to the social. We like to think that we take social, biological, and political considerations into our management philosophy, but when it comes down to where the power is, it is with the people through their elected representatives. I think the reason the legislature delegates power to the resource agency is because of a clear-cut recognition that the power cannot be adequately handled in the legislature. They simply have too damn much to do.

"I don't resent being in the middle. We belong in the middle. Like Harry Truman said, 'If you can't stand the heat, get out of the kitchen.' Hell, if you're successful in developing a fishery where there was nothing before you're going to have conflicting interests. Twenty years ago they didn't have anything to conflict about." (64)

Pennsylvania

"You cannot downplay the contribution of eutrophication and water quality degradation in Erie. The mayflies went at an early date. The stock compositions changed as the highly desired fish declined while less marketable fish increased in response to the changing environment. The blue pike are gone and you can say that smelt and overfishing played a part. There is the standard profile of a collapsing population where, in the last years the commercial fishery took many large individuals and then, abruptly, nothing. It is true this is the pattern of a population on its way down but I don't think it was fished down nor do I think anyone else seriously believes that. I think the habitat went. (65)

Pennsylvania borders on only forty-two miles of the Lake Erie coastline. The great population centers of the state are far from this area and thus some of the burning political pressures present in other jurisdictions are absent, as are great demands on fish populations.

Consequently, the state has not felt the need to initiate a limited entry program although it is under consideration as a possible response should greater stress be placed on stocks by commercial fishermen coming from other jurisdictions, notably Ohio. In 1978, fifty-nine commercial licenses were issued. Thirty-one of these were for gill nets, fifteen for seines, and three for trawlers. In addition ten were issued for outlines (trotlines) which have a minor impact on the fisheries.

Controls are mainly centered around gear and geographic or zonal restrictions. The minimum size of gill net mesh is set at 2½ inches. No mesh sizes are allowed in the range from slightly over three inches to 4½ inches, the minimum

allowable for whitefish and lake trout. Similar mesh restrictions apply to trap and pound nets which are presently not utilized.

Geographic and zonal controls allow gill nets no closer than three miles from Erie harbor in the winter months and four miles during the summer. In all other shoreline areas, the seasonal variation ranges from three-fourths to 1½ miles. This protects the walleye, generally close to the shore in summer, and prevents conflicts with sport fishermen. Seines and outlines are prohibited within three hundred feet of streams or tributaries.

Beyond prohibitions against the taking of traditional sport fish and various endangered species, commercial fishermen are not severely regulated. They are not prohibited walleye although the zonal restrictions greatly limit the potential catch, and, most amazing, they are not denied lake trout. The rarity of the fish in these waters has meant that no organized effort is specifically aimed at the fish, although a few are caught in nets set for perch.

Regulations are set by the state Fish Commission, a politically appointed, non-salaried board of nine members. The state resource agency generally proposes rules and a public meeting is held before the board. Regulations are then published officially for a ninety day period to allow public response and input before final consideration. The Commission meets quarterly so that they may vote on proposals which were published after the last session. Commission appointees serve staggered eight year terms with eight members representing various districts of the state, and one member selected at large.

Chinook, coho, and steelhead are planted by the state and although there is some natural reproduction, there is little expectation that stocks will become self-sustaining. Chinook and coho spawn in the fall when stream bottoms and winter ice scour are not conducive to successful reproduction. Lake trout, planted in cooperation with the federal Fish and Wildlife

Service, are hoped to eventually re-establish populations in the eastern basin of Lake Erie.

The Pennsylvania shoreline has been significantly improved by control of domestic sewage from the city of Erie, and industrial effluents from a nearby papermill. The problem is that the state coastal areas could be a North American model for water quality and still basically be at the mercy of events elsewhere. As in other jurisdictions, the lowering of PCB standards could have an impact on state stocking efforts. Another current concern is the possible construction of a large steel plant that would straddle the state line near Conneaut, Ohio, and could imperil the extensive and increasingly successful sport fishery along the small coast. The environmental impact of the proposed operation is presently being considered.

In recent years sport fishing has centered on good perch and walleye catch. Recently, deeper offshore salmon angling has begun which allows summer utilization of the fish and avoids the uncertain weather of the fall spawning season.

As everywhere else, the future of the commercial fishery is uncertain. The small state shoreline was once the center of a surprisingly large fishery that recorded harvests of between one and three million pounds until the early 1960's. It was, however, focused almost exclusively on the blue pike and when that fish collapsed the state industry was particularly hard hit. The remnant commercial operation, now averaging three to four hundred thousand pounds per year, is still basically a single specie fishery, now targeted on perch. The recent unsteady nature of Erie perch stocks may indicate further trouble. Management options in such an event include quota management or limited entry.

Because of its limited lake shoreline, Pennsylvania is necessarily in the position of reacting to the initiatives of others, rather than setting its own long term goals. This means that any state efforts must be geared to cooperative arrangements with other jurisdictions. The need to work in a cooperative framework has given managers a long perspective on the multitude of agencies and committees set up to achieve that goal. Attempts to establish coordinated programs on the Great Lakes rattle and echo through the history of the region and there is only one modern effort that consistently receives high praise. The following comment from Pennsylvania is seconded throughout the management, scientific, and fishing community of the Great Lakes:

> "The only common point we have with the larger jurisdictions where things can be accomplished in a comprehensive or constructive way is the Great Lakes Fishery Commission. You've probably heard it from others. If not, you can hear it from one cynic in the east. There are dozens of commissions but the only one that really functions constructively, that we feel comfortable working with, and that is actually doing something, is the Great Lakes Fishing Commission." (66)

New York-Erie

Perhaps the most surprising thing about the eastern end of Lake Erie is the relatively low level of chemical contamination. There are generally lower contaminant levels in fish currently common to the lake such as walleye, perch and smelt. What is surprising is the low levels present in the salmonids that have been planted in this area. Mercury and DDT levels have declined. Even the larger trout have shown levels of PCB's less than the current U.S. standard of 4 parts per million. The majority of these fish could even meet the 2 ppm standard. Tested fish have contaminant levels as low as, or lower than, those taken from inland lakes.

Nonetheless, chemical contamination remains a persistent threat:

141

"It seems like we are collecting more fish for the damn chemical analysis than for the traditional management purpose of determining species composition, age, growth, or population dynamics. You get by the PCB's, the DDT, and the mercury only to wonder what will be the next thing off the chemists' shelf. Some of the fish we are sending to EPA are being tested for 98 separate chemicals." (67)

New York is currently attempting to enhance the sport potential of Erie and in recent years the lake has been estimated to be the most heavily fished area in the state. As elsewhere the purpose behind plantings of lake trout has been the creation of self-sustaining stocks. The eastern basin was the historic home of that fish in Erie. Although there has been some evidence of limited rainbow and chinook reproduction, they and the other planted species, coho, brown, and steelhead, have been viewed primarily as the center of a put, grow, and take sport fishery.

There has been considerable abatement of local pollution sources as three large industries recently began utilizing new sewage treatment facilities. Despite relatively favorable conditions, it is thought that the widely publicized contamination crisis in other parts of the state has been the cause of the current decline in license sales.

Although there is no official limited entry policy in the New York waters of Erie, it is an unwritten rule to issue commercial licenses only to state residents. Approximately thirty of these licenses are issued to what is basically a part-time fishery, and of this number there are estimated to be only a half dozen serious operators in the New York waters. Gill nets are about the only gear currently in use and the minimum mesh size of 2¾ inches, the toughest on Erie, is designed to protect perch through at least one spawning. These nets must be at least 1½ miles offshore from May 1 to October 1 and outside the 24-foot

depth contour the remainder of the year.

The power to determine the time, location, and manner in which commercial fishing is permitted rests with the Department. Mesh restrictions, however, are set by the legislature.

Twenty-five years ago the blue pike provided the mainstay of a commercial catch that sometimes exceeded a million pounds per year. Today two to three hundred thousand pounds, primarily of yellow perch and walleye, is the best that can be expected. All salmonids are barred to the commercial licensees.

Recently the Department was given the authority, on a three-year experimental basis, to regulate the sport fishery as to size, season, and limit. A persistent problem in the Erie area is the lack of an adequate profile of the current sport fishing opportunities. Recently a station has been established at Dunkirk to more adequately serve the recreational needs of the region.

The New York agency participates in the attempts to bring minimal management coordination to Lake Erie and the situation has improved considerably in recent years. For instance, Pennsylvania recently cancelled plans to stock striped bass after obtaining the opinion of the other jurisdictions that the present species mix should first be evaluated. Often, however, the parties simply agree to disagree. The large Canadian commercial smelt fishery is at odds with the U.S. salmonid stocking programs for the obvious reason that salmon like to eat smelt.

New York—Ontario

Ontario has been the Great Lake longest exposed to the effects of white settlement. Most of its high valued fish have disappeared, alien species continuously introduced, and its watershed subject to steady visible and invisible pollution.

The invisible pollution has begun to make headlines. Love Canal has graduated from a place name to a symbol and raised the uneasy sensation in many people that we may have entered a technological cul de sac.

Consider the fish managers of New York. Plans were laid for a vast expansion of the lake sport fishery after the successful Michigan salmon plantings of the late 1960's. Lake Ontario seemed particularly well suited for such a venture, having experienced the loss of its cold game fish at an early date. Enthusiastic sport groups provided a supportive political structure for these new programs. Coho, chinook, lake trout, rainbow, steelhead, and brown trout were planted. Plans for an eleven million dollar hatchery were drawn up. A strongly motivated management crew looked forward to the opportunity and challenge of creating a viable fishery. Then one day they came to work and were told that their programs had been suspended.

Their plans had been halted by the effects of the spreading chemical plague. In this case the principal villain is Mirex, developed to slay the fire ant which has overrun large areas of the southeastern United States. Mirex has done little to halt the progress of the fire ant but has demonstrated a great ability to enter the food chain.

On September 14, 1976, possession of coho and chinook salmon was banned. Trout Unlimited and other powerful sport interests threatened a court suit. The state health department wavered on the question of immediate danger to human beings and the sport ban was lifted. The fishery opened with the familiar warning label as to possible dangers on March 31, 1978.

Nonetheless, it has at least temporarily meant the end of chinook planting.

Coho, once planted by the hundreds of thousands, have been reduced to a token forty thousand, and the main function of this small number is to serve as a living contaminant monitor.

What do you do when planted fish have been declared inedible? This question, which may soon face all U.S. jurisdictions, is an extremely difficult one. It is one thing to discontinue a put-and-take fishery. Despite the political uproar, managers know that stocking may be resumed if contaminant levels improve. It is quite a different matter if your aim is to create a self-sustaining population. The planted fish may continue to carry unacceptable contaminants for years. If discontinued, however, whatever progress has been made toward establishing reproductive populations will likely be lost, and there is some evidence of limited lake trout reproduction in Lake Ontario. New York has chosen to continue the planting of this fish, as well as browns and rainbows. In response to the possible human health problems, managers swiftly developed specific recommendations to move the emphasis of the stocking program away from Pacific salmon to fish that are not as prone to heavy contamination.

Nonetheless, plans to reconstruct the fish populations of the lake are in limbo between political pressures and chemical realities. Managers are understandably frustrated at the difficulty of penetrating this dilemma. Their responsibility is the management of fish, and this is what they would like to do.

Increasingly precise chemical analysis may be detecting contaminants in fish that were previously unnoticed. The problem is not simply Mirex. The channel catfish, for instance, remains under a ban after having shown an unusual contaminant sophistication by concentrating both PCB's and Mirex. The synergistic (combined) effects of these chemicals is suspected to be particularly sinister.

The remnant commercial fishery, ironically, has been little affected by the contaminant problem. Banned from all salmonid catch, only the prohibition on channel catfish has affected operations. American eel also contain unacceptable levels, but one of the major destinations of this species is foreign markets and these markets continue to be available if the importing country permits higher contaminant levels than those allowed by the United States.

Only four of the twenty-one commercial licensees are considered full time operators. Gill, fyke, and trap nets are used. Bullheads are sought in the spring and yellow and white perch in the summer and fall. Annual landings are in the two to three hundred thousand pound range.

The commercial activity on the lake has often been characterized as that of a mosquito fleet. The political climate is no more favorable to commercial fishing here than in the western jurisdictions. Sport fishermen vastly outnumber commercial operators and tend to prevail when conflicts arise. The money comes from sport fishing and so does the management emphasis. The main hope for expanded commercial activity lies in utilization of what are presently regarded as lower value fish.

In addition to problems with chemicals, Ontario managers are working with the least adequate data on the Great Lakes. The early decline of the Ontario fishery and the limited research done on the lake has meant there is a blank in the lake's ecological history. Most early sampling efforts were directed at desirable food fish, so agencies were unable to keep tabs on the total biomass of the lake. Thus, for all the limitations, one is aware of how important commercial statistics have been when confronted by their relative absence on the U.S. side of Lake Ontario.

Further, one student of the New York fisheries indicated that the state was thirty years behind in lake research partly because of a stand-off with federal officials. The basic New York position for years was that they would be happy to conduct research if the federal government would provide the funds. The Bureau of Commercial Fisheries, for its part, demanded a larger role in the conduct and direction of such research. The unproductive nature of this conflict has been of educational value to present U.S. and state officials. Cooperative research is now the order of the day.

This attitude extends to Canada, despite differences in attitude toward commercial fishing. Stocking programs are reviewed by state and provincial officials and there is an informal exchange of information on all aspects of fisheries research.

In New York, resource managers have been caught in the bind of biological politics to a greater degree than their colleagues in other states. They have felt the adverse effects of the Niagara River chemical complex for years. It was always difficult to make headway against the economic and political clout of the polluters. Now publicity and exposure of the problem has given them some of the clout. Considerable patience and skill will be needed, for the fight is just beginning.

Interview with Claude Ver Duin

Commissioner, Great Lakes Fishery Commission
Publisher, The Fisherman

"We had sports fisheries back in the early days, and I told the fishermen many times in the meetings, 'The sport fishing business is going to expand. We're going to have a shorter work week. We're going to have more leisure. People are going to have money over and above the necessities of life to spend on recreation. In the industry we should recognize this and make room for them. Join your local conservation club so when they talk about these things you can explain how and where they would work and where they wouldn't. Let's get this done in an orderly way.

"But the commercial fisherman by virtue of his way of life is an individualist. They leave the dock and they're in a world of their own until they come back. After a hard, long, day on the lake I had a rough time reading the local newspaper before I'd fall asleep. Particularly in the early days these men lived in a world of their own making. They couldn't see that there were going to be inroads made in the industry in the interest of sport fishing. Even today there are commercial fishermen who can't recognize that the sport fisheries have a claim. They sure as hell do.

"The only thing I feel bad about is that the people who are paying the bill, the American public, are not getting their share of the benefits. The general taxes of the United States support the lamprey program and without it there could be no fishery of any consequence. These same taxes also support lake trout hatcheries. Today the sport fishermen are the only ones getting the benefit from all that money. That has got to change. There has got to be a sharing of the resource among the principal users.

"The public should understand that when a commercial fisherman goes out in the lake, he is going for fish that belong to the public. They're not his fish. He didn't plant them. When he brings them in, they should be available to everybody. All he can claim is that he should be paid for going out and getting their share of the fish. Actually, the commercial fisherman is operating a consumer fishery. They have another choice. They can go out, buy a boat and license, and catch their own."

"I've actually called fishermen and said, 'I've talked to your representative in Lansing. He is going to be home for Easter vacation and would love to have you come over and talk to him about your problems. Do you know him? No, well then here is his address. Here is his name. For God's sake get involved.'

"A month later I'd go back and talk to the representative. He'd shake his head and say to me, 'Joe Blow never came to see me.'"

"John Van Oosten's writings have been used very selectively. It's like quoting the Bible. You can take any one verse out of context and simply say that it came right out of the Bible. A lot of people will believe you on that basis alone. But if you read the paragraph ahead of it or the verse behind it, the meaning is changed.

"Van Oosten recognized that the resource could be overfished and conducted a lot of investigations to determine if it was being overfished. I'll tell you one thing: he was an advocate of a multi-species fishery, each species being a seasonal fish.

"We fished lake trout in the winter, and we fished with hooks because we couldn't afford to risk losing a gang of nets. They were too expensive. In the spring we fished perch, and in the summer we fished chubs and whitefish. In the fall we went back to lake trout. While you were fishing one species, the others had a chance to recuperate.

"The DNR, by their own actions, forced the remaining fishermen on the east shore of Lake Michigan to overfish the chubs when that was the only species left to them. As long as we had a multi-species fishery, and that is what we want to get back to, each fishery was more or less seasonal.

"When you get down to a one-specie fishery and have four months of effort on it, I don't give a damn what specie it is, it's going to be overfished."

"I recall sitting in the meeting when the first proposal was made to the effect that we might be able to find a specific poison. When I heard somebody say that a chemical had been developed which controlled the corn borer without affecting other things, I said that if it could be done for the corn borer it could be done for lampreys. Six thousand and some hundreds experiments later they had it."

"I think the pendulum has begun to swing the other way. Tanner, who was death on gill nets, got up in a public meeting and declared that he could envision the day when there would be self-sustaining stocks of lake trout in the offshore waters. Then, he felt, we will need a commercial fishery with gill nets to harvest those fish; to do less would be a waste of a natural resource."

"One of the things about a gill net is that it is set on the bottom. It obviously doesn't take fish except those near the bottom and therefore takes very few salmon because they occupy the mid-strata.

"Now, if you want to take a gill net and buoy it, or 'can' it, as the fishermen say, you can fish it at any level. You can slaughter the salmon by simply setting it at their depth. That is what they did in Indiana, and they took a tremendous number of salmon. This is what actually gave the gill net such a bad name.

"In a very short period of time the Indiana fishermen, and there are few of them, shipped about 80,000 pounds of salmon to the Chicago market. Immediately the word got out that the fish were being slaughtered with gill nets. Naturally, when you point out that a gill net set in a small area took 80,000 pounds of salmon in a short period of time—hell, no wonder the sportsmen were up in arms. I would've been too.

"Our Michigan DNR never took the trouble to point out that regulations in Michigan would have made that technique illegal. It was expedient from their point of view not to tell the whole story."

"I think the Wisconsin limited entry bill was fairer than Michigan's and certainly a hell of a lot fairer than Illinois'. Wisconsin just said that anyone who has a license this year can have one next year. Next year eighty percent of your livelihood must come from the industry—you can't be a retired fireman who fishes for fun—and you must have an investment of at least $5,000 in the industry. If you meet that criteria you can be licensed the following year.

"That is pretty reasonable. The person has to make a decision whether he wants to be a fisherman or whether he wants to be something else. The decision is up to him, not the state agency."

"There is a lot of talk about uniform regulations. One of the fishermen got up at one of our meetings and said, 'When you talk about uniform regulations, and you mean by that if eight inches is the legal size for a fish in Michigan, it has to be the legal size in Wisconsin, it won't work. The situation under which we are fishing is not uniform; the habitat varies from place to place.'

"What you have to talk about is how we manage a fishery so that we achieve a balance by perpetuating a healthy population while harvesting the harvestable resource. Perhaps the harvestable population in Michigan waters can be cropped in six months while that in Wisconsin waters takes nine months. Suppose you have a uniform season. If you make it six months, you are not harvesting what you could in Wisconsin. If you make it nine months, you overfish in Michigan for three months. Instead of talking so much about uniform regulations, we should be talking about uniform management of the resource.''

''There is going to continue to be a strong emphasis on sport fishing, but there will come a time when there will be self-sustaining stocks of lake trout in the offshore waters. I am sure that these will be reserved primarily for the commercial fisheries for three reasons:

''First, there has got to be a commercial fishery in order to regulate some of the species in which sport fishermen have no interest. You can't use this, however, as an excuse to make them garbage collectors. They can't survive as garbage collectors, simply fishing for underutilized species.

''Second, the public is entitled to some of these fish. They're paying the bill.

''Third, and of equal importance, the average sportsmen has no damn business being forty miles from shore. There are plenty of places for him to fish without jeopardizing his life and equipment in any one of the Great Lakes.''

''We have to have a complete inventory of stocks. We must know the complete composition of the biomass. How many alewives are there? How many lake trout? How many salmon? How many more fish could be supported by the forage base without putting it in jeopardy? Have we gone far enough with planting and should we now take a look at these four billion odd pounds of alewives as human food?

''In the Bay of Fundy there was a substantial herring fishery. An inventory showed that too many of the small herring were going to waste in the food chain. The solution was the creation of a sardine industry with the small herring. They developed a tremendous fishery in which the production of all species went up.

Claude VerDuin

''What our Commission (Great Lakes Fishery Commission) had been concerned with is the lack of knowledge on what constitutes the biomass of a given lake. You can't regulate a fishery without knowing all the component parts. We know there is an interaction between species. When alewives exploded, perch and herring declined. It doesn't make a lot of sense to rebuild a herring fishery unless the alewife population is going to be reduced to the point where the herring have a fighting chance. In the future management of the fisheries, we have to manage the total biomass.''

Chapter 6:
The Canadian Attitude

"The future for Ontario's commercial fishery appears bright. A growing demand for fish and fishery products has created strong markets and fish prices are rising. With this increased demand for protein, the world is entering a period of technological innovation that can lead to revolutionary advances in the techniques of harvesting fish and the production of new fishery products. The challenge in the face of these advances is to use the renewable fishery resource wisely and rationally to maintain stocks for the future." (68)

Michigan stressed her dominant position in the 1966 statement on the future of the Great Lakes fishery. Her 41 percent water ownership is, however, closely followed by Ontario's 36 percent. Michigan is a distant second, moreover, in shoreline ownership. The Canadian shorelines add up to nearly 5,000 miles, while Michigan's are just over 3,000.

The massive Province of Ontario with 413 thousand square miles of land reduces Texas' 267 thousand to a welcome humility. The Province stretches from a point on Hudson Bay at nearly the same latitude as Anchorage, Alaska, to Point Pelee at a latitude south of the northern border of California. Its western boundary is north of western Minnesota and its eastern, nearly due north of New York City.

This single political unit contains all the Canadian waters of the Great Lakes while the U.S. side is shared by eight states. In addition, a tenth of the Province, excluding the Great Lakes, is covered by fresh water. In talking to Canadian fishermen and fish managers, one is aware of a wider perspective.

Ontario has been the center of much of the scientific investigation of the Great Lakes, including the pioneering international symposium on Salmonid Communities in Oligotrophic Lakes (SCOL) which is widely regarded as a great advance toward understanding the effect of stresses placed on lakes by man's activities.

Canadian attitudes toward use and abuse of the Great Lakes has varied significantly from those of the various U.S. jurisdictions. One of the notable differences has been its policy on use of the fisheries. Limited entry is a control of long standing and there are additional restrictions centered around open and closed seasons, size limits, quotas, and specified fishing areas.

The license itself is a means of control. The document describes the exact privileges of each user, and the fee is based on the type and amount of gear used. Under the prevailing philosophy, controls are aimed at accommodating commercial fishing to the point of "maximum sustainable yield," the point beyond which additional effort results in fewer and smaller fish:

"The primary industry takes an active interest in new fishing gear and techniques. Both the federal and provincial governments assist the industry in developing more efficient and economical gear and handling techniques. Joint ventures between government and industry have resulted in the adoption of the otter trawl, the development of a fish meal plant, the development of a bulk handling technique for smelt and numerous exploratory fishing operations throughout the Great Lakes." (69)

It is thus apparent that both the provincial and federal governments have taken a hand in aiding the commercial fishing industry. In the early 1960's a weak market for perch led to the Fisheries Prices Support Board which provided a form of price control. This helped the extremely large perch fishery, particularly on Lake Erie.

The economical harvest of smelt was another problem faced by fishermen. Traditional methods made the harvest of this fish a marginal proposition. Existing nets were simply unable to gather enough of the fish to cover labor and overhead. With government assistance, the otter trawl was developed. A large cone-shaped net is carried on the trawl until electronic fish-finding gear locates a large school of fish. The net is then ''shot'' and towed through the concentrated mass of fish which are gathered in the tapered end. It is stated that a day's fishing can then be completed in an hour. By 1971 there were over 200 trawl nets being utilized by the Ontario fishery.

This increased fishing ability produced handling problems. The traditional 25 to 30 pound boxes require as many as 14 men working up to 12 hours. Boxes were often broken and icing was insufficient to preserve fish quality because of the time involved. Federal and provincial governments combined efforts with the fishermen and tested polyethylene and wooden totes with capacities of up to 250 pounds. It was discovered that the wooden totes were more efficient. Polyethylene liners were used to prevent fish contamination and layers of fish were alternated with ice. The liner was then folded across the top to keep out air. The totes are constructed so as to be interlocking and are piled four high. For unloading the boat, lifting equipment is used to remove the stacks of totes. One operation estimated that it saved over $85,000 in a single year using this technique. (70)

The government has also sponsored exploratory trawling operations to determine the economic feasibility of fishing in underutilized areas. It was discovered that smelt operations in western Lake Ontario would be of a marginal nature and similar experiments in Huron revealed problems because of the rocky lake bottom.

The federal government has also sponsored a program whereby the cost of boat modernization and repair is partially subsidized. The Ontario government has maintained a program to assist fishermen in the more remote northwestern part of the province, away from the Great Lakes proper. There, in order to encourage the harvest of unutilized fish, fishermen are reimbursed a portion of their high transport costs.

The closure of fisheries due to contamination appears to be a persistent threat on the Great Lakes. In Ontario, the Fisheries Loan Act, which ended in 1973, provided loans to fishermen who were forced out of business by contamination closures in 1970. The loans were forgiven in 1976.

In addition, fifty percent of the cost of chilling equipment for vessels and processing plants has been subsidized by the government. Insurance, a large cost item for commercial operators, has been provided at below-market interest rates under the Fishing Vessel Insurance Plan. There were 110 Great Lakes vessels with an insured value of $3 million covered during 1976–77. The plan is designed to be self-supporting and is not considered a subsidy program.

The effect of this attitude toward the commercial fisheries can be seen on Lake Erie. In 1976 the Ontario fishermen harvested over 17 million pounds of smelt, while the combined total of the four U.S. jurisdictions totaled 39 *thousand* pounds. Until the mid-fifties, the U.S. production of all Erie species exceeded the Canadian totals, but in recent years they have sunk to a quarter of the amount harvested in Ontario. Several Ontario fishermen credited a good deal of their success to the restrictions placed on their U.S. counterparts by the various state governments. It is obvious that policies have been working in

two different directions.

The various programs of government assistance, while significant, are only part of the story. Equally important is what Ontario has chosen *not* to do. There have been no major efforts to institute limitations on efficient gear such as the gill net. Also, the province simply did not enforce the eight-inch limit on Lake Erie perch for a number of years. Declining catch and alarms about conditions of stocks led to tighter controls in 1977. Populations are being monitored to determine what future controls may be necessary.

The vastly different attitudes of the Canadian governments led the U.S. General Accounting Office (GAO) to the following conclusion in its 1977 report on the Great Lakes:

> "We believe the relative success of Canada's commercial fishing industry compared with that of the U.S. industry can be attributed, in part, to the fewer and less restrictive regulations imposed by Canadian authorities." (71)

This spirit of accommodation will be tested as the Ministry of

Natural Resources moves toward a more comprehensive definition of allowable harvest. Ontario commercial licenses are issued annually and at one time there were approximately 2,000 such licenses issued in the province. This number has been reduced to about 1,000 as the inactive operators have been phased out. Once the question of allowable yield is resolved, the ministry plans to negotiate with the user groups to determine allocation. In order to provide the province with flexibility in determining what is an allowable harvest, there may have to be a mechanism to compensate for increases in gear efficiency.

Stocking policies in Ontario also reflect a different philosophy. The province has aimed rehabilitation programs at the goal of natural reproduction. In Superior the goal is the establishment of a self-sustaining lake trout population and stocking efforts have been directed toward this end. In Huron this goal is limited by the fact that native trout have been wiped out. Efforts with kokanee salmon provided stocking through two life cycles of the fish (six years) in hopes that it would become established. Stocks are now on their own. Efforts with the splake, discussed earlier, are aimed at producing a fish that achieves sexual maturity at the maximum allowable size and longevity before becoming a target of the lamprey. In Erie, a small number of rainbow trout are planted.

Lake Ontario presents the greatest challenge as managers have tried to determine whether water quality problems are so severe that they presently preclude natural reproduction in splake and lake trout. The long-term effort is aimed toward establishing those species in the healthier eastern basin. Only around Toronto are coho stocked in large numbers. Even here, these fish will provide recreational fishing opportunities only until a "put-and-take" fishery can be established for splake and/or rainbow trout. The streams of the Great Lakes in general are not regarded as sufficient to provide enough lakewide production, and it is believed necessary to establish shoal spawning populations.

Not only is the primary provincial goal directed toward self-sustaining populations, it is directed toward native fish. As in the states, growing recreational demands may produce political pressures toward stocking:

"If we do get forced into this artificial fishing business on a long term basis we're much better off to do it with species that are native to which we have access over the long haul." (72)

Why such a difference in attitude? In terms of political reality, the main reason has to be that commercial fishermen in Ontario possess a degree of economic power in relation to the province that U.S. fishermen did not, and do not, have in relation to the various states. The fishery is scattered throughout the province with a large portion of the catch going to an export market and, consequently, favorably contributing to the balance of payments. With the exception of Lake Ontario, the lakeshore areas are generally more lightly populated than those of the U.S. side, so the industry also plays a proportionately greater role in the local economy.

There is also a different philosophy toward utilization of the resource. Canadian managers seem to be more aware of the food value of the fish and the growing world need for protein.

There is more to it than this, however. Ontario has a much smaller population in relation to its recreational resources than do the states to the south. There are vast inland areas available for fishing and water recreation. Some Ontario fishermen are aware of this difference and have stated that it is primarily the lack of pressure from sport fishing, manufacturing, and outfitting groups that has allowed them to flourish. If that attitude were to change or perhaps be actively altered by management agencies, their position could deteriorate rapidly. Some of these pressures are building and many stem from U.S. attitudes.

Most, however, come from Canadian experiences with depleted coastal and inland fish stocks.

All of this is still insufficient to explain the relative good will that seems to prevail among the sport, commercial, and fish management interests. There seems to be a great deal of civility in dealing with the problem. In the fall of 1977, I talked with a commercial fisherman who, as a representative of the regional fishing association, was about to meet with spokesman for sports and tourist interests to discuss problems which had arisen in a portion of Georgian Bay. Their goal was to work out a mutually acceptable solution to then be presented to the Ministry of Natural Resources for approval or comment. There was an air of accommodation that was startling to anyone aware of the bitter battles that have raged in some of the states.

The Canadian approach has some obvious implications for U.S. policy. Why is it possible for such a rational adjustment of conflicting interests between the two main user groups attainable in Ontario and seldom south of the border? Why is the food value of the commercial catch frequently stressed by provincial officials but seldom mentioned in the states? What sense does it make to limit harvests and fishermen on the U.S. side if fishing effort is redoubled on the Canadian side? What sense does it make to eliminate the gill net in one place while the otter trawl is being developed in another?

These are questions that will be discussed at greater length in the concluding section. The odd thing is that while all the questions about the proper use of the fishery were being debated in the late sixties and early seventies, another issue arose which may make all of them quite academic. It arose slowly as governments and individuals became aware that the chemical and industrial wonderland that had fostered our high-rolling standard of living had a darker side. Suddenly fisheries began to close for reasons that had nothing to do with management philosophies or sports and commercial interest conflicts.

Aerial photograph of Green Bay NASA/USGS-EROS Data Center

SECTION 4:
THE LAG FACTOR

". . . In the present century, species have become rare or have disappeared from sections of lakes or entire lakes during periods of accelerated changes in water quality. These conditions have often developed after fishing had ceased to be profitable or was virtually absent, and after marine species had had their full effect." (1)

". . . It worries me that we keep losing the battles of the mining operations, pulp and paper mills and what not, because of the economics of the situation, so I think we have a major job in getting a handle on this value system by taking the issue more intelligently to the public . . . I think we need to seriously present the people with a better knowledge of what this value system is all about. It is not enough to say that we must have a nice clean environment because we all want that. We have to get down to some dollars and cents and compare our economic or environmental values too, even if we have to develop a new, comparative value system." (2)

" There is no doubt that we are still playing a catch-up game." (3)

Chapter 1:
The Second Stage

The first stage of pollution was the almost inevitable accompaniment of the life style of the European settlers. Wherever new settlement occurred, the land was cleared and the environment altered. Wildlife had always retreated in the wake of expanding populations. The destruction of the ancient forests, the building of dams, and the crude disposal of wastes were a by-product of settlement and the higher the concentration of people, the greater the effect.

In many parts of the Great Lakes basin the first stage of pollution was followed by a period of recovery. The land adjusted to the new regime and accommodated it, new growth slowly reclaimed the soil and root structures of the obliterated forests, the sawmills closed and the dams that had served them disappeared. Marginal farms were abandoned and the forests slowly recovered. Portions of the nothern basin saw population drop steadily from the early years of this century until after 1940.

The second stage was the product of forces that accumulated through this century and were to result in the lifestyle that emerged during and after World War II. The population was not only growing but concentrating in greater numbers in urban areas. The economy was steadily shifting to an intensive mass production that utilized increasing amounts of raw materials. These forces, held in check by the Great Depression, became dominant during the massive expansion of industry during the second World War. In years following the war, the rising standard of living pushed the process to an almost geometric progression.

The great cities of the watershed grew and dumped their sewage into the convenient lakes and their tributaries. Industries did the same with increasingly complex substances that fueled the industrial miracle. Households now had the washer and dryer. A dash of detergent, the press of a button, and good-bye to the wringer, hand scrubbing, and waiting for a sunny day. The automobile had to get to work as the system depended on efficient daily maintenance of industry and commerce. Life could no longer stop to accommodate the seasons, so snow and ice are banished from the auto's path by ordinary rock salt. Life is increasingly comfortable. No more mosquitoes on the front porch, flies in the bedroom, or worms on the tomatoes. Spray it and forget it. From the same acre three times the yield without that smelly manure. Spray the much more presentable chemical fertilizers and forget them.

The City of Green Bay closed its beaches in the 1940's. Dangerous during the polio season. Along Lake Erie recreation areas were closing during the early 50's. Massive algae blooms change the color of the water, large stringy masses of weeds wash up on the shore, and mix with alewives. Where did *that* come from? The water tastes funny. Very irritating.

All the snaphot memories of a time when these events seemed separated from one another. Annoying, but isolated incidents. Part of the small price to be paid for the great improvement in the standard of living. Actually lakeside residents were watching the accelerated deterioration of the lakes; an increasing destruction of water quality, recreational areas, and aquatic environment. The term used to describe this process is "cultural eutrophication."

Lakes exist in various trophic states. A shallow inland lake may be surrounded by dense plant growth. In summer the waters warm to the bottom, encouraging the rapid turnover of large amounts of small plant and animal life. The decay of such materials maintains a high nutrient level and these euthrophic lakes are generally highly productive in terms of plant and animal life. Oligotrophic lakes, on the other hand, are generally colder, deeper, and less productive. During the summer season they do not warm to the bottom. Warm surface waters of uniform temperature, the epilimnion, form over a zone known as the thermocline where water temperatures drop rapidly. Bottom waters, the hypolimnion, are of uniformly colder temperature and inhibit the rapid turnover of life forms. Nutrients are generally less abundant in these lakes and the total population, the biomass, is most often lower than that of eutrophic lakes.

This is a very general picture of a complex and somewhat vague concept. At one time it was generally believed that in the course of the "natural" aging process lakes moved from oligotrophic to eutrophic. This concept has largely been supplanted by the belief that the trophic state of the lake tends to remain the same over the bulk of its history. Thus eutrophication is not synonomous with aging. Basically an oligotrophic lake is nutrient poor and a eutrophic lake is nutrient rich.

Cultural eutrophication occurs when nutrients increase in a lake because of human activities. The major sources of this increase are expansion of industry, agriculture, and population in the watershed. Nutrients are added to the system and changes begin to appear at the level of microscopic plants and animals. These changes gradually affect more species in a progressively larger area. In the past they were generally perceived only when they began to seriously affect desirable fish species and drinking water quality. By that time serious damage had already oc-

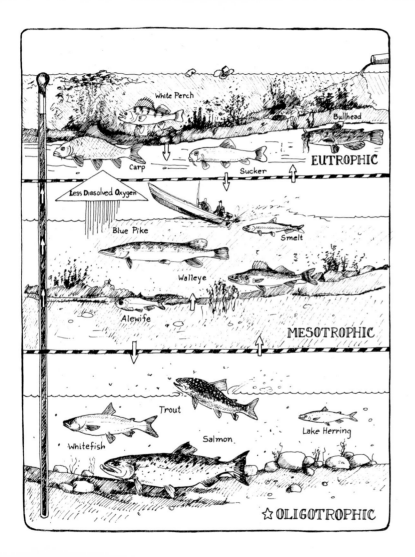

White Perch

Bullhead

Carp

Sucker

EUTROPHIC

Less Dissolved Oxygen

Blue Pike

Smelt

Walleye

Alewife

MESOTROPHIC

Trout

Salmon

Lake Herring

Whitefish

☆ OLIGOTROPHIC

curred. Thus the lag factor has historically meant that efforts were directed at preventing or limiting further damage, rather than at maintaining or restoring a healthy aquatic environment. A search, therefore, has been made to find an early warning system of changes before major damage occurs.

Cultural eutrophication affects different bodies of water in different ways. The following description illustrates how the process might affect a hypothetical lake. There are a number of ways to chart the change in the lake by actual changes in the chemical composition of the water and by species changes in small plants and animals. Let us picture the oligotrophic state. Phosphorous is present at less than ten parts per million, chlorophyll at 0 or 1 to 2 parts per million, and water is highly transparent and tastes and smells pure. There are certain plankton that thrive in this nutrient poor environment with its high quantities of dissolved oxygen.

As various lakeside sources pour nutrients in the water, the lake enters a mesotrophic state. Phosphorous approaches 10 to 15 ppm and chlorophyll 5 and 10 ppm. The taste, transparency, and odor, of the water begin to change. A species of mayfly, hexagenia, becomes less abundant, and the amount of dissolved oxygen begins to decline.

As the lake becomes eutrophic phosphorous and chlorophyll exceed 15 and 10 ppm respectively, complaints become common about the taste, appearance, and smell of drinking water. Plankton species change yet again to those best able to thrive in the nutrient rich waters. Dissolved oxygen falls below 6 ppm. A filamentous green algae, cladophora, or a red algae, bangia, may appear while a small oppossum shrimp, mysis relicta, disappears. (4)

Cladophora may have a major impact on local environments. It may become so dense as to be an obstruction to pleasure craft.

156

Cladophora and similar growths can destroy sport fishing areas as has happened in the Thousand Island Region of the St. Lawrence River. Large masses of cladophora frequently wash ashore in summer causing costly clean-up problems in park and recreation areas. The value of lake front real estate on the north shore of eastern Lake Erie has been reduced up to 15 to 20 percent, with the presence of cladophora. (5)

These measuring devices have various advantages and disadvantages. Chlorophyll and phosphorous have been measured for over fifty years and are conservative and reliable indications of water quality changes. They may not, however, reflect increasing nutrients for five to forty years while plankton changes may show up within a year. (6) There are also indications that the amount of phosphorous needed to produce environmental changes may be smaller than previously believed:

> "The magnitude of the phosphorous increase needed to produce the change is not known, but it could result from an average increase of only a few tenths of a microgram per litre, which might be impossible to detect in the lake. Processes of this type in large aquatic systems with relatively long residence times point to the need of limiting phosphorous inputs as much as is practically possible." (7)

The Great Lakes are so large that they do not respond in the uniform, overall manner of smaller lakes. Changes will occur in one part of the lake and only gradually appear in the other sections. Changes tend to appear first in harbor areas and then show up in onshore waters, and only gradually affect the open waters. The problem is that these nearshore waters are "of the greatest importance to us for fish production, water supply, waste disposal, and recreation, but they are first to be altered by pollution." (8)

The entire Great Lake system must be understood as just that; an interconnected flow of water from the western areas of the basin to the St. Lawrence outlet. Viewed in a relatively unpolluted state, about 1900, the flow can be traced by the concentration of various ions in each lake. Superior and Michigan flow into Huron. Superior reflected low values for the calcium, sulfate, chloride, magnesium sodium, and potassium ions in its basin. Limestone in the Michigan basin added calcium and magnesium. Erie added more of these two substances, plus sulfate. The chloride content of the lower lakes was not much different than that of the upper lakes.

Fifty years later it can be seen that there have been great increase of calcium, sulfate, and chloride. There have been no corresponding increases of magnesium, and magnesium is not normally an important constituent of waste water as are the other materials. (9)

The process of increasing concentrations of wastes as water passes through the system has produced the worst deterioration in Lakes Erie and Ontario. Ontario is slightly better off, even though the ultimate recipient, because its greater depth allows for more dispersal of pollutants. There are signs, however, that it is being severely affected. Michigan is also in a deteriorating condition. Its southern portion is the site of massive pollution and Green Bay holds the dubious distinction, along with Saginaw Bay in Huron, of being in the Erie class. The rest of Huron is in relatively good shape. Superior is the standard.

Superior

"... Lake Superior is a 'pristine' lake and its 'ultimate fate' is directed toward maintenance of this condition." (10)

Superior remains a magnificent example of the oligotrophic lake. Deep, pure, cold waters form the beginning of the Great Lake system. The continued protection of Lake Superior is important for several reasons. It has survived the long period of our inattention and ignorance. Any environmental degradation that would be allowed would be inexcusable because we would be aware of the consequences. Any degradation would be seen as a great defeat for *any* program to restore the water quality of the lakes. Further, it would deprive the lower lakes of one of the factors that has muted the full effects of the massive abuses that have occurred in their basins. The unpolluted waters continually dilute the concentration of industrial, agricultural, and human wastes.

Superior may even be the unique example of a lake that recovered, that actually reversed some of the environmental damage done to it. As has been noted, Superior suffered from widespread first stage pollution, primarily through stripping the basin of its forests. By contrast, it has been largely spared second stage disruption. The shores remain lightly populated, cities few and widely scattered, and farmlands relatively rare. Vast portions of the northern coast have the feel of a wilderness preserve and are virtually uninhabited. The Superior basin has been "blessed" with poor soil and a truly dismal climate. Portions of the Upper Peninsula of Michigan rank close to the rainforest areas of the Pacific Northwest in the percentage of possible sunlight received annually.

There has actually been a small decline in dissolved solids and other pollution indicators in the last 50 years:

"... It has been generally considered that the slightly declining trend in total dissolved solids, sodium plus potassium, and perhaps chloride is not significant and that present conditions are primitive. Considering the history of timber exploitations in the basin which ... must surely have dislocated the pattern of nutrient supply to the lake, those long term trends may be real though very slow and reflect a return toward a pristine condition as a consequence of forest regeneration. Considering the enormous volume of the Lake Superior basin such a return would be expected to be slow." (11)

The outlook for maintaining the integrity of the basin area, given even a small dose of common sense, is good. Nonetheless, the 1976 Report of the International Joint Commission, which has been coordinating water quality data, listed 21 problem areas on Superior shores. Ten of these are concentrated in the Duluth-Superior harbor area where dissolved oxygen, fecal coliform (an indication of sewage treatment adequacy), and industrial wastes do not meet goals. Five other areas are in the Thunder Bay, Ontario, region and the difficulties there are much the same as those of Duluth.

The biggest controversy arose over the taconite tailings at Silver Bay, Minnesota. The problem or, more correctly, potential problem is the presence of asbestos fibers in the waste materials being dumped into the lake. Asbestos fibers enter the water and are circulated by currents to the Duluth-Superior area where traces have appeared in the drinking water. Tests from 1939–40 and 1949–50 showed little of the materials which, in 1964–65, had come to constitute 31 percent of the total inorganic solids of City of Duluth water samples.

The debate has centered around the significance of these fibers. It is well known that inhaling asbestos fibers may lead to a variety of lung disorders including cancer. What is not known is whether ingesting the fibers poses major health hazards.

''It has been shown by experiments in rats that asbestos fibers can penetrate through the digestive tract and be carried to other organs of the body, accumulating especially in the brain and omentum (tissue surrounding the small intestine). The feeding of large concentrations of asbestos in the diet may cause malignant tumors in the kidney, brain, lymph-nodes and peritoneum of rats and evidently also in baboons. . . . Asbestos-like fibers are widespread. Through ordinary sand filtration 90 percent of the individual fibers can be removed. It is the remaining 10 percent, the very small fibers, which according to some medical authorities, may represent the greatest health hazard over the long term. There is growing concern that these minute fibers may be absorbed from drinking water through the gastrointestinal tract and into the bloodstream. . . . The picture is by no means clear since a recent report summarizes evidence that shows short-fibered asbestos dust . . . is not capable of causing fibrosis or cancer. . . .''(12)

The whole affair has been rattling about the courts since 1969. Repeated delays and appeals have focused on a fundamental dollar and cents issue. Reserve Mining is a large employer in an area of chronically low employment. Reserve countered demands that it change its methods of waste disposal by stating that such changes were economically impossible. If pushed on the point the company might be forced to close. The miners scream. The businessmen scream. Everyone's screams are understood politically. A closure would result in great economic hardship. Are the threats to close real? Is the threat to human health real? How do you balance these two things? It is becoming easier for public health agencies to move in matters of imminent health hazard. In such a situation the offending operation knows it is likely to be closed down if something is not quickly done.

When the hazard has delayed effects, the problem is more subject to emotion and politics. There is often a pattern of delay and negotiation spread out over a longer period. The most difficult case is one where there *may* be serious effects but no one is exactly sure. As noted above, the case against Reserve presented contradictory evidence. Asbestos fibers inhaled are dangerous. Ingested asbestos fibers (may be) (are likely to be) (could be) (are almost certainly) dangerous. If push comes to shove, should the company be closed? You take your pick depending on where your value system triangulates the potential health risk, potential economic upset, and its effect on you and your community.

The people of Duluth wisely determined not to wait for the results of the experiment on themselves. The city has completed construction of a filtration plant that removes the fibers from drinking water. Other municipalities do not as yet have this advantage.

The U.S. District Court lifted a July, 1977 closure date from Reserve after an onland disposal site was finally ruled suitable by the Minnesota Supreme Court. The Court order states that construction of the site must be completed and discharge to Superior terminated by 1980.

Michigan

". . . These four criteria indicate that the open waters of the southern basin are on the border between oligotrophy and mesotrophy. The nearshore waters are clearly mesotrophic. The open waters at the extreme southern end are definitely mesotrophic. The open waters in the transition areas between the northern and southern basins of the lake are still somewhat oligotrophic." (13)

". . . The most heavily polluted area is southern Green Bay, a large area of the bottom of which is covered with anoxic gray sludge . . .(14)

Michigan is the transition lake and, as illustrated above, it is possible to find all three trophic states in its waters. The position is far more precarious than this statement would seem to indicate. Michigan is the slough, the backwater, of the system. The direct flow is from Superior through Huron-Erie-Ontario and the flushing time of these lakes allows hope that if changes are made, improvements will move in a fairly rapid fashion through the system. This is not so in Michigan, for it is estimated that the flushing time, the amount of time needed for a complete replacement of existing waters, may be as much as 100 years.

As noted, one of the great plus factors for the lake is the fact that the sanitary canal has diverted Chicago waste water to the Mississippi system. Milwaukee does release treated sewage into the lake, and Chicago recently sued successfully on the grounds that sewage treatment was inadequate and the results were drifting south to Chicago. Milwaukee, in turn, has considered suing Chicago for polluted air which drifts northward. One wishes both parties the best of luck.

There are indications that the level of total dissolved solids increased by 30 ppm in the ninety-year period preceding 1966 (15). Both chlorides and sulfate increased during the same period. There is some indication that sulfate is no longer increasing because of declining use of high sulfate fuels and industrial waste discharge abatement programs. Chlorides are a different matter. Industrial discharge of the material has decreased but is still present. Moreover, it is still used in large amounts as a deicer in winter. At the current rate of increase it is estimated that the quality standard for Michigan and Indiana will be violated by the early 1990's. The Indiana standard is 10 mg/1 (milligrams per liter) and this was once thought to be more than adequate, since chlorides were not thought to affect water quality until they reached 350 mg/1. Recently, it has been hypothesized that at levels as low as 7.5 to 10 mg/1 a plankton shift occurs which favors species tolerant of brackish waters. These species are filamentous and may end up clogging water intake filters and causing odor and taste problems in the drinking water. (16)

The trouble spots on the lake are Green Bay and the Indiana Harbor ship canal. The IJC (International Joint Commission) lists 34 problem areas in Lake Michigan. An amazing twenty of these are in Green Bay while eleven are in the Indiana Harbor area.

The small area of the lakeshore occupied by Indiana is the site of an incredible concentration of steel, chemical, and petroleum operations. In the middle 60's this area was the source of a pollution mixture so nightmarish that it was speculated that it, alone, could lead the lake to a rapid and irreversible deterioration. The canal is the most important discharge into the lake and is more than 95 percent municipal and industrial waste. (17)

The turnaround has been impressive. Major industrial waste control programs were instituted. Ten years after the pessimistic assessments the area does not meet standards but great progress has been made. There have been improvements in the dissolved oxygen, sulfate, nitrate, suspended solids, and impressively in the fecal coliform rates (18). Merchant seamen who have regularly docked at steel plants in the harbor, state the change has been substantial enough to be noticeable to eye and nose.

The pollution that pours into Green Bay is awesome. It comes from a wide assortment of paper plants and inadequate sewage facilities. Most of it is dumped into the Fox River which flows into the southern portion of the Bay. Water degradation existed for so long in this area that it had been accepted by the population as the standard condition. Minimum oxygen levels in the southern bay declined from an already low 2 to 3 ppm in the late 30's to 0 to 1 ppm by the mid-50's (19). The problem is aggravated by the fact that the shallow bay is temperature stratified in summer and ice-covered in winter. This situation prevents vertical mixing and aggravates the oxygen depletion. Cladophora is found throughout the southern bay and extensively on the western shoreline (20).

In short, the area has been subjected to severe alteration. Progress has been slow as the industries involved gradually construct waste treatment plants. There are, nonetheless, noticeable improvements in some of the tributary waters.

Huron

". . . If remedial measures are not applied, the water quality of Saginaw Bay and other inshore areas will decline. Because these shallow areas are important to the life cycles of many fish species of Lake Huron, this decline will undoubtedly have adverse effects. Conditions in the open waters of the lake will largely depend on the quality of inflows from Lakes Michigan and Superior." (21)

The water quality of Huron is second only to that of Superior whose waters contribute greatly to this healthy condition. The lake has recorded increases in dissolved solids in the past 70 years though the increase is slight. It is probably real, however, since Michigan contributed 30 percent of the inflowing water. Chloride and sulfate levels are higher than could be accounted for by waters coming from the two feeder lakes and point to sources within the basin itself. The figures indicating high quality water may be somewhat deceptive as it may take over twenty years for nutrient increases to be felt throughout the lake. (22)

There is a color photo in Appendix B of the 1976 Great Lakes Water Quality Report. It was taken on July 31, 1976 by Landsat satellite. On the same day the Environmental Protection Agency collected 16 samples from the same area and photo and sample data were combined by computer. The subject of the study is one of the problem areas of the lakes and *the* problem area of Lake Huron, Saginaw Bay. Of the 24 problem areas in the lake, 14 are clustered about Saginaw's watershed. They comprise the now familiar stew of chemical, sewage, and industrial pollutants.

Aerial photograph of Saginaw Bay
"NASA/USGS-EROS Data Center"

163

The varying temperatures of the water are represented in colors that range from vivid magenta and red through orange, green, and blue. The swirls and eddies of the colors indicate the interactions between the summer warmed waters of the bay and the colder waters of the lake proper. The temperature range is between 20.6 C (blue) and 27.3 C (red). There is also a great range in the corresponding pollution indicators. What may be seen in this photo is the process by which warm and nutrient rich waters are processed through various life forms.

"... Dissipation of nitrogen and phosphorous in these waters is not a matter of simple dilution, however, since biological uptake must be considered. An example is the inflow of Saginaw River water, with high concentrations of total dissolved solids and phosphorous, into Saginaw Bay, Lake Huron. ... Contoured distributions of the major ions and conductivity showed that these decreased 35–40 percent in 30 miles as the inflowing river mixed with bay water and that this decrease could be attributed to simple dilution by bay waters. The phosphorous content decreased about 72% in an equal distance, indicating a great biological uptake. The large plankton blooms observed in the inner part of the bay were probably maintained by the continued inflow of nutrient-rich river water." (23)

The messy cladophora flourishes in the bay and now extends into the lake itself. The Saginaw River appears in the Landsat photograph as a magenta thread and it influences Saginaw Bay in much the way the Fox River affects Green Bay. Fecal coliform standards were exceeded in 19 of 23 samples taken from the river in 1976. There are also disturbing indications that the nutrient load is increasing. Between 1974 and 1976 there were gains in the amount of chlorophyll a, chloride, and total phosphorous (24). Investigations as early as 1943 indicated

that pollution was affecting fish and it appears that the current condition of the bay is serious and may pose a threat to a greater area of the lake. There is a bright spot in the analysis of the bay and that is the fact that the flushing rate is less then 200 days. Control or elimination of discharges affecting the waters could therefore, bring a fairly rapid improvement.

Erie

"... In a little over 200 years, the drainage basin of Lake Erie has been completely altered from what was mostly wilderness populated by about 100,000 people to a watershed used intensively for agriculture and industry in which the population has increased to approximately 12 million. ..."(25)

The IJC prints maps of the five Great Lakes in its annual reports pinpointing pollution sources. There is barely room on the Erie map for the listings. The waters of the Great Lake system flow southward from Huron into the St. Clair River through Lake St. Clair, and south through the Detroit River to the shallow western basin of Lake Erie. It is a short journey that subjects the waters to the effects of 31 problem areas, more than the total found along the vast shores of Superior. In fact, there are 88 such areas in the Erie basin, more than the combined total of the upper lakes. Into the western basin pours a massive soup of domestic, industrial, and commercial wastes, coming primarily from the Detroit and Maumee Rivers. The Detroit River alone has accounted for 6.1 billion liters of such waste (26).

The western basin has been classified as eutrophic, the central basin as mesotrophic-eutrophic, and the deeper eastern basin as oligotrophic-mesotrophic (27). Total dissolved solids have soared from less than 140 ppm to close to 200 ppm in

1968 (28). There have been sharp increases in calcium, sulfate, and chloride ions. The major nutrients have tripled since 1900. Much of this nutrient loading comes from detergents discharged through municipal waste systems. These increases were first noticed in nearshore areas but have since spread into the open waters of the western and central basins.

The calcium, sulfate, and chloride ions increase as waters move from west to east through Erie, while the nutrients decrease. Here we see the same phenomena observed in Saginaw Bay; nutrients are decreasing because massive amounts are being utilized by expanding populations of plankton. The plankton, in turn, are exploding as the nutrient food source increases. This uptake is so intense that it is estimated that the plankton biomass has increased twenty times since the 1920's. The creatures are not only more abundant but their population pulses are lasting a longer and longer time.

Massive algae blooms settle to the bottom and place greatly increased oxygen demands on the water during decomposition. This draws huge amounts of oxygen from the system. The situation has led to the summer collapse of dissolved oxygen in the central basin. We have seen that this situation first became critical in 1953. The frequency and duration of depletion increased in the 60's and 70's and anoxic conditions spread more extensively through the basin. The severity of the problem has generally increased although the extent of the oxygen starved area depends on the climatic conditions in any given year. The hypolimnion, the deeper and colder water, is the area affected. In 1973, 94 percent of the central basin was anoxic. This dropped to 70 percent in 1974, a mere 4 percent in 1975, and then rose to 63 percent in 1976 (29). As noted, this destruction of oxygen had widespread effects on fish populations. Certain cold water fish are unable to endure oxygen levels below 3 to 4 mg/1. Obviously such years as 1973 would be calamitous for remaining population in the central basin

The source of pollution may be understood by examining the 1976 figures of one aspect, phosphorous loading. Michigan contributed 5,799 tons, Ohio 3,699, and Ontario 1,476 (30). Some progress has been made on the Detroit River. Phosphorous loading has decreased from 90,000 kg/d (kilograms per day) in 1968 to 28,000 kg/d in 1976 due to remedial industrial measures and municipal phosphorous detergent control programs. The progress is still slow for the basin as a whole. Municipal loadings dropped from 21,180 kg/d to 17,880 kg/d between 1975 and 1976, but this is still 10 thousand kg/d above target levels (31).

Cladophora now covers vast portions of the island area of the western lake as well as large areas of the southern shore and smaller portions of the northern (32). It is a regular subject of complaints along south shore beaches where decaying fish and vegetation have somewhat diminished the lure of a day at the beach. Water intakes of industries and municipalities become clogged. Lines carrying water to the Ontario nuclear hydro plant were obstructed and led to a revenue loss of $40,000 each time they had to be cleared. Finally a 2.7 million dollar heat exchange unit was built in an attempt to solve the problem.

Deterioration in Lake Erie has reached the point where it can be seen, smelled, and tasted. Perhaps most important in terms of changing the situation, it has begun to cost, cost visibly and measurably. The fight to salvage Erie will be difficult, but when it is made results may be quickly noticeable, for Erie has a flushing time of only three years. There is, however, a long way to go and it remains to be seen if clean-up efforts are affected by increasing energy demands and costs.

Ontario

". . . Lake Ontario is characteristic of the more eutrophic of the large lake ecosystem of North America. Situated downstream of productive Lake Erie, it is influenced both by nutrient inputs from that eutrophic system and its own . . . tendencies towards oligotrophy. . . ." (33)

The waters that tumble over scenic Niagara Falls are on their way to the last of the Great Lakes. They carry pollution souvenirs from all of the other lakes and as they pass through the Niagara River they acquire another substantial dose. Twenty of the thirty-seven pollution problem areas in the Ontario basin contribute their wastes to inflowing waters before they reach the lake itself. These sources are particularly important as they contribute 80 percent of the water draining to Ontario. As a result of these additions the total dissolved solids, sodium, calcium, and sulfates are the highest in the system.

Despite this burden from the upper lakes and the considerable contributions of its own basin, Ontario is in better condition than Erie. Since the lake's surface area is the smallest of the system and it is the second in greatest average depth, the waters absorb the pollutants with greater ease than those of Erie.

Nonetheless its vital signs are deteriorating and it is regarded as approaching the mesotrophic state. An example of the problem is the amount of phosphorous received by the waters. In 1976 it was estimated that Erie contributed 5,613 metric tons. Basin sources added another 7,082 metric tons. By comparison the same estimates credit Michigan and Superior with a gift of only 657 metric tons to Huron which presented Erie with 1,080 (34). This downstream loading can be extended by analogy to some of the other pollutants.

An increase in plankton activity has been noted since 1973. There are two plankton pulses, one in the spring and another in the fall. During the summer lull the populations fall to a lower level. Recently the spring period has increased with the result that the summer minimum is higher and the mass increased (35).

The nasty cladaphora has occupied nearly all the shoreline areas of the lake. Studies since 1970 have indicated continuous growth from Hamilton to Toronto.

From Toronto to near Kingston, most of the northern shore of the lake, it occupied about a third of the shoreline. On the south side it was two-thirds of the shoreline from Niagara to Rochester, and 79 percent east of Rochester. As mentioned, the recreational damage has already been considerable. Further diminution of beach and sport fishing areas may be expected (36).

Certain areas are severely polluted. The Bay of Quinte, discussed as a fishing center of the lake, is the worst area and has problems with dissolved oxygen and algae. Toronto and Hamilton harbors have experienced similar problems, plus those of industrial wastes and coliform.

Something else, however, was threatening to destroy *all* fishing for certain species not only in Lake Ontario, but in large sections of the Great Lakes. In the fall of 1977 New York State announced it was suspending further salmon planting in Lake Ontario due to health hazards.

Chapter 2:
The Third Stage

"If you have any reason to believe that the fish you are using harbors objectional amounts of DDT or other chemicals, filleting is the safest approach. Chemical residues tend to be concentrated in the fatty tissues, namely the belly flesh and the dark areas at the sides. These areas may be cut away during the filleting process. . . ." (37)

"The world used to be a simpler place, before science began creating two problems for every one it solved and the ecology movement kidnapped the alphabet. The seasons came and went, crops were either good or disappointing, the human life cycle proceeded more or less on schedule, and nature's delicate balance was maintained. Then came the marriage of science, which is impersonal and precise, and man, who is neither. Among the offspring of this imperfect union has been the proliferation of frequently bewildering new threats to life and the planet itself. Today only the scientifically trained or the most dedicated of environment-watchers could possibly keep track of all the new perils identified by initials taken from their chemical composition. . . ." (38)

"We have, in the name of compromise and acceptance, already allowed ourselves to be carried too far down this hazardous road. We have been regulated by a malignant belief that things will work out, that better substitutes will be found and used, that American know-how and technology will lead us to the light. We have until recently condoned the use of such chemicals even in the Department of Conservation, and we have in the past used them to combat forest insects, park pests, and fish and game problems. We are all sheep in the same flock, and the real fight is not against some distant state or federal bureau, or lone farmer, or crop dusting pilot. The real fight is against ourselves. Are you, as an urban, or suburban householder, willing to pay twenty-five cents a pound for apples where you now pay twenty cents? Will you accept higher prices when costs of crop production rise? Individually and collectively we enjoy big, luscious wormless fruits and vegetables available at every market, and we fail to question the individual farmer or rose grower when crops and flowers are dusted, several times a year." (39)

Bioaccumulation. Unlike so many of the words spit out of the bureaucracy this one has a very distinct meaning. Let us take an example that was probably repeated many times in many places. In a place called Clear Lake, California, a chemical called DDD was sprayed to rid the area of midges. The mixture was .02 of one part per million parts of water, a solution of 0.02 ppm. It is pointed out that this is the equivalent of a few drops of the material in a railroad tank car full of water. Thirteen months later there were 10 ppm in plankton, 903 ppm in the fat of plankton-eating fish, 2,690 ppm in the fat of carnivorous fish, and 2,134 ppm in the fat of fish-eating birds who did not generally survive the experience. In short, the fish-eating birds ended up with a proportion of one hundred thousand times greater concentration in their body fat than had been placed in the water (40).

The technological catechism of the post World War II era announced endless horizons of enhanced comfort and productivity. One of its tenets stated that farmers would no longer suffer the peril of crop destruction by predatory pests. Further, acreage yields were to be greatly increased by substitutes for the older, cruder, organic fertilizers. If there was a problem, a chemical could be found to take care of it. Increased agricultural yield meant that fewer and fewer farmers could produce more and more food. Great benefits would flow for farmers and consumers alike.

It was not only in the area of food production that this attitude prevailed. It seemed that long standing medical and industrial problems could be eliminated or alleviated by something from the chemical goodie box and, as the man said, we were all sheep in the same flock. The attitude peaked in the 1950's, a strangely insensitive time in many respects. I went to a high school located next to a chemical test field. When the winds were right great clouds of chemical waste products would blow over the school and surrounding neighborhoods. There were certain other annoying things; paint flecked off cars and women claimed that nylon stockings seemed to suffer from the effects of the chemical wind. Yet I remember no one suggesting that such things might be bad for us, for humans. We were already aware of pollution and the beaches were occasionally closed in the summer, but such events seemed a part of the season. As for the chemicals, they appeared to bring great benefits to the city. The company involved was one of the few expanding industries in a region of chronic unemployment and, most important, it was one of the few that paid a decent wage.

Eventually trees in the area of the school began dying and the test field was moved to a less populated area. Years later a new high school was built—next to the new test field. I am unaware of what effects those chemicals may have had or whether the effect on humans was significant. It is symbolic, however, of the efforts to control damaging chemicals. Every time we think we have escaped their effects we find that the can of tuna, the apple, or that great steak we had yesterday contained something extra.

The unfortunate truth is that there is little room for escape. DDT was one of the first of our miracles to be called into question. By the time its possible dangers had reached widespread public attention, it was showing up in the Antarctic Ocean, deep sea fish, and, ominously, in human tissue. It was being passed through mother's milk to nursing infants. It was reaching humans by water, air, and by bioaccumulation with ourselves serving as the top predator.

The issue exploded in the late 60's as an imminently dangerous threat to human and animal life. The first chemicals to cause great alarm were the so-called hard pesticides such as DDT, Dieldrin, Aldrin, Heptachlor, Endrin, Lindane, and Chlorodane. Also identified as an immediate threat were the industrial by-products of mercury.

The substances can actually fall in the rain. Lake trout from Lake Superior and a small lake on Isle Royale were tested and compared. There was a ten-fold increase in one of the chemicals in the Isle Royal trout over the open lake fish. It is suggested that the difference may have resulted from rainwater concentrating the chemicals in the small lake (41). A 1976 test showed Lindane, Dieldrin, and DDT residues in rainfall samples (42). The substances were discharged through industrial and municipal sewage systems, they were washed off fields and orchards by rain and entered streams and rivers. The vast and pervasive use of many chemicals led to their circulating through air, water, and the food chain.

It was only a few years after the enormously popular salmon and trout stocking that many people began to realize that the fish were being seriously imperiled by the build-up of these chemicals. The higher up the food chain, the more accumulation. As early as 1970 mercury contamination caused the closing of Lake Ontario to northern pike, eel, and yellow perch, while white bass and walleye were prohibited on a portion of Lake Erie for the same reason. All Canadian fisheries on Lake St. Clair were closed in 1970. There were partial closings of walleye on Lake Huron and the entire fishery of Thunder Bay on Lake Superior.

What was the effect of this on human health? It was known that mercury was dangerous. That had been proven when a large number of the villagers of Minamata, Japan, had been exposed to high concentrations of the material from a nearby corporation. In the early 60's fish died in droves, and cats went mad after eating the dead fish. The effects soon appeared in fishermen's families as the central nervous system was affected and hideous deformities crippled individuals. Children were poisoned in the womb and doomed to a life as retarded invalids. The corporation resisted the suggestion that it was the cause of these tragedies. Eventually it came under siege as protests became nationwide and stockholders meetings were disrupted. After twenty years of litigation money was finally paid to the victims.

"When exposed to quantities of DDT as low as one-half of one part per million . . . cells of human origin showed changes. Microscopic observations showed increased granulation, elongation, and vacuolation, all of which are manifestations of irregular cell growth and cell destruction. Dieldrin had a similar, but lesser effect. Dieldrin and DDT affected synthesis of both RNA and DNA in cells of human origin, although the pattern of change was inconsistent. These findings suggest a possibly fundamental influence on mammalian cellular biochemistry. . . ." (43)

The known and potential effects of the hard pesticides and mercury were enough to sound the alarm and bring various agencies into action. DDT was phased out and substitutes found for the other pesticides. There were varying effects to these bans. DDT responded quickly and its progress through the food chain was swift. In 1969 chubs from southeastern Lake Michigan contained 9.9 ppm while by 1976 this had dropped sharply to .9 ppm. In coho salmon the drop had been from 11.8 ppm to 3.0 ppm and in lake trout from 19.2 ppm to 5.6 ppm. Thus within seven years even the largest fish were approaching the guidelines of 5 ppm and residual problems appeared to remain only in Lakes Michigan and Superior.

Mercury sources in the St. Clair-Detroit river system had been reduced and large portions of the mercury-bearing sediments had moved into Lake Erie. The decline was encouraging but concentrations in fifteen species remained above 0.5 ppm. Dieldrin was another matter. It was banned in Ontario in 1969 and in the United States in 1974. Levels appeared to drop in coho salmon but in Lake Michigan trout and chubs, they have fluctuated close to the Food and Drug Administration guideline of 0.3 ppm (44).

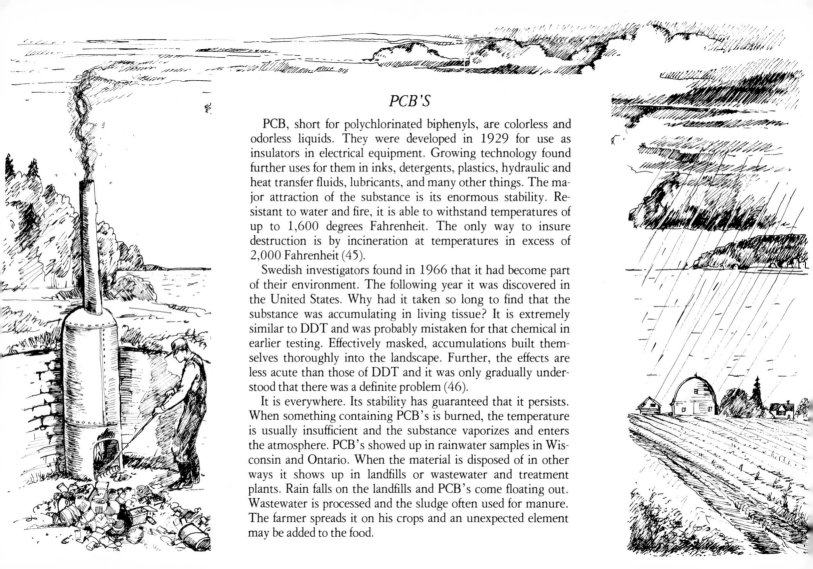

PCB'S

PCB, short for polychlorinated biphenyls, are colorless and odorless liquids. They were developed in 1929 for use as insulators in electrical equipment. Growing technology found further uses for them in inks, detergents, plastics, hydraulic and heat transfer fluids, lubricants, and many other things. The major attraction of the substance is its enormous stability. Resistant to water and fire, it is able to withstand temperatures of up to 1,600 degrees Fahrenheit. The only way to insure destruction is by incineration at temperatures in excess of 2,000 Fahrenheit (45).

Swedish investigators found in 1966 that it had become part of their environment. The following year it was discovered in the United States. Why had it taken so long to find that the substance was accumulating in living tissue? It is extremely similar to DDT and was probably mistaken for that chemical in earlier testing. Effectively masked, accumulations built themselves thoroughly into the landscape. Further, the effects are less acute than those of DDT and it was only gradually understood that there was a definite problem (46).

It is everywhere. Its stability has guaranteed that it persists. When something containing PCB's is burned, the temperature is usually insufficient and the substance vaporizes and enters the atmosphere. PCB's showed up in rainwater samples in Wisconsin and Ontario. When the material is disposed of in other ways it shows up in landfills or wastewater and treatment plants. Rain falls on the landfills and PCB's come floating out. Wastewater is processed and the sludge often used for manure. The farmer spreads it on his crops and an unexpected element may be added to the food.

So what does this shit do? Once again the Japanese, who seem to have had more than their share of experiences as test cases for the latest products of science and technology, were the first to discover. A heat exchanger leaked PCB fluids into rice oil. This was later eaten by approximately 1,200 people. The special oil contained 2 to 3 *thousand* ppm of PCB's. A debate is currently being waged over whether the present U.S. standard of 5 ppm is adequate. About half the people were affected with:

". . . skin lesions, blindness, hearing loss, systemic gastrointestinal disorders, jaundice, edema, and abdominal pain. A few birth abnormalities were noted, some babies being born with decreased birth weights and skin discoloration, a problem which fortunately regressed later on. Surveys of the incident showed that the severity of each victim's reaction depended on the amount of oil consumed." (47)

No doubt about this one. A warning label was now slapped on large trout and salmon. A curious one. Do not eat fish more than once a week. If you are pregnant, however, do not eat them at all.

Meanwhile unpleasant things were happening to another creature that consumed Great Lakes fish:

". . . DDT is a good example because we were looking at it from the wrong angle all the while. It wasn't so much later that we found out about the egg shell problems. The investigators were looking at it from other points of view; then all of a sudden over a period of 3-4-5 years, it became evident that it was dangerous from a totally different point of view. . . ." (48)

The egg shell problem was simply the discovery that some bird eggs had become so soft that a simple touch was sufficient to dent them. The herring gull has become the victim of another lesson in bioaccumulation. Tests of herring gull lipid revealed concentrations of 16 pollutants, including PCB's, DDT, Mirex, Chlorodane, and Dieldrin. PCB levels stood at 3,530 ppm, ten times the concentration of the next major pollutant. The food chain progression is visible in a series of samples taken from Lake Ontario species. Alewife and salmon averaged 1.11 ppm, coho salmon 5.8 ppm, while herring gull eggs averaged 133 ppm. No decimal point (49).

What has this done to the gull? It has affected the reproductive ability of the birds and the problem is most acute in Lake Ontario. In 1975 observations of herring gull nests were made in Lakes Superior, Huron, Erie, and Ontario. In Lake Superior 79.6 percent of the eggs hatched, in Erie 63.1 percent and in Ontario only 18.6 percent. The embryo failure in the Superior sample was 9.4 percent while in the Ontario it was over one-third, 35.1 percent (50). There has been almost total reproductive failure in Lake Ontario colonies. There are fewer eggs, fewer of these hatch, and fewer of the chicks that hatch survive. Adult gulls show "behavioral abnormalities," namely they don't tend nests or properly attend to incubation. Implicated as probable causes are "hormonal and genetic changes." (51)

Other birds have been affected. The population of double crested cormorants has declined by 90-95 percent in Lake Ontario, and in Georgian Bay by 50 percent. There are growing numbers of deformities in lower lake birds such as terns and herons. The deformities include crossed bills, skeletal disorders, and eye lesions (52). PCB's have spread throughout the bird populations of the lakes. Tests conducted on gull eggs in 1974-75 showed 142 ppm in Ontario, 91.3 in Michigan, 65.8 in Erie, 60 in Superior, and 51.5 on Huron (53).

It is obvious that there is a very dangerous substance loose. The implication for the fisheries is obvious:

". . . The contaminants problem is really a double-barreled one in that they not only affect the utilization of the fish but probably also play a subtle role in their growth, reproduction, survival and long term potential. . . ." (54)

Indeed it is a problem. If reproductive failure is a result of this contamination, it may put the collapse of some of the Great Lake fish stocks in a different light. It certainly puts the reproductive failure of many of the planted fish in an interesting light. The nightmarish aspect of PCB's is the long time that PCB's take to break down once there is no further source. Early estimates ran as high as 84 years. Recent estimates are more optimistic.

The mercury contamination had put 240 Canadian fishermen, 12 percent of the Provincial total, out of work in 1971. Four million pounds of fish had been destroyed and a million dollars in revenue had disappeared (55). That closing, however destructive, had been partial and temporary. It was nothing like the horror that the State of Michigan now regarded. A $60 million commercial and sports fishery was endangered by PCB's. The state had invested $30 million since 1965 in hatcheries, boat launching facilities, fish passage devices, and vessels for management personnel (56).

The danger is very real. The Canadian standard for PCB's in commercial fish is 2 ppm and the Food and Drug Administration of the United States has wrestled with the idea of lowering the current U.S. standard of 5 ppm to that level. This may have been done by the time you read this book. Many of the fish in the lakes will not meet the standard. A further reduction of the disappearing commercial fishery on the U.S. side of the lakes is more than likely.

Many trout in the lakes have been off-limits to commercial fishermen even on an incidental basis since the PCB level was pegged at 5 ppm by the Food and Drug people in May of 1976. Nonetheless, federal funds are being used to stock salmon and trout, two of the fish with the highest concentration of PCB's:

> ". . . In 1975 American taxpayers contributed $148 million to the federal fish and wildlife service. A hefty percentage of the department's total annual budget of $235 million went into fish stocking programs. Of that amount (the total amount) only 18 million came from taxes on fishing gear." (57)

It is a pretty difficult situation to sustain. The fish are regarded as so dangerous that they must be banned from commercial sale and the very fish that acquires the highest concentrations continue to be planted in vast numbers. If the situation continues, there will be more editorials such as the one above which is entitled, "Why are fish unfit to eat still being planted?"

Michigan, Minnesota, Wisconsin, and Indiana have passed measures banning PCB uses. Canada has passed the Environmental Contaminants Act and intends to prohibit the use of the material in all goods except electrical equipment. Other acts may not be all that restrictive. The Wisconsin law prohibits the manufacture or purchase of PCB's after July 1, 1977, but the law exempts waste paper and electrical components as well as products for which no alternative is available. Some manufacturers were taking other steps to make sure their supplies were adequate:

> ". . . Although Monsanto has been ordered to stop producing PCB's, a study undertaken by Rep. Les Aspin shows that 316,585 pounds were imported the first eight months of 1976 and custom figures indicate manufacturers are building up stocks." (58)

It is not only the eating of fish that is a potential health hazard. The FDA is checking the invasion of PCB's into other familiar food products and proposing to reduce the standard for milk from 2.5 ppm to 1.5 ppm and for poultry from 5 to 3 ppm on a fat basis. Meanwhile we are bioaccumulating just like the herring gull:

> "This past year an Ellison Bay commercial fisherman underwent surgery. Whatever part of his body he was forced to part with was tested (at his request) for PCB's. The lab test showed 7 ppm." (59)

The editorial that has been extensively quoted is a response to another editorial. A commercial fisherman had been acquitted of bootlegging fish. The first editorial expressed displeasure with this result and stressed that the state had a vital interest in keeping contaminated fish off the market:

> "Again, no mention is made of why this food fish is being turned into an inedible commodity but concern that the trout stocking program may be jeopardized is strongly expressed. The writer apparently fears that once the limit is cut to 2 ppm, trout will be banned, period. Even sportsmen will be discouraged from eating them. The fault, of course, the editorial points out, lies with the commercial fishermen (referred to as bootleggers) and not the polluters. It's obviously a lot easier to put the hooks in Johnny Olson, a rowboat fisherman, than the Monsanto Company or paper mills." (60)

And that, my friends, may be the nut. It may indeed be easier to eliminate the result of the pollution or the contamination than the source. Think why. A move against any large polluter is generally a move against a large employer. As in the Reserve case, an employer who is the source of substantial community income may claim that remedial measures are so costly that he may not be able to continue. He may threaten to leave the community or simply shut down. Pressure is brought against the state which either officially or unofficially exerts pressure on the control agency. It is a terrible situation until it happens to be our job and then the extenuating circumstances are very clear.

There is more to it than this, however. We don't know where the hell our technology is going. We haven't for a long time. It leads and we react to the consequences. PCB hid behind DDT until it had saturated every corner of the environment. Perhaps PCB's will settle out faster than anticipated when their wide-spread use is curtailed. Perhaps not. In the meantime there is mirex. It is a carcinogen certified by the U.S. Cancer Institute and is known to be so in mammals including primates. It has shown up in amounts as high as ten times the FDA guideline of 0.1 ppm in white perch, smallmouth bass, trout, and salmon species in New York inshore waters of Lake Ontario (61) (62)

It has begun to feel as though we have all been given an involuntary membership in the Chemical of the Year Club. Even when a substance is identified we seem to be unaware of what the effects may be until the Japanese or some other unwilling group has suffered the torments. The weariness is even beginning to show beneath official language:

"The Water Quality Board and the Research Advisory Board, in response to the seemingly perpetual discovery of new and hitherto unknown toxic substances in the Great Lakes, held a series of discussions with representatives of public health agencies in the basin in an attempt to establish procedures for early identification of human health related water quality problems. As a result of these discussions, the Boards have taken steps to facilitate exchange of information between themselves and the public health community.

The Board expressed concern that public health agencies have difficulty evaluating this information in terms of significance to public health." (63)

Now in case you think that anyone, including you, knows what they are doing, consider this. Once, long ago, in the early days of the ecology movement it was correctly pointed out that we were wasting enormous forest resources by not recycling paper products. Certain paper companies responded to the situation by initiating recycling programs. The companies won widespread applause and the programs were largely successful. One day someone pointed out that one of the reasons the fish in the nearby bay were contaminated was the large quantity of PCB's coming from the mills. It was soon discovered that the PCB's were coming from the recycled paper. Fish or trees? Alice would have understood after her visit to Wonderland. The Mad Hatter is in charge of the script as the circle closes.

At the mouth of the harbor, Green Bay

SECTION 5: CRISIS AND OPPORTUNITY

April 25, 1978:

"The price of the PBB incident continues to rise five years after the calamity. The State Legislature recently appropriated $2.25 million for a general study of the state's population. Last October a separate PBB unit was established in the Agriculture Department with a budget exceeding $16 million."(1)

August 3, 1978

"Twenty-five years after the Hooker Chemical Company stopped using the Love Canal here as an industrial dump, 82 compounds—11 of them suspected carcinogens—began percolating through the soil. The problem has become so serious that the New York State Health Department recommended Wednesday that pregnant women and children less than 2 years old move out of the area as soon as possible." (2)

September 3, 1978

"Wisconsin's industries are generating an estimated 29.8 million gallons and 149,000 tons of potentially hazardous waste—including acids, heavy metals, caustics, solvents, paints, and pesticides—a year, a new state survey has found.

"The wastes are presumably being disposed of privately and safely but some may not be. Some may haunt us later, like the Hooker Chemical Corporation wastes that threaten Niagara Falls, New York, or the Ansul Company's arsenic wastes that are seeping into Green Bay, or the PCB's that contaminate Lake Michigan trout." (3)

Sunday, October 1, 1978

"Dioxin, a chlorinated compound in a popular weed killer is a lot more deadly than most scientists have thought, tests on rhesus monkeys at the University of Wisconsin-Madison indicate. . . .

"Monkeys on a dioxin diet of 500 parts per trillion suffered lesions and cellular changes in stomach mucus membranes and other duct tissues, Allen reports. Their ability to produce blood cells broke down. Eyelids swelled grotesquely. They lost eyelashes and body hair, and menstrual cycles lengthened. Allen suspects the immunity system was attacked, too.

"After seven months, the first death from advanced blood abnormalities occurred. In the next five months, five of the eight test animals died. . . .

"The 500 parts per trillion dosage was a minute fraction of the amount of PCB's that produced some similar effects in earlier experiments. . . .

"There are no federal restrictions on the sale or use of 2,4,5-T. Wisconsin requires no permit for aerial spraying of the herbicides which are widely used." (4)

Chapter 1:
A Question of Control

"A piecemeal approach to toxic substances control would only delay and hamper our efforts to stringently regulate the occurrence of poisons in our environment.

"Philosophically, we must consider man's role in his environment. Thoreau urged that we 'probe the earth to see where our main roots run.' The health of our fish and wildlife acts as a pulse indicator for human health.

". . . all medical and environmental gauges indicate this pulse to be unsteady and irregular. The irony of our position today is that our left hand is spending millions of dollars and thousands of man-years to establish crucial resources, while our right hand renders each new growth of this resource malignant. Our new resource will not only self-destruct, but will place the human population in mortal danger.

"As a final thought, let me stress that we should consider all alternatives. Since drastic action is needed, we should not be afraid to step back from industrial efficiency if we can step forward to environmental health.

"Quite frankly, I am thoroughly disgusted by the gnashing of teeth, wailing, and rubbing of hands. To the agencies which have the enforcement responsibilities—a word on behalf of the bewildered but concerned American people, 'Get on with it!' (5)

The problem is not simply what value we put on the Great Lakes, nor what value comes first among competing values. The philosophical problem is whether or not we are willing to subject technology to some scrutiny before we enjoy its benefits or suffer its detriments. The trick is that its benefits are usually the first apparent, while its detriments tend to remain hidden up the sleeve of the cosmic joker for years. One estimate states that there are 600 *new* chemicals produced or used every year in the Great Lakes basin.

The primary method of surveillance to this point has been to watch fish to see what they have picked up from the sewers or dumps of North America. It seems a bit after the fact, but it is certainly necessary to keep abreast of the current situation.

A step toward control was taken with the passage of the Toxic Substances Control Act in October, 1976. The act stresses four main points: (a) It is to enable the EPA (Environmental Protection Agency) to obtain better information on toxic substances, (b) prevent future problems with those substances by screening them before they get to market, (c) "balance costs, risks, and benefits in environmental decision making, (d) "and to better coordinate the government activities with regard to toxic substances." As an aid toward compilation of the initial inventory of possibly dangerous compounds, the EPA published a list of *34,000* chemical substances. (6)

How is it possible to evaluate 34,000 chemicals on a predictive basis? With essentially the same technique used to discover the larvacide for controlling the lamprey and currently used to evaluate chemicals in the pharmaceutical industry. The method is known as "structure-activity correlation" and uses existing knowledge of the structure and physical characteristics of chemicals to predict their toxic and bioaccumulative potential:

> "We, therefore have to make an environmental decision on many compounds or at least develop some trends so that we can more efficiently predict which compounds have less environmental hazards. In this type of approach we generate a regression curve, for a group of compounds and, in this case, all of the compounds considered for one new product are very, very similar. They have only minor structural modification in order to increase efficacy. In these particular cases, I can see a tremendous application with this type of effort, where the selection of five or six compounds in what may be an "infinite" number of possible formula developments is made to get some toxicity and correlative data . . . We then are in a position to direct the synthesis of compounds which would be not only . . . effective as products, but also safe in the environment. I think this is very much like the "two-peak" situation in the pharmacology industry where they want to have an effective compound and they want to keep the compound from causing toxic reaction. Our two peaks are efficacy in the product and not something in the environment . . ." (7)

Basically the goal is to isolate potential groups of chemicals that *may* have toxic or bioaccumulative potential and then test further to discover what aspect of the substances is dangerous. There seem to be two goals. One is to determine which chemicals already in the environment have caused, or are likely to cause, trouble. The other is to screen chemicals that may have dangerous properties and determine whether they are safe *before* they are used. In short, the purpose is to (a) catch up, and (b) get ahead, of the chemical plague.

It is an attempt, one of the first, to put a bridle on technological excesses. Whether it will be a success is another question. The problems are immense. Some of them were highlighted at a symposium held in March, 1975. Much of what is quoted comes from the general discussion which followed the symposium. Here, government, industry, and research participants struggled with the problem of translating the structure—activity concept into administrative controls. Here are some of the problems they discussed, as well as others which have appeared subsequently:

1. *Combinations of chemicals*—Let us suppose that considerable predicative skills are developed in determining the danger from particular chemicals. What about the combination of two or more of these compounds? There are a number of things that can happen when such substances are combined. First, they may have a simple additive result (1 + 1 = 2). They may actually have an atagonistic or cancelling effect (1 + 1 = 0). It is also possible that they may have a synergistic response. This last possibility is best illustrated by the warnings against combination of alcohol and prescription drugs. Thus a relatively small amount of alcohol and an otherwise safe intake of barbituates may be fatal in combination. In the world of synergistic reaction, 1 + 1 may equal 10. Waste products from municipal and industrial sources now form a great chemical stew. What is the possibility of being able to anticipate the effects of this variety? There are several views:

"Vieth: The structure-activity could be used to determine the relative toxicity of new organic compounds. The second more complex question is how to predict the toxicity of a mixture of these compounds given the relative proportions. It is difficult to foresee the application of structure-activity correlations to complex mixtures except in the simplest cases. Complex effluents are probably within the realm of predictive toxicology, but require different types of models.

"Anderson: There have been at least two long-term studies which have shown that the toxic unit concept is not applicable.

"De Freitas: There is indeed a probability that prediction of multiple toxicity would not involve many more parameters than are already under consideration. There is a strong possibility of linearity of response." (8)

2. *Toxicity and Accumulation*—The problem here is the creation of a method that is wide enough to consider both factors. Some compounds may be toxic, but not accumulate in the systems of living creatures. Others may accumulate, and yet have no toxic characteristics. If danger to the life system is considered to be the paramount issue, both elements have to be considered. A toxic substance may pose a short term, acute danger to individuals. Accumulated substances may or may not pose a long term threat to individuals or communities.

3. *Residual Sources*—Some chemicals have entered the environment in such a way that control of production sources may not control the substances. The pervasive aspect of PCB's is an obvious example. The search for the source of Mirex pollution on Lake Ontario may be another. There are apparently two sources, one in the Niagra River and the other in the Oswego River. Sediment samples in the Oswego confirmed a discharge. A further effluent sampling is now necessary to determine the source. In 1976 the EPA conducted sampling tests that indicated that Hooker Chemical Company was the source of Mirex discharges. This is occurring despite the fact that Hooker has not produced the chemical since 1967 and has not ground or packaged it since April of 1975.

Officials of New York, EPA, and the chemical plant tested fourteen sites. The general consensus was that it was not present. Here is an example of a chemical known as dangerous, and no longer being manufactured, somehow showing up in the environment. Even with cooperation of the company involved, detection of the source is proving difficult.

4. *Airborne Pollution*—One problem is setting up an adequate framework for dealing with air pollution on the basis of its resulting pollution of water. The far deeper problem may be locating the sources and evaluating their impact. They may be many miles away. As we shall see in the next chapter, they may be the result of whole areas of industrial concentration. Further, as with PCB's, the sources may be so widespread and diffuse that controls would be near to impossible. Some scientists believe that the primary remaining source of PCB's may be atmospheric. Finally, there is the all-important political consideration of how much control people in a given area will tolerate.

5. *National or Regional Standards*—It may well be that because of industrial techniques, methods of waste treatment, the sensitivity of an area, or the nature of the compound, that chemicals may be safe in one area, but not in others. In such a case, blanket federal or even state standards might cause unnecessary difficulties. Further, priorities of danger vary from one area to another. Mirex is a definite problem in Lake Ontario. Mercury continues to be a potential problem in Lake Erie, while PCB's are probably at the top of the list in Lake Michigan. Regional standards, therefore may be in order. The obvi-

ous hassles are determining the area, setting the priorities, and assigning the responsibility to an authority that may have to cross state or international boundaries.

6. *The Translation of Scientific Data into Regulatory Guidelines*—The preceding question illustrated the interaction of scientific, political, and legal problems. This is the real heart of the matter and the difficulty is awesome. The following quotation is long, but worth the reading. Here we are allowed an unusual glimpse through the fog of bureaucratic language at an official struggling to find a way out of the technological cul-de-sac. The speaker is J. E. Amson of the EPA:

Amson: . . . ''I'm bothered, speaking as a person who is in the legislative-regulatory field, by the inability of the researchers and the poor sons-of-guns, like me, that have to write the law, to mesh. When you put together a model, it's fine if it holds true. Let me give you an example of one that did not. I am sure that most of you are vaguely familiar with the famous water law—Public Law 92-500 . . . Section 307 says in effect, 'there are a few substances that are so toxic that their discharge ought to be totally banned.' We became involved in it over a period of time, and we tried to solve the problem from a hydrodynamic model. We talked to the people we presumed knew a lot about hydrologic models, and we rapidly found that for specific waterways such as Vicksburg, Mississippi, the Corps of Engineers does a superb job of modeling a particular estuary or a particular river between two points. But applyiing that model to another estuary, which may be next door, doesn't work (expletive deleted). Because the model is so exact, it can't be generalized. We ended up with four very bad models . . . they're not really very good but they're all we've got.

''Let me go on to the third section. Section 311 deals with hazardous materials and the problem . . . of spills, extraordinary instances, such as when a railway car goes off the track and a chemical is spilled or a tanker truck rolls of the highway. There are some 375 different substances on that list in the advance notice of the present ruling. Let me come full circle now, back to predictive toxicology. There are four points to that Section 311. One of them says, 'designate them—what are they?' This is where the 375 chemicals come in. The second one says 'tell us what constitutes a hazardous quantity.' A tank car is leaking a drop an hour of this substance—if that doesn't constitute a hazardous quantity, what does? The third part says 'Tell us what the penalty should be for spilling it' bearing in mind that the penalty is not the same for any of the 375 substances. It just has to be 'in a common unit of measure.' The fourth clause says 'tell us if it is removable or not removable' because the penalty is different whether it is removable or not removable. I don't want to get into the legal/economic hassles involved here, but let me say that the possible penalties under Section 311 are huge. For example, if a vessel carrying a hazardous material spills it in a hazardous quantity, it is possible to fine up to $8,000,000. If the insurance company refuses to carry insurance for $8,000,000, the vessel will refuse to carry, and there will be many other ramifications.

''Let me get back to where I was. If we have to define hazardous quantities and write the legislation for 375 different substances, we'll be doing it from now to the year 2000. Isn't there a simple way . . . to predict on the basis of not so much of toxicity . . . but on the basis of some innate physical-chemical-structural properties of the substances themselves? Are we really at the point that we cannot do a prediction of hazardous or toxic materials? Are we really back at step one and a half?'' (9)

183

It is a wonder that there weren't more expletives to delete. The EPA has been charged with the interpretation and enforcement of a wide range of environmental acts. They have been under heavy fire recently on the very point of toxic substance control. At congressional hearings in February of 1978, an EPA official admitted that the organization's track record left a lot to be desired. Even admitting this, it must be remembered that the truth about chemical miracles is just beginning to penetrate the minds of a wide sector of the public. The chemicals have likely already penetrated their bodies. On February 13, 1978, a spokesman for the Environmental Defense Fund stated that the invasion of milk, fish, and poultry by compounds such as the ones we have discussed will have effects that may take fifteen to forty years to manifest themselves in the human population. He raised the possibility of a great increase in cancer in the last quarter of the century. One of the congressmen at this hearing charged "that nothing we eat is certifiably safe." Another brought up what he thought was a particularly flagrant example of EPA neglect. The EPA spokesman responded that "if you applied the law literally, you'd ban the food supply."

The congressman seemed to have forgotten the charge in the Toxic Substances Act to balance costs, risks, and benefits. Effectiveness of the act depends not only on the awesome scientific problem of evaluating the chemicals, but also on the relative weights assigned to risk as opposed to cost and benefit. The cost item is likely, as always, to be more important than anyone will admit. Will the control of toxic substances cost businesses a great deal of money? As an example, the pesticide Chlordane cost approximately 18¢ per unit. Its replacement now costs the orchard owner $1.03. If a vast number of substances are controlled, will it put U.S. businesses at a competitive disadvantage with less restrictive nations? Possibly not. The channelling of energies into other, safer substances or, in agriculture, non-chemical techniques, will probably lead to effective substitutes. Industrial users will eventually learn which areas provide the safest directions in new product development. Standards will become familiar and gradually environmental considerations will be a decisive factor in the introduction or rejection of new substances or techniques. It will certainly be a lot easier to pull a chemical, or alter a process in the test stage than to recall a product in full production.

Actually the economic arguments against chemical control must eventually become secondary. If the health of the general population is imperiled, the solution may demand alteration or loss of certain things we have come to expect. In the end we have the right to demand certain minimum standards from those producing the goods:

> "Anderson: This sounds like a game of Russian Roulette. While the gun is to our head, we are trying to develop models whereby we can predict in what chamber the bullet is. I think we should, in relation to organic chemicals anyway, take a look at the finger that is on the trigger. Maybe the emphasis should not be to try to determine the toxicity for every organic chemical and set some sort of standard based on dilution for that particular chemical in the environment, but simply eliminate it altogether."

> "Amson: I'm not sure whose head and what the gun stands for.

> "Anderson: The head is, of course, the ecosystem. I guess we are part of that. The persons who are holding the gun are those who are contaminating the ecosystem with synthetic materials (organics)." (10)

Quetico Provincial Park, Ontario   T. Uttecht

Chapter 2:
The Acid Rain

Something was wrong. Salmon had been stocked in George and Lumsden Lakes the previous year, and University of Toronto researchers had returned to monitor the growth and survival of the fish. The problem was that there were no survivors.

It was 1965 and the university team was in the La Cloche Mountains, an area south and west of Sudbury, Ontario. The mountains, actually a series of four ridges of quartzite hills, are part of the Canadian Shield. The Shield is the vast landform which dominates the northeastern quarter of North America, mainly consisting of granite, slates, and quartzites. It, like the Great Lakes, is the result of glacial activity. The ice eroded and scoured the ancient mountain range that once occupied this area leaving a rocky plateau covered with thin stony soils. The soils, as a result of the vast evergreen forests that still dominate the area, are acid podzols and very poor for agriculture.

A notable feature of the Shield is its countless lakes which range in size from ponds to Lake Superior. The La Cloche area, north of the North Channel arm of Lake Huron, alone contains over two hundred lakes. It was in this area to all appearances far distant from the pollution problems of more southerly lakes, that salmon were stocked experimentally in the 1960's.

Professor Harold Harvey had himself stocked pink salmon in Lumsden Lake and was puzzled by the total failure of the fish to survive. Taking a closer look, he discovered another curious thing. Suckers in Lumsden were maturing as small as fifty-five grams, while the same species in nearby George Lake at the same age weighed in the more normal range of one to two kilograms.

Harvey wrote to the Fish and Wildlife Management districts across Ontario stating that he had found what appeared to be a population of dwarf suckers, and asking whether similar populations existed in other lakes. Replies from nine districts indicated that other such populations did, indeed, exist. No one was sure whether they were actually a smaller strain of suckers or simply fish whose growth was being affected by some unknown factor. Seven of the lakes with dwarf suckers were reasonably accessible, and Harvey asked a graduate student, Richard Beamish, to examine the situation:

"I told him that I had an interesting problem. Were these fish responding to nature or nurture? Was it a genetic or environmental result? I asked him to collect a random sample of suckers from these seven lakes. I wanted to know the age and growth composition of the population.

"When he returned, Beamish said he would be interested in doing the research for his thesis and took over the project. The first year he tagged suckers in Lumsden and George Lakes and did a recapture which gave estimates of 1,200 and 950 mature suckers respectively. He had tagged roughly a quarter of each population." (11)

From this initial survey another element was added to the mystery. In Lumsden, age classes of the suckers were not complete. There were two, three, and four-year olds, no fives but a number of sixes and sevens. That year the fish failed to spawn at all.

The nurture factor was then examined. An investigation revealed that food for suckers was twice as abundant in Lumsden Lake. Scratch one possible explanation.

The unusual events of 1965 were nothing compared to what Beamish found the following year when he returned to study the tagged fish. The entire population of the Lumsden Lake suckers had disappeared. It was simply, and abruptly, extinct. Lumsden Lake has a falls on its outlet stream such that fish cannot enter from below. There were no suckers upstream from Lumsden Lake. Thus these fish could have gone extinct from this lake only on this one occasion since the last ice age.

As we have seen, it is not unusual for a lake's species balance or composition to change. Normally, however, researchers can only measure natural and man-made changes by yearly observations over a long period of time. Each observation is similar to a single frame of a motion picture. Only when large numbers of these frames are placed in sequence does motion, changes or trends through time, become apparent. Here, however, the changes were occurring before the very eyes of the researchers. They began to question nearby residents:

"There are many commercial fishermen in the local town and they are very familiar with the area. The town of Kilarney is at the end of a road that was only a few years old when we got there. It had been an isolated fishing community for almost a hundred years and those people know their fish.

"Over the years they had fished for sport in Lumsden Lake. They gave us dates for the disappearance of yellow perch and burbot. Trout were fished up to the year we began working in the area. There were none caught that year, and it was the last year the local residents bothered to fish the lake.

"We caught a few trout in our surveys and then they

were gone. In all, we were able to determine the years in which all eight species disappeared from the lake." (12)

Changes in George Lake, the larger of the two under examination, were occurring more slowly. It lay at the end of a chain of lakes and was not responding so quickly to whatever was happening. Even here, however, bass were extinct and walleyes disappeared during the research period.

Simultaneously some members of the research group were collecting environmental data. One of the factors examined was the pH of the water. The pH of any solution is measured in units that reflect its relative acid or base nature. The deviation of ground or surface water from the standard norm of rainwater, 5.9, indicates its general acid or alkaline character. The lower the pH, the higher the acid content. The pH of the first lakes tested showed them to be acidic. Strangely, the lake surface became *more* acid after a rainfall. This clue was followed as the group spread out to 160 lakes for the purpose of examining the water chemistry. It was discovered they were remarkably acidic. Obviously, the entire situation warranted a closer look.

Harvey and Beamish then did two things. First, they went back through the records of the Ministry of Natural Resources and identified lakes in the La Cloche where old data was available. They then compared the old and new results and established a rate of change for area waters of 0.16 pH units per year, a frightening rate of decline. For example, one of the larger lakes had declined from a pH of 6.8 to 4.5 in fifteen years.

The decline varied from lake to lake and was generally a function of its size, flushing rate, and the type of rock and soil in the watershed. Lakes north of the La Cloche had nearly twice the ionic content and were changing more slowly. Even there the rate was 0.08 pH units per year.

The team next selected a group of sixty-eight lakes for closer study. In the course of this two-year project, they tried for a good cross section to avoid the tendency to examine only those waters accessible by road. It was found that headwater lakes had been affected to the greatest degree and, almost without exception, were discovered to be without fish. In all, *nineteen* of the sixty-eight had lost their entire fish population, and fauna in more than half of the remaining lakes was greatly reduced.

The university group knew that the acidification phenomenon was not limited to the study area. Efforts, however, had been aimed at discovering the effects of the changes rather than their origins and a series of papers on the acidification of the lakes and the loss of their fish populations resulted. It was felt, naturally, that the media would be interested in the alarming discoveries made to that point. Such was not the case:

"We found it quite difficult to interest people in our findings. We wrote them up in the form of a popular article and sent them to the big national news magazine. At first they said they'd love to have it. A couple of weeks later they checked and asked how much we wanted for it. We told them we didn't want any money, we just wanted to get the story out. They eventually phoned back and said their advertising department might not like it.

"We then sent it to one of the weekend newspaper magazines. They wrote back and said that if it was as important as we said it was, someone else would have seen it first. An interesting argument.

"We next tried another weekend magazine and they told us that somebody in their office had once caught a fish in that area. Finally we got the thing into the popular press through the *Globe* and *Mail* as a letter to the editor. It was a very slow and painful business. We found out nearly all we really needed to know by 1968, but it wasn't until 1972 that we convinced people that we were on to something." (13)

Unknown to the Canadians, the same events were unfolding elsewhere. As early as 1961-62, atmospheric environment officials in Scandanavia began flying danger signals. They had become concerned about increasing amounts of sulfates and acidity in precipitation. In the early 1960's, Swedish scientists first reported that the acid and sulfate content of rain and snow was increasing. By 1968 Sven Oden had mapped the distribution of acid precipitation on the European land mass. By 1971 the Norwegians documented their situation and what it implied for the future of their fresh waters. Sweden presented its report on the effects of pollution across international boundaries in 1974. In it, they implicated the major industrial nations of western Europe, especially Britain, France, and Germany, as the principal sources of the sulfur dioxide and nitrous oxide which were altering their environment.

The alteration of these substances into sulfuric acid is the function of a series of events. As air masses move north toward Scandinavia, changes take place with them. The sulfur dioxide emissions of western Europe are gradually oxidized into sulfuric acid. This falls in solution with precipitation or as a dry deposition in the absence of rain or snow.

There followed a long series of Scandinavian publications, primarily from Swedish air and environmental researchers, on the known and predicted effects of the acid rain. One group was concerned with the soils of the region. Some areas of Sweden and Norway were taking delivery of two grams of sulfuric acid per square meter per year. The more alkaline soils in the north of the two countries, and in other sections of Europe, can expect to withstand this type of loading for a century before soils are destroyed. In southern Scandinavia, as in the Canadian Shield, soils are podzols containing little calcium and already acidic.

Here they may last only one to two decades.

Others mapped the effects on the fresh waters of the area. It was estimated that by the turn of the century *one quarter* of those waters would be inhospitable to desirable fish species. Already rivers in the southern tip of Sweden and Norway are too acidic to support salmon and trout. The possibility of placing lime in these waters to offset this condition was examined by Sweden. In addition to the difficulty of finding the great amount of material that would be needed, massive logistic problems would have to be solved in delivering it to the lake.

Normally, as female fish mature, they double their blood calcium level in the form of protein bound calcium. With suckers in the acid lakes this did not happen. It was not simply lack of calcium in the waters themselves, as lakes with one-half the calcium were found to be producing normal fish. It is speculated that the problem is an acid related phenomenon involving calcium metabolism.

Professor Harvey notes that many of these events have been observed but not explored in detail. Further information and a complete understanding of the environmental impact of the acid rain in North America is still a number of years away. The university team felt that the next order of business was to identify a point source for the events they had observed. This was one of the few steps of their investigation that did not prove too difficult:

"Historically, smelting of sulfide ores consisted of roasting, that is oxidation that yielded sulfur dioxide. For example, in the Sudbury area, commencing in 1885, nickel ores were roasted in the open and the fumes destroyed plant life for miles around. (Nineteen eighty-five will mark 100 years that people have been complaining about pollution in the Sudbury area.)" (14)

At the time of investigation, three stacks of the smelting complex were throwing 2.6 million metric tons of sulfur dioxide into the atmosphere each year. In the mid-70's they were replaced by superstack, a 1,200-foot monster, and sulfur dioxide output has been reduced to about 1.3 million tons per year. SO_2 is released too high for local downdrafts. There has been a return of some species, especially plants, grass, and trees in the immediate area. The trouble is that the problem hasn't been solved, simply transferred to other locations. The superstack plume can be seen extending for hundreds of miles and has on occasion been observed holding together as far as the Atlantic Ocean. The company argues that it is too expensive to completely intercept the material.

Investigators were aware that Sudbury, while an obvious source, was likely only one of many. They have begun the attempt to apportion these sources. This task is simplified by the fact that sulfur 34 isotopes are more common in igneous rock than in the natural environment above ground. Thus the ratio of sulfur 32 to sulfur 34 can be used as an indication of source.

Many of the first University of Toronto findings have been confirmed by other researchers. Current efforts are aimed at developing an early warning system that acidification is underway. What is the first signal? Observers in the La Cloche had been examining ecological basket cases. There were simply no control lakes to be found in the region. Now five of the most sensitive areas in Ontario, selected on the basis of known water chemistry, have been identified for special study. They extend from the Manitoba border, along the north shore of Lake Superior, to areas north of North Channel and Georgian Bay, then eastward along the Algonquin and Haliburton highlands and southward to the Muskokas. One of the primary aims of this project is the collection of more accurate chemical information. There are strong restraints on the existing data base; traditional tests to determine the pH of lake water often required the presence of an indicator. Investigators ended up titrating the buffering capacity of the indicator as well as the actual lake sample. More sophisticated tests have to be developed to correct this weakness.

What makes the whole issue such a time bomb is that problems may not become apparent until the buffering capacity of a particular lake is exhausted. In short, the acid is neutralized until the neutralizing ability is used up. At this point a small additional increase in acid produces a rapid series of changes in the lake waters. For example, in one experiment a lake in northwestern Ontario was deliberately acidified. The following year the pH had apparently returned toward its original level but the addition of only a portion of the acid administered the first year, drove the lake back to an acid condition.

Swedish scientists have found indications that if acidification reaches a certain point, simple addition of nutrients may be unable to reverse the condition. In this ultimate situation the metabolism of the lake turns from bacterial to fungal recycling of detritus. The bottom of the lake is eventually covered by a fungal mat and it becomes increasingly oligotrophic. The image is chilling. A pure, clear lake, visually delightful but hostile to many life forms.

Much of the Sandinavian work has not been repeated on this continent and it is too early to predict which of their experiences are pertinent to us. How the acid environment destroys fish populations is only partially understood:

"Is it the failure to spawn that is preponderant? Is it the failure of their eggs to hatch and produce viable young? Is it the fact that young larvae are lying close to the substrate and are exposed to adverse conditions as, for example, heavy metals freed by the acid environment? Is it due to the acid pulse coming down streams where the fish tend to spawn? There are several mechanisms that can affect this phenomenon. There are only a few for which the data base would permit meaningful inference. The rest is highly problematical." (15)

Much of the current research is centered north of Lake Superior, an extremely sensitive area. The buffering capacity of fresh waters of the region is extremely modest and there is some speculation that small lakes and rivers will be hostile to aquatic life in one to two decades. The acidification of rivers and streams of this area has an enormous implication for the supply of fish in Lake Superior itself because many lake dwelling species historically spawned in their waters. Their elimination would be a blow to hopes of widespread re-establishment of the fish.

The key factor in determining the vulverability of a given lake is, as mentioned, its buffering capacity. Two major determinants of buffering capacity are the soil depth in the surrounding lake basin, and the amount and quality of inflowing waters.

Dr. David Schindler is currently involved in research in northwestern Ontario. One of the targets of this research is development of an adequate method of measuring this capacity. There is a vast range. If an arbitrary unit of ten is used to represent the bicarbonate of the most vulnerable lakes, others in less sensitive surroundings may range up to 1,000 and some as high as 100,000. Thus the effects are highly variable. With sufficient soil depth, the acid rain can bombard a watershed for fifty years without noticeable effects. The bad news is that the process appears to be happening faster in North America than in Europe. Some lakes in Ontario have shown a shift of .09 pH units per year, three times the Scandinavian rate. (16)

In the United States there are some highly vulnerable areas in the Quetico and other regions of northern Minnesota, upper Michigan, northern Wisconsin, and in the Adirondack Mountains. It is estimated that some of the Minnesota lakes may lose fish populations in little more than five years, and estimates for a number of Adirondack lakes range from ten to fifteen years. By contrast this took an average of ten to twenty years in Scandinavia.

Effects on plant life are manifested more slowly. Lacking a central nervous system, they are mainly affected by the decrease in soil nutrients. As acidification continues, forest growth will slow up to fifty percent in scattered areas with shallow soil, while in areas with deeper soil the effects may be negligible. In Norway 5,000 lakes have lost fish populations while there has been only a ten percent reduction in forest growth.

The effects of acid rain are much less completely documented in the U.S. than in Canada. Many lakes lack baseline data on their chemistry so it is difficult to establish a rate of change. Only in the Adirondack area are there measurements that cover several decades and pH levels are on their way down.

While the effects in U.S. lakes have been less completely noted, the chemistry of the rain has indicated a widespread tendency toward acidification. The impact of Sudbury was obvious. It was a distinct, sharp, point source and the effect in the immediate area was acute. General input is more widespread and diffuse. Sulfur dioxide is drifting north, as in Europe, from major industrial centers hundreds of miles distant.

Industrial sources are only part of the problem. There are disagreements among scientists on how much loading is the result of the internal combustion engine, with some estimates running as high as fifty percent. The automobile has been found to be the cause of many urban air problems and may now be contributing to damage that extends far beyond the cities.

Alleviating factors? There may be one in form of dust particles moving eastward from the prairies to western areas of the shield. The deposition of this wind-transported soil might add extra buffering to some regions. Further, some of the

pollutants themselves may have a nutrient content that offsets, to a degree, the acid timetable. Information and data are only now being pulled together in an attempt to discover what compensating forces may be at work.

Nonetheless, vast lake areas in the northeastern part of the continent are in peril. Solutions after the fact? Liming has been mentioned. Dr. Schindler points out that in order to be effective the entire lake watershed would have to be limed, since the constant wash of acid into the lakes would soon exhaust the added buffering capacity.

There are, of course, the obvious solutions. With reduction of industrial pollution—the addition of 'scrubbers' in the stacks of power plants—loading would be limited. But the automobile is unlikely to be checked in any way. It is the center piece of technological affluence, the symbol of the good life. It is part cliche, part truth, that the automobile has given greater personal freedom to a greater number of people than any other invention of man. It has liberated rural areas while destroying urban neighborhoods. Suburbs are planned around it and people seek to move to the country, away from it. Our economy depends on it, and our foreign policy is in hock to its fuel needs. The systematic destruction of alternate mass transit in cities, and railroad passenger traffic between cities has made it a necessity. It is unlikely that anything short of a catastrophe will produce an alternative to it, and the end of fish populations in northern lakes is unlikely to qualify.

Controversy over the significance of acid rain may soon be an international issue. The Environmental Protection Agency is preparing a report, concerned in part with the dangers from a proposed Ontario power plant to be built just across the Minnesota border at Atikokan. This is near some of the most vulnerable shield lakes. Researchers found out more than they wanted to know. The Atikokan plant may not pose a great danger, but the cumulative effect of various sources of atmospheric acid looms as a major environmental threat.

Quetico Provincial Park, Ontario

T. Uttecht

Trace the implications to the current debate over nuclear power plants. One of the arguments against them is that discharge of waters used to cool plants will so warm lake waters as to increase the choking effects of eutrophication to intolerable levels. On the other hand we have seen the animated maps on television which illustrate that we are the Saudi Arabia of coal. There are already major efforts to convert to coal and a delicate shift in middle east politics could turn this into a stampede.

We have seen two opposite chemistries at work, one leading to the destruction of aquatic life through suffocation with an overabundance of nutrients and the other leading to the same result through the obliteration of nutrients. One solution poses the threat of an accidental nuclear disaster and the problem of storing deadly wastes for thousands of years. The other promises a likely deterioration of air and water quality that may be as deadly in the long run.

The pleasant alternatives have disappeared. We are facing choices which we are not prepared to face but, if they are not faced, decision will come by default.

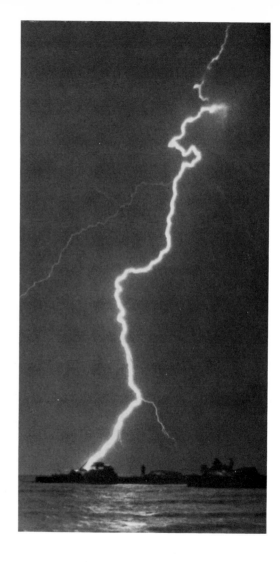

Chapter 3:
What Happened?

Various man-made activities of the last two hundred years have altered the face of the Great Lakes and changed or destroyed the life within them. Researchers have only recently begun to separate and evaluate the results of individual stresses. This has been extremely difficult because so many of them have acted in unison, particularly during the devastating period of the last forty years. What follows is based partially on speculation and is an attempt to briefly reconstruct the impact of successive aspects of European settlement on the Great Lakes. A general understanding of what we did, and how we did it, is a necessary preliminary to an attempt to rehabilitate or enhance the Lakes.

Settlement

This is the most underrated and least documented of the forces that changed the region. It involved nothing less than the systematic destruction of the original basin environment and construction of a new, made-man order.

The original white settlers cleared the land for farming and, later, large scale lumbering clear-cut the forests. These changes had a major effect on the watershed.

"Initially the effect of forest removal on stream flow was controversial . . . but by the end of the 1800's it became clear that stream flows were greatly reduced. It was observed that thousands of water powered mills were abandoned and that 'creeks and rivers in which water hardly flows in dry summer give mute evidence that

forests play an important hydrologic role.' (Hedrick, 1933). Some tributaries that previously supported Atlantic salmon runs became dry or intermittent, the summer flows in rivers where juvenile salmon spend their early life became very low during dry periods, and the magnitude of seasonal or short-term flunctuations in stream flow increased greatly . . . The consequences of such changes were to widen and flatten stream beds and increase the silt loading during periods of heavy run-off. The springs that contributed to sustained flow throughout the year dried up . . . undoubtedly as a result of drainage of swamps and loss of the forest floor which retained water from melting snows and summer storms." (17)

Lumbering and early manufacturing also spilled waste products into the streams, covering spawning areas with massive deposits of sawdust and other debris. These wastes were carried into the lakes and concentrated along shoreline spawning areas by currents and, in the spring, by the thermal bar.

Early individual and commercial fisherman seined at the mouths of streams and rivers and captured portions of stream-based spawning runs. It is stated that fish were so plentiful that farmers netted wagonloads for use as fertilizer, as well as for food.

Enormous marsh areas along the margins of the lakes acted as filters for inflowing river waters, reducing turbidity and silt, and eventually supplying clean water to the lake. They also provided refuges and spawning areas for fish. Human beings, by and large, find such areas uncongenial, and their drainage has been the object of massive engineering projects throughout civilized history. In the Great Lakes conversion of marsh and swamp to 'useful' land was accomplished with speed and efficiency.

Thus, in the first impact of settlement, the natural regime which had prevailed for thousands of years was torn apart. Massive areas of forest and marsh became farm land, runoff clogged streams, and the character of the water flowing into the lakes from many streams was degraded by industrial and human wastes. This and the construction of dams must have contributed to the elimination of whole stocks of river and marsh spawning fish.

The effects of this period are, however, impossible to measure as the original state of the lakes is largely a mystery. Because of this changes cannot be precisely measured. What we have are personal observations and occasional detailed descriptions of the awesome abundance of the early lakes, followed by later accounts of the reduction of this abundance, often noticeable over a period of several decades. (18)

Warming

Though generally recognized in scientific writings, this may be the factor least understood by the general public. There have been two major sources of this warming. As mentioned, the destruction of the forest cover over vast portions of the lakes, resulted in much warmer summer stream temperatures. Secondly, there has been the general climatic warming of the last century which may now be coming to an end. Temperatures necessary for successful hatching and survival of a number of fish have been shown to be extremely precise and there has been a strong tendency for those needing low temperatures to be the most severely depleted.

"It is also possible that the general climatic cool period in the Northern Hemisphere from the late 1500's to 1900 could have suppressed sea lamprey populations, and the sharp warming after 1920 . . . may have enhanced lamprey production throughout the Great Lakes drainage in recent decades. This could in part, explain why lake trout did not become extinct in Lake Ontario and the Finger Lakes in the early part of this century, but have had greater difficulty surviving to maturity after sea lampreys became abundant in Lakes Superior, Michigan, Huron, and Ontario in recent years, prior to artificial sea lamprey control." (19)

A third source of warming is a result of thermal pollution and has become increasingly important in recent years. Warm industrial wastewater has visible local effects and there are scientists and fish managers who fear this input will be vastly increased by construction of nuclear power plants. Warming of waters by only a few degrees could lead to vastly expanded algal blooms and alter spawning conditions so that some fish would be severely affected. One manager conjured up the vision of pea green, instead of sky blue, waters.

Exotic Species

The lamprey made its destructive presence felt in Lake Ontario by the end of the nineteenth century, perhaps entering by canal from the south. If resident in the Lake, its effects may have been masked by the fact that earlier, larger fish could withstand attacks or by lower stream temperatures which inhibited spawning. They multiplied in Ontario and destroyed large numbers of predator fish.

Alewives may have always hovered on the periphery of the Lake Ontario. While Atlantic salmon and lake trout were plentiful, they were naturally held in check. Freed of predation by the salmon, populations exploded. Initially, some other fish such as chubs also expanded, but the enormous range of the alewife allowed them to occupy the entire lake at one point or another during the year. By predation on the eggs of other species, or the sheer mass of their food competition, they reduced the numbers of herring, emerald shiner, perch, and finally chubs.

The alewife and lamprey passed through Lake Erie with relatively minor effect. In Huron and Michigan, and to a lesser extent Superior, the lamprey obliterated the lake trout and greatly reduced whitefish and burbot. Management agencies were slow to perceive the threat posed by the lamprey.

"The research needed by fisheries managers to stem or counteract effect of the sea lamprey . . . was not initiated until 1946—more than fifty years after problems caused by the sea lamprey in the Great Lakes were fully recognized and after it had spread throughout the Great Lakes . . . In fact, the first documented concern about the destructiveness of the sea lamprey in the late 1880's and 1890's went unheeded. It was not until 1929, after the lamprey had entered the upper lakes via the Welland Canal and long after it had ravaged the fisheries of Lake Ontario, that the information was consolidated and reviewed for Lake Ontario . . . or fear for the future of the fisheries of the Great Lakes expressed . . . Although fishery problems had been more thoroughly documented for Lake Ontario than for any of the other Great Lakes, evidence of the sea lamprey was never mentioned before the 1880's." (20)

In the wake of the lamprey's destruction, the alewife rose to dominance in Lakes Huron and Michigan, repeating the pattern established in Lake Ontario. The threat of the alewife was early understood and much research undertaken. It was not the quality or timeliness of this research, but its relevance which was questioned in 1973 by Dr. Stanford Smith:

"The research on the alewife has not been primarily concerned with determining how and why this fish affected the fishery resource, or with measures for its use or control, or with the reduction of its effects on the stability or productivity of fish populations. Instead, the main objective of alewife research has been to learn why alewives die in large numbers each spring where they are abundant in large fresh water lakes . . ." (21)

Carp were introduced throughout the Great Lakes in the burst of nationwide planting fever in the late 1800's and their arrival proved to be the high point of their popularity. The pollution tolerant fish has become very abundant and occupies many bays and shallows. Smelt populations escaped from the inland lake where they had been planted and exploded at various times in each of the Lakes with likely adverse effects on native fish. More recently, the pink salmon 'accidently' introduced into Lake Superior has become abundant and is moving south. Likewise, the white perch has become more extensive after having apparently used the canal route to invade Lake Ontario. It has become more abundant and will likely expand its range to Erie and the upper lakes. Which of these fish will become the newcomer of the decade in the 1980's is not yet certain.

The century long attempt to establish salmon in the Great Lakes culminated in the massive stocking programs of the last decade. Various Pacific salmon were imported for this purpose and currently form the basis of an extremely lucrative and popular sport fishery.

Eutrophication

The effect of 'bad' water was recognized early but it was felt that the lakes were so vast that effects would be confined to river and near shore areas. After the collapse of the Lake Erie herring in the 1920's the possibility of a lakewide threat from pollutants was considered. Studies that followed were very encouraging, noting that the enrichment of the waters made more food available to some fish populations and thereby balanced the adverse effects to other species. This complacent attitude became widespread and left officials poorly prepared for what was to happen later.

"These conclusions seemed valid but the interpretation needed by the managers was lacking, i.e., that conditions, although not considered distressing, would become progressively worse if corrective action was not taken. Thus, neither fishery nor resource managers were stimulated to initiate action. Severe problems had extended throughout the western basin of Lake Erie by the early 1950's and spread through the central basin by the early 1960's . . . By 1970 all of the most valued species of fish of Lake Erie were either declining, scarce, or extinct." (22)

The growing wash of fertilizers and municipal and industrial sewage greatly enriched the waters and favored a shift from such fish as lake trout, whitefish, and salmon to walleye, blue pike, and perch. As the process continued, these latter fish were increasingly affected and began to decline or disappear in the most polluted areas. The final stage appears to be the collapse of dissolved oxygen, an event which affected fish in a variety of ways:

"The terminal declines of the lake herring and lake whitefish in Lake Erie started in 1944 and 1949,

respectively, in the same sequence that they disappeared earlier from Lake St. Clair and the Detroit River . . . During the period of their terminal declines, the herring and whitefish lived mostly in the eastern and central sections of the lake. The initiation of the terminal declines preceded the first occurrence of oxygen depletion in the central basin by about a decade. Thus, the stress that contributed to terminal declines must have involved factors other than anoxic conditions in the water. High oxygen demand at the mud-water interface, where the eggs incubate and hatch, may have impaired reproduction, and the reduction of habitat or food for fry or fingerlings may have contributed to the stunted growth that has been recorded for lake herring." (23)

By the mid-1970's the most badly affected areas were Green Bay on Lake Michigan, the southern portion of that lake, the western portion of Lake Erie, Saginaw Bay on Lake Huron, and the Bay of Quinte on Lake Ontario. In some streams and rivers the process reached its ultimate conclusion.

"The Cleveland area is one of the greatest steel producing and manufacturing areas in the world and thus the industrial pollution of the Cuyahoga River which flows through Cleveland is no surprise. For example, the oil released by industries which floats on the surface of the water has resulted in the river being considered as a major fire hazard. At one time, the problem reached such proportions that fire breaks were built to separate the surface waters into sections so that oil fires could be contained within a certain area . . .

"A description of the eleven mile reach of the Cuyahoga River from the lake to the Southerly Sewage Treatment Plant follows and serves as an illustration of what can happen to a river flowing through an industrial area in the Great Lakes basin . . .

"In the biological survey of this reach, only a few sludgeworms and midge larvae were found in the occasional riffles upstream. Some aquatic life was also detected at the bottom in the extreme downstream reach . . . where the lake water extends under the river due to density stratification. The environment is also unsuitable for nitrifying bacteria and thus ammonia is carried out into the lake where it eventually exerts its oxygen demand. This reach of the Cuyahoga presently does not meet water quality criteria for any use . . ." (24)

By 1978 some encouragingly swift improvements in water quality were seen in some areas as advanced methods of sewage treatment and industrial waste treatment became operational. The response of some of the rivers in the basin was rapid and fish not seen for decades, have returned to some. Nonetheless one expert summed up the situation by saying that "Things are getting worse at a slower rate." Given previous conditions, even this must be regarded as a major milestone.

Microcontaminants

During and after World War II a growing number of chemical products and wastes were released into the Great Lakes basin where they concentrated in fish, wildlife, and human beings. A number of mysterious and disturbing occurrences indicated that something was wrong but for a long time these symptoms were either regarded as isolated events or conscientiously ignored. Finally, the publication of *Silent Spring* by Rachel Carson, and a series of catastrophes brought widespread attention to the problem. Statistical correlation between use of these substances and disease, notably cancer, forced a number of widespread warnings and, in some cases, an outright ban on their continued use. Once again, if we had been listening, the fate of aquatic and bird life could have told us something:

"During the period since 1940 there has been a succession of species to extinction or near extinction in Lake Ontario. These declines were most abrupt, earliest, and most extreme in the main body of Lake Ontario (excluding the Bay of Quinte and adjacent shallow, eastern area of the lake), and occurred during a period when exploitation was virtually absent in most areas of the lake . . . The deepwater sculpin, a small deepwater forage fish that had never been exploited, declined to near extinction during this period following the decline of its major predators—lake trout and burbot. These declines occurred, however, during a period of accelerating increases of chemical constituents of the water . . ." (25)

There can be no certainty as to why this small fish has virtually disappeared from Lake Ontario but a growing number of individuals believe contaminants are the key factor. This is particularly sinister for it means that these substances have penetrated the deepest parts of Ontario. It also means that we may have just begun to discover how widespread and dangerous these contaminants may be.

The spread of these substances has imperiled fish stocking programs throughout the Great Lakes and may be affecting the reproductive ability of fish, as it has demonstrably affected that of fish-eating birds. These substances may have a singular, cumulative, or synergistic effect on human beings. Effects may not be felt for years. Some substances might simply have no effect in the amounts now present, but no one is certain of what 'safe' levels may be.

This is, by near universal consensus, potentially the most dangerous problem facing human and animal life in the Great Lakes Basin. The danger lies not so much in what has been discovered, as in what is not known and what may be discovered. There is a sensation here, more than in any other environmental problem, of loss of control. The lag factor is fully at work with substances buried long ago bubbling from dumps or, as with mercury, combining with other substances to present a sudden danger. Toxic substance control legislation may provide some help in the future, particularly if structure-activity proves a tool sufficiently accurate to predict safe or dangerous directions for research. It is likely that far more stringent controls will be necessary, however, to master the situation.

"One of the most retrograde principles currently implicit in environmental management is that any suspected polluter or chemical compound or project is innocent until proven guilty. This is a basic tenet of human justice in our soceity, and it expresses a willingness to accept risk or alienation to what is usually the greater number of people. There is an onus on environmental agencies and/or affected parties to marshal evidence. Even if resources to do this are allocated, by the time that strong evidence has been obtained, the resource may have been so depreciated that the users have faded away and the only voice left may be that of the investigator himself. Obviously, fisheries agencies and others have to press for a number of changes. They should plan to do more complete work at fewer sites to establish the sound knowledge for broader application, to respond firmly on the basis of inductive reasoning, and to act while there are still affected parties with standing. Funding levels for such work are inadequate at present." (26)

Fishing

No other factor has been subject to as much political manipulation as that of fishing. In recent decades it has been actively promoted in some quarters as the sole, or major cause of the decline of fish species. A case in point is the relative roles assigned to the lamprey and commercial fishing in the matter of lake trout disappearance in the upper lakes. During, and immediately after the event, there was an almost universal consensus among those who studied the problem that the lamprey was the obvious villian. The U.S. Fish and Wildlife Service investigated the situation and the results of their deliberations were published in a 1951 report. The researchers utilized catch statistics from the individual districts of Lake Michigan and weighed the factors of abundance and fishing intensity. They reached some rather definitive conclusions.

"Some factor other than overfishing caused the lake trout to disappear in Lakes Huron and Michigan. The best evidence points to the sea lamprey." (27)

James W. Moffett of the Bureau of Commercial Fisheries writing in 1958:

"Did something else cause these declines? Extensive studies indicate as follows:
    Overfishing did not. There was no increase in fishing intensity in Lake Michigan preceding 1945. In fact, for three years prior to 1945, fishing was ten percent below normal. In Lake Huron the story was the same. The lake trout fishery has not existed in Lake Huron for ten years and in Lake Michigan for seven years; still there is no sign of lake trout stocks.

"Evidence that sea lampreys did cause the collapse of the lake trout fishery is ample. The collapse progressed from

Pound net fishermen

Ellison Bay, Wis.

lake to lake in order of their geographical proximity to Niagra Falls. During severe storms, thousands of dead trout and burbot, all with fresh lamprey scars were lifted from the bottom by currents and entangled in gill nets.'' (28)

By 1971 what had seemed clear in the 50's was no longer so. John Scott of the Fisheries Division of the Michigan DNR carefully noted that the cause of the lake trout disappearance was not a clear-cut issue. The idea was developed, however, that the lamprey administered the fatal blow to already declining lake trout stocks.

"However, a major factor in the collapse of lake trout stocks was the introduction, about 1945, of synthetic fibers used in the manufacture of commercial fishing gear, notably gill nets. The nylon gill nets, being inexpensive, rot-free, and requiring little or no care, permitted more commercial fishermen to enter the lake fisheries at less cost. The truth is borne out by the fact that the number of fishermen increased from 1,200 to 1,600 during the decade 1940-1950. Nylon gill nets, since they do not readily absorb water, weighed less, required less room, and enabled fishermen to haul more gear to the fishing grounds. Finally, and most importantly from the commercial fisherman's viewpoint, the nylon gill net was two to three times more efficient in catching lake trout than were the old cotton and linen nets . . .'' (29)

The point of all this is not that such a thing as overfishing does not exist. It quite obviously does and the experience of coastal marine fisheries bears this out. With the use of sophisticated gear and factory ships some stocks were severely depleted. The stripping of the U.S. grounds was a major factor in the adoption of the two hundred mile limit by the United States. In the Great Lakes the statistical correlation between the collapse of the whitefish stocks and the use of the deep trap net, as well as its bitter denunciation by fishermen of the time, shows that abusive technology is always a distinct possibility. What, however, is overfishing? The term is used so widely and in so many situations by opponents of commercial fishing that it is difficult to understand what is meant. It would seem that fishing would become overfishing only at the point that it endangered a stock of fish. A certain acceptable level of fishing may become dangerous when stocks are imperiled by other causes but overfishing, in that case, is not the source of the peril. This is *not* to say that fishing should not be controlled when stocks are endangered by other factors. It would seem, however, that integrity or simple fairness would demand that the primary factors be recognized as such.

It must be pointed out that of all of the stresses discussed in this section, fishing, the use of the resource for food, remains the only legitimate one as long as stocks are not imperiled by it. It must be noted also that commercial fishermen historically have recognized the need for controls. Further, what is regarded as overfishing in a time of peace and prosperity, may actually be encouraged in a time of crisis.

"By 1900 the Erie fishery was generally recognized as overintensive; some fisheries had been forced into bankruptcy and others relocated to less heavily fished lakes. Some regulations restricting catches were enforced on all parts of the lake by 1905; the low catches during 1901-10 reflect both depressed stocks and reduced effort. Restrictions were largely relaxed for patriotic reasons during World War I resulting in increased catches. During the next decade, a very efficient new gear, the bull net, was used widely, but the value of catches dropped. The bull net was outlawed but World War II again resulted in relaxation of new regulations . . .'' (30)

Thus the perception of commercial fishing has depended on the prevailing national or local priority of the time. If it conflicts with another priority and debate centers on the priorities, the process is a legitimate political one. What is offensive is the manipulation of scientific data and the image of environmental concern to create a picture of rapacious exploitation when the actual issue is something quite different. The following exchange took place at the Petosky hearings.

Mr. Thornton: "I have noticed an inconsistency in one basic element of your argument; namely, that is that on the one hand it said that the Indians are depleting the resource and yet you seem to now have testified that really the problem is an economic problem rather than a biological one; that is that the State of Michigan gets more bang for the buck through the recreational fisheries than it does through the Indian fisheries.

"Is that an accurate summation of your testimony?"

Dr. Tanner: "Your summation of it is inaccurate. There is—there are two questions: one, a biological one and that is assurance of the basic principle, . . . that you try to permit a fish species to live long enough to spawn once and in order to achieve that you need regulations, in the case of the lake trout, of Lake Superior, to protect the female fish, from anywhere from 7 to 9 years. That is a part of my testimony.

"The economic portion of it . . . is a somewhat separate question; but it is within the definition of conservation, the greatest good for the greatest number; and that is that unless you maintain a level of abundance suitable to support a recreational fishery which must be substantially above that necessary to support a commercial fishery, then you have, in fact, lost a recreational resource.

Mr. Thronton: "That is different, however, from depleting the resource."

Dr. Tanner: "Well, you destroy its value. I determine that to be depletion.

"You see, depletion of the resource is not strictly a biological point. That is what I take at issue; because it is so very important. Go back to the definition, and it is mentioned in the judge's words, if necessary for conservation and conservation defined, I believe by everyone is generally accepted, is the greater number for a longer period of time. So now when you destroy a recreational fish worth $80 for the purpose of selling it at a $1.25, to a point where the charter boat fisherman could no longer operate, a motel can no longer fill, the boats are no longer sold, the licenses are no longer sold, then that, in effect, is effective depletion and I am afraid people are going to miss that point." (31)

So we see that economic factors, quite apart from conservation or depletion as generally understood, are at work in the guise of those terms. Plainly presented, these factors are legitimate. They raise the question of allocation.

None of the foregoing is meant to present an argument for uncontrolled fishing of any kind, but simply to indicate that the impact of commercial fishing, basically consumer fishing, should be judged by scientific criteria, not by political or economic criteria masked as biological criteria. The consensus of scientists is that fishing is simply one of a number of stresses visited on fish stocks.

"Overfishing has seldom been clearly indicted in the collapse of Great Lakes fish stocks. The loss of lake sturgeon and some stocks of whitefish were chronicled for the last century, before such factors as eutrophication and the

205

introduction of exotic fish became problems, so they represent exceptions. In latter years extremes of fishing pressure on premium stocks in the lower lakes coincided with the emergence of these problems. Even though its exact role cannot be specified, it has been accepted . . . that overfishing figures prominently in the family of recent stresses man has imposed. (32)

Jurisdictional Fragmentation

This matter is seldom emphasized in public as strongly as it is in individual conversations with the parties involved. The simple reason for this is that tranquility is a necessary prerequisite for whatever cooperative action can be achieved. I have been told that, on occasion, either of two competing programs would have had more beneficial effects than the delay caused by the disagreement over which course to pursue.

Fumbling, bumbling and fragmented controls allowed the perils of eutrophication, lamprey, and toxic substances to build to crises. Only then, under the gun of public indignation, was action and coordination forthcoming. Intelligent individuals, programs, and actions were sucked into the black hole of jurisdictional chaos, never to be heard from again. If you think this is an exaggeration, consider your own experiences with a single government agency and then contemplate the following:

"Given the geographic range of the Great Lakes and the diversity of uses, a large number of formal agencies are involved, in resource policy, resource planning, and resource management. For example, in terms of fisheries alone there are some 32 government agencies involved on the Canadian side. For the United States, there are at least 25 state and federal agencies with direct fisheries responsibilities. If one considers governmental units with jurisdiction over Great Lakes shoreline, there are over 650 separate units of government at the local, regional, state province level in the U.S. and Canada which have such jurisdiction . . ." (33)

With this in mind, it is easy to see that accomplishment of anything on the Great Lakes is a truly remarkable achievement. Special awards should be designed for those officials, scientists, or politicians who are able to achieve concerted action. There are those that consider the jurisdictional situation of the Great Lakes to be the single most destructive factor in their history:

". . . Whatever the reasons, the lack of a concerted and compatible approach toward taking the appropriate action to regulate the fisheries or control undesirable species and manipulate fish stocks at the right time may have been the single most dominating factor that has contributed to the deterioration of the fisheries of the Great Lakes. Liberal regulations of some jurisdictions may contribute to overexploitation of some stocks of a lake despite research or theory that might support the more stringent regulations of other jurisdictions. Stocking programs of some agencies can be incompatible with stocking programs of others or cause conflict in management theory or objectives. Under present hatchery techniques of mass production, uncoordinated introductions without adequate research could result in serious and detrimental overstocking of lakes particularly under the present unstable conditions." (34)

Against this background the accomplishments of the Great Lakes Fishery Commission in gaining consensus on certain objectives is a landmark. Evolving from its position as the international agency designed to coordinate lamprey control efforts, it has provided a nucleus for lakewide and lakeswide cooperation in other matters. All parties agree that there has been improvement and a semblance of order has been achieved.

The other major international agency, the International Joint Commission, has attempted to deal with water quality issues. They have gathered valuable data, pinpointed problem areas, and achieved some effect by naming some of the worst offenders, industrial and municipal, on the lakes. They are also involved in research on the formidable problem of toxic substance control.

Pensaukee, Wis.

Raymond Tuttle, Suamico. 1978 is his sixty-fifth year as a commercial fisherman.

Chapter 4:
What Can Be Done

Before we begin to alter the present unsatisfactory state of the Great Lakes, we must determine our goals. At a symposium held in Windsor, Ontario in May of 1978 the feasibility of lake restoration and rehabilitation was examined. H. A. Regier outlined some of the general options.

Begin with the present state of the Great Lakes. There is the possibility of *restoration*. Using this approach, an attempt would be made to duplicate the lake environment of some point in the past, perhaps that of 1940 or earlier. A purist pursuit of this cause would, however, lead to the suppression of certain desirable man-made additions. It is doubtful that a program involving the extermination of the rainbow or brown trout would attract widespread support. Further, no one is certain what ''original'' conditions were.

Enhancement would proceed without reference to the original state of the lakes. Here we might add desirable man-made features and suppress undesirable natural features. Used without reference to the whole ecosystem, this method is often piecemeal and shortsighted. What is thought to be desirable today, may be condemned at some later date when unforeseen side effects become apparent.

There is always the possibility that the present destructive course will continue and lead to further *degradation*. The economic and political forces which have encouraged this course are familiar and well-entrenched. They will likely promote the idea that environmental quality is an indulgence.

Rehabilitation has been defined as ''a pragmatic mix of non-degradation, enhancement and restoration.'' Using this concept, we can begin to set the priorities for simultaneous moves to halt further degradation, restore water quality, and retain or add desirable man-made features.

By general agreement, the first priority must be the termination of further loss of water quality, particularly by chemical contamination. The strongest possible position must be taken on this issue. The goal should be that waters returned to the lake not significantly differ from those taken from it. Any attempt to zone waters for ''acceptable'' pollution must be opposed as should propaganda indicating that contamination is necessary, inevitable, or unimportant.

Microcontaminants

Further chemical and heavy metal contamination must be stopped, and new contamination prevented. Failure to meet the threat of these substances could invalidate any other efforts to rehabilitate the lakes. The problem is incredibly difficult as each of the microcontaminants pose special problems. Some are amenable to easy control, while others may be so pervasive that decades may be involved in tracing sources.

PCB's may be an example of the latter. Recent evidence indicates that there may be two pathways by which this substance enters the aquatic food chain. The major route seems to be from water and suspended particles through small plants and animals, and to final predators, including man. The minor route involves the cycling of PCB's from sediments through small organisims to the predator chain. Supposing an end to all new introduction of the material, there would likely be a rapid reduction of the contaminant in the water column. Materials in the sediments, however, will be reduced at a much slower rate. Thus with DDT there was a swift, initial, drop followed by stabilization at a lower level. If no new PCB's entered the system, it is estimated that there might be a fifty percent reduction of the amount found in the water column in as little as six to twelve years. Because of sediment cycling, it would take a longer time for fish concentrations to diminish. However, there are special problems with PCB's:

> "... Unlike DDT, which was purposely released into the environment in a controlled fashion, PCBs have been introduced accidently. Diffuse PCB sources, such as landfills, are expected to release PCBs for years. Point sources to lake systems can conceivably be removed by discharge elimination and dredging. Since the effects of pollutant input reductions should be apparent in a relatively short time, a clear need exists for a comprehensive program to evaluate and remove contaminant sources." (35)

Control of PCB's is symbolic of the far larger problem. It is apparent by now that new chemical dangers are cropping up faster than old ones can be contained. Some dangerous substances will have to be simply banned outright. Those of potential danger must be put through testing so rigorous that the time and cost involved will constitute a barrier. There may be general resistance to some of these controls, particularly when they result in economic disclocation. Sadly, some restrictions will not be politically feasible until human effects are graphically portrayed on Sixty Minutes.

The prospect for control of chemicals is doubtful at present. They are showing up faster than their potential danger can be tested. Moreover there is some question about our *ability* to control some airborne contaminants. There is certainly, at present, a question about the will to do so. Eventually, however, something will have to be done. Discussion about fish and animal life should not obscure the fact that the ultimate threat is to human beings. In the summer of 1978 Rachel Carson's dark vision of a society in a continual state of environmental crisis has come close to reality.

Eutrophication

Economic techniques should be utilized to demonstrate how much loss of water quality is costing the average lakeside community and consumer. The message must be loud and clear for when economic conditions deteriorate, environmental measures are often successfully attacked. Many view them as a luxury to be reserved for times of prosperity:

> "We should 'depolarize' the issue of environmental and socio-economic benefits. Environmental benefits are now poorly recognized, largely unquantified in any useful terms and, as a substitute, heavy emphasis is placed on water quality objectives. These objectives are in fact methods rather than social goals. Others consider environmental benefits in very relative terms,—something to achieve in times of economic booms, but surely something to forego when hard times come. Parenthetically, much gross pollution has been sanctioned in time of war, even in the Great Lakes. We must simply recognize that environmental benefits *are* socio-economic in both the short and the long term." (36)

Wastewater treatment is the most common means of controlling the input of nutrients. There have been numerous problems. Some industries have resisted adequate treatment of waste products, while others realize that the long-term impact of loss of usable water could be disastrous. These latter operations do a lot of pointing with pride. They should be encouraged in this pride by praise and recognition from the media and, most importantly, by environmental groups. Pollution Probe, an Ontario organization, issues awards to those industries that come up with innovative, environmentally positive techniques or products. Some industrial leaders have found that meeting water and air quality standards without having to be dragged kicking and screaming through the courts has given them added prestige and political clout.

Municipalities often have a different problem. Some of the largest cities, such as Detroit and Cleveland, have both severe pollution and economic problems. U.S. federal assistance on these matters is often long in coming and some treatment centers may be outdated or inadequate by the time they are built.

Some way must be found to speed up the system. Perhaps a sliding scale of economic incentives might be utilized in encouraging both industrial and municipal controls. Grants for cities and tax writeoffs for industries could be geared to the length of time taken to make facilities operational. For those who feel that the Divinity has granted them the right to use the environment as a sewer, fines and court actions appear to be the only answer.

Further, there must be a more open attitude toward new sewage treatment techniques. One method, land treatment, avoids the use of waterways. Other methods have been devised which might avoid the traditional rural dependence on septic and holding systems. The principle underlying many new approaches is recycling. If effluent could be safely and adequately treated without being injected into waterways, nutrient loads might be quickly and dramatically reduced.

There are also methods that have been developed to provide after the fact improvement in smaller lakes. It is a tremendous technical leap to apply these to bodies as large as the Great Lakes, but they might be used in appropriate harbor and bay areas. There are some interesting implications from a technique used in Lake Washington, in Washington state where diversion rerouted contaminated water away from the lake. There have even been suggestions that industrial wastewater be constantly recycled through a series of canals. This self-contained system would keep a substantial part of the worst effluents entirely away from the lakes and might be particularly effective in regions of intense industrial concentration.

There are other things that might be used in limited areas of the lakes where nutrient rich sediments have been deposited. Dredging of these sediments has proven successful in some small lakes. There is, unfortunately, the question of what to do with contaminated dredged materials. Moving your problem elsewhere is no longer viewed as an enlightened means of solving it. Nonetheless, in certain circumstances it might be necessary. Another technique, used in Sweden, involved injection of nitrates into sediments, thereby preventing nutrient recycling.

It is difficult to find many optimistic notes in the current situation. One of the few is recent evidence indicating that time required to clear the Great Lakes of some pollutants may be less than originally predicted:

"The *response time* of the Great Lakes system to decreased phosphorous loads was recently reviewed by the IJC Technical Group to Review Phosphorous Loadings . . . Current estimates of response time are now much more optimistic than many previously thought. The response times for Saginaw Bay and Lake Erie are now estimated to be in the order of one to two years or less. The response time for Lake Ontario is estimated to be about six to seven years. The response time for Lake Superior is estimated to be 15 to 20 years, while Lake Michigan and Huron have response times of about five years. Thus, it appears that

off the Door Peninsula

rehabilitation and restoration of the Great Lakes in response to reduced phosphorous loadings may be relatively fast despite the size of the lakes.'' (37)

Political Action

There are two forces which will help accelerate the move toward rehabilitation. One will be the continuing crisis which will fuel public outrage. Environmental groups in the United States and Canada must use every means at their disposal to see that information on dangerous substances and environmental degradation is kept before the public. There will be resistance to this exposure since some newspapers, radios, and television stations are owned by individuals or corporations who have direct or indirect connections to profits from pollution. In some small towns, simple economic self-preservation may result in the supression of unpleasant information.

It is also not uncommon for governments to attempt to suppress, or simply dismiss, findings that convenient or useful substances may be dangerous. Often, this stems from a desire not to alarm the public before testing has been completed. In other cases it is more difficult to explain:

> "Within Environment Canada excessive and unnecessary secrecy surrounds much of the data on the environment. This is viewed as a major constraint in the search for understanding of the effects of contaminants on the aquatic environment . . .
>
> Parenthetically, the present system of keeping the results of fish inspection data secret is extremely wasteful of federal resources. Many other agencies require the same information in the legitimate development of their own mandates. The result may be two laboratories side-by-side generating the same data, at least in part. Ofttimes other agencies are obliged to turn to less

satisfactory measurements on environmental pollutants. Thus when the International Joint Commission was refused data on contaminants in Great Lakes fishes, it was obliged to launch a costly and not altogether satisfactory alternative study of contaminants in fish-eating birds and mammals.'' (38)

In the United States the dangers of 2,4,5-T were first brushed aside. If current research findings hold, however, the government may be faced with a real horror story. Of all the pieces of insanity that stem from the collective insanity of Vietnam, none is more difficult to understand than the belief that the widespread use of defoliants would not harm humans. By the mid-sixties data was present that should have indicated the potential danger of these substances. The use of 2,4,5-T and its possible effects on soldiers and civilians, is the stuff of nightmares.

The other major force for rehabilitation will have to be in the form of political action. Not the action of those who appear to be opposed to anything man has done since he emerged from the stone age, but well-organized, well-financed, continuous pressure. It is a fact that a major political contributor is often able to accomplish more over cocktails in an hour than several thousand people with letters and petitions in a year.

In researching this book, I found no topic on which there was more agreement than water quality. An international group whose sole objective is the rehabilitation of Great Lakes water should focus on political pressure. For this purpose, groups presently opposed on allocation matters should join forces. Without a solution to the contamination problem there may be no usable resource to allocate.

Fish and game allocation causes many antagonisims to be directed at state resource agencies. It is vital to remember that these same agencies are often charged with pollution and contaminant control. People interested in preservation of the environment should get used to the seemingly illogical position of fighting their point of view on allocation matters while supporting the agency's environmental moves. A widespread, blanket hatred of these departments could have disasterous results. I can think of nothing that would bring greater joy to some major polluters than the dismantling or political crippling of these agencies. They will need support or pressure to take on politically powerful corporations and municipalities.

Nonetheless state efforts may be insufficient. If significant progress or commitment is not made by these local jurisdictions the condition of the lakes might require the creation of a federal or international organization equipped with the power to override states or cities on the matter of pollution and contaminant control. An action group might actually be designed to self-destruct. Only the worst areas would be pin-pointed and target levels set for water quality and contaminant control. When acceptable levels in these target areas were attained, control would return to local agencies or officials. A strong desire to avoid or get rid of such a super-agency might prove to be a strong incentive to self-help.

Reconstruction of the Fisheries

Control of pollution and contamination is a basic prerequisite to any long-term rehabilitation efforts. There must be a broad recognition that single species management must be replaced by ecosystem management. This will require a general understanding of the relationships between all elements of the lake ecosystem. A complete biomass study of each lake should be initiated so that present conditions are clearly understood.

The goal should be the creation of a stable, self-regulating order that would operate with the least possible external interference. As desired water quality goals are reached, rehabilitation efforts should be conducted in limited areas and re-

sults monitored before being applied on a lake-wide basis. Such a program is currently being conducted in the Bay of Quinte. Project Quinte featured a five-year period of observation of all biota before application of phosphate control in 1977. There will now be a five year observation of the natural recovery process. At the end of that time active management intervention to improve fish stocks will be made. Such an approach allows management moves to be made from an understood baseline rather than from instinct and prayer.

There should be no major moves for massive utilization of the forage base until the needs of a restored and stable order are understood. It would seem that native fish would generally provide the best hope for reaching that goal. During the period of transition it may be necessary to intervene by regulation and stocking to sustain lake herring or other fish. The past history of the lakes has shown that fish may recover from severe depletion but once lost, re-establishment is extremely difficult.

The concept of discrete stocks must become an active management concept. Such a stock is differentiated over a number of generations so that it is imprinted as to spawning location and does not interbreed with stocks spawning in other locations. Such a stock may also develop distinctive physical characteristics and habits which promote its survival in a particular location. If stocks are identified and enumerated, their numbers and health can be monitored. If hatcheries were geared to maintain a genetic "file" of various stocks, planting interventions might be far more effective.

The top predator in the biomass in all lakes except Superior, is now being maintained almost exclusively by stocking efforts. There is uniform disappointment over the lack of natural lake trout reproduction. The reason for this reproductive failure is a mystery. It may be that failure to utilize the stock concept has resulted in fish that are not genetically adapted to reproduction in their new environment. Microcontaminants, such as PCB's may be the controlling factor, though some recent evidence tends to indicate this is not the case. Perhaps the population pressure of the smelt and alewife have made it impossible for eggs or fry to survive. Perhaps degradation of the aquatic habitat is responsible.

What is believed to have been a major error in stocking technique has been corrected. Trout are now released on traditional and favored reefs, rather than from shorelines or docks. It is hoped that they will evolve discrete stocks in this manner.

It is also possible that not enough fish have been planted. The number of yearling fish is believed to be far less than that of the pre-lamprey days. It has been suggested that at least one major attempt be made to massively increase trout plantings, to literally saturate the system with fish from a variety of stocks. This would have the effect of driving down the alewife population and allowing the formation of new discrete stocks.

In any case, establishment of a self-sustaining top predator is the key. The alewife would be extremely vulnerable to such a new regime. It is a schooling fish, and this trait is not found in native fish. Thus heavy predation should favor chubs and herring. Some non-native fish will likely become part of the new balance. The pink salmon seems to have a reasonably bright future. Smelt are at least a partially schooling fish, but they seem to have done reasonably well in the face of large trout populations in earlier years. The coho and chinook appear to pose no threats to restoration efforts. It is possible that they will share the position of dominant predator with the lake trout. They are, however, not native and perhaps less likely to take root in a restored system featuring a greatly reduced number of alewives. These fish could be sustained for sportsmen by continued planting.

Anything beyond the establishment of a key predator, is, however, speculation. If a key predator takes hold, much of the subsequent restoration may be automatic. There is one artificial element that will have to be maintained for the foreseeable future. The lamprey must be kept in check if any new balance is to be maintained. There has been some concern expressed over TFM, the chemical larvacide. No substantial adverse effects have been detected but in the current environmental climate, control by chemical tends, quite naturally, to make people nervous. Dr. Stanford Smith has suggested that reforestation of immediate stream and river banks might lower water temperatures enough to make them unfavorable for lamprey spawning.

The above suggestion raises another issue, that of enhancing the environment of a reestablished system. Perhaps one of the best methods would be to identify key spawning areas for various species and establish sanctuaries for them. It is believed that relatively small regions, off-limits to *all* fishermen might supply necessary insurance for survival of populations. Another aspect of ecosystem management would involve restraining further development of marsh and wetland areas. These features should be recognized as valuable buffer zones and maintained, or restored.

Finally, the allocation of fish from a rehabilitated system should be fair to all user groups, including consumers. A resource agency should never be allowed to become the philosophical or economic captive of a single user group. Systematic destruction of a commercial fishery removes an important regional resource which might become a valued source of food in time of crisis. Recreational fishing also has widespread beneficial effects, including transfer of revenue to previously depressed lakeside cities and villages. It is not necessary, however, to set aside the entire mass of the Great Lakes for this purpose.

From a strict management viewpoint, obliteration of the commercial fishery is a foolish move. Integrated into a broad program of ecosystem management fishermen could make a

living while helping to fine tune the system. Subsidies would encourage the removal of undesirable species and direct payments could finance needed biomass and monitoring surveys.

We should use great care to preserve *both* our natural and human resources.

Lack of Regional Identity

This is the fundamental issue which underlies fragmented efforts to manage the lakes. We have been so separated by arbitrary boundaries that they have overcome the natural physical unity of the lakes in human perceptions. These fresh water seas are unique on the face of the globe, yet tours haul people to less interesting but better publicized regions. The physical beauty and diversity of our region is stunning, yet Aunt Jenny trucks off to New England for the Autumn tour.

Literature and song celebrate the New England heritage. There is even said to be a Yankee personality. We are bombarded with characterizations of the American west and the mythology of the American south. In Canada the issue of French culture and language has led to a crisis of national unity.

The history of the Great Lakes dates back to the sixteenth century, when English settlements consisted of scattered enclaves on the east coast. Yet the saga of the Voyageurs and Jesuits is largely unknown. Even the latter history of this region is confined to local libraries and historical societies. The heroic and rapacious tale of lumbering and mining has seldom entered literature or song. It is only very recently that the maritime history of the lakes has been examined in any depth. The magnificent Sierra Club volume, *The Faces of the Great Lakes,* is a major breakthrough in that it portrays the region as a unit.

It is hard to explain some of this lack of regional perception. The U.S. media largely ignores events in Canada. We are far more likely to hear a report on the political tribulations of Europe or South America than we are of the issues and attitudes of the massive Province of Ontario with whom we share a common environment.

The themes of our literature and music are largely imported from other parts of the continent. Even local songwriters are more apt to set bluegrass and country lyrics in a part of the country they have never seen, than to explore regional themes. The rare exceptions, such as Gordon Lightfoot's song, *The Wreck of the Edmund Fitzgerald,* point up the rule.

There are some things that can be done about this. We can demand better regional coverage by the media. We can focus private groups on lake issues and recruit membership across jurisdictional boundaries. If there were a demand, tour operators might well provide an expanded lakewide itinerary. We can fight the termination of transportation links. It is amazing that some of the remaining ferry connections across Lake Michigan are in peril of cancellation. Such connections should, in fact, be increased and, if necessary, subsidized. The cost would be a tiny fraction of supports tendered to the airline industry for decades. In the United States, we should encourage cable operators to carry the Canadian network (CBC) in place of one of the duplicated U.S. networks. There should be a more active media exchange between the two countries on themes of area interest.

All of these are suggestions aimed at promoting a degree of regional self-awareness. Without such an identity, it will be impossible to sustain any long-term rehabilitation of the lakes.

Sources

A variety of materials were used in this book. I have relied heavily on the *SCOL* reports, published by the Great Lakes Fishery Commission. These landmark works pulled together scattered original sources to provide individual portraits of the Great Lakes. These reports were also part of the large SCOL Symposium, reprinted in the *Journal of the Fisheries Research Board of Canada.* In this symposium the individual efforts of many researchers and observers focused on the ecosystem impact of modern development and technology.

The research and coordinating efforts of the International Joint Commission have produced valuable studies that form the basis of much of the Sections dealing with pollution and microcontaminants. In addition to the *SCOL* reports, I have utilized Great Lakes Fishery Commission studies of Lake Erie Management and their compilation of catch statistics.

One periodical allowed insight into management attitudes and the growing official concern over the contaminant problem. Here *Michigan Conservation,* later called *Michigan Natural Resources* was the key publication.

The Fisherman is one of the least-known treasures of the Great Lakes. Published intermittently since the early 1930's, it has been far more than a commercial trade publication. In its pages it is possible to trace the concerns and debates of scientists, managers, and fishermen. It provides one of the few running accounts of recent Great Lakes history and, as such, should be available in regional libraries. *The Journal of the Fisheries Research Board of Canada* provides a vast amount of wide-ranging information. The scope of the publication is remarkable.

The bottom line of research has, however, been the personal and telephone interviews. The willingness of scientists, fishermen, and managers to express their views and share freely of their findings and resources, was the most rewarding part of this project. We have on the Great Lakes a poorly perceived, but immensely valuable heritage that has been protected by a very few individuals. Their dedication should be celebrated.

Footnotes

Section 1

1. *Robert Wells, Fire at Peshtigo,* Englewood Cliffs, New Jersey: Prentice-Hall, Inc., 1968, 194.

2. Fred A. Westerman, "The Lake Whitefish," *Michigan Conservation,* July-August, 1958, 19.

3. John Van Oosten, "A New Immigrant Comes to Michigan," *The Fisherman,* June, 1936, 1.

3a. Great Lakes Basin Commission, *Great Lakes Basin Study,* Appendix 8, 230.

4. G. F. Adams and D. P. Kelnosky, *Out of the Water,* Ontario: Ministry of Natural Resources, 1974, 4.

5. P. J. Colby, G. R. Spangler, D. A. Hurley, and A. M. McCombie, "Effects of Eutrophication on Salmonid Communities in Oligotrophic Lakes," *Journal of the Fisheries Research Board of Canada,* June, 1972, 29:6, 981.

6. Justin Leonard, "Looking Ahead in Conservation," *Michigan Conservation,* September-October, 1952, 5.

7. Wilbur Hartman, *Effects of Exploitation, Environmental Changes, and New Species on the Fish Habitats and Resources of Lake Erie,* Technical Report No. 22, Ann Arbor, Michigan, Great Lakes Fishery Commission, 1973, 1.

8. Henry Regier, Vernon C. Applegate, and Richard A. Ryder, *The Ecology and Management of the Walleye in Western Lake Erie,* Technical Report No. 15, Ann Arbor, Michigan, Great Lakes Fishery Commission, 1969, 27.

Much of the information in this chapter with regard to Lake Erie management and fishing techniques is distilled from information found on pp. 27-47 of this publication.

9. *Ibid.,* 39-40.

10. Hartman, 25.

11. *Ibid.,* 26.

12. W. B. Ellis, *Land of the Inland Seas,* New York: Weathervane Books, 1974.

13. A. H. Berst and G. R. Spangler, Lake Huron, *The Ecology of the Fish Community and Man's Effects on It,* Technical Report No. 21, Ann Arbor, Michigan, Great Lakes Fishery Commission, 1973, 11.

14. John Van Oosten, Ralph Hile, and Frank Jobes, *The Whitefish Fishery of Lakes Huron and Michigan with Special Reference to the Deep-Trap-Net Fishery,* Fishery Bulletin 40, Fishery Bulletin of the Fish and Wildlife Service, 1946, 50, 299.

15. "The Deep Water Trap Net," *The Fisherman,* October, 1934, 1.

16. *Ibid.*

17. *Ibid.*

18. Van Oosten, *et al.,* 319.

19. *Ibid.,* 333.

20. *The Fisherman,* October 1934, 3.

21. Berst, *et al.,* 27-28.

22. LaRue Wells and Alberton McLain, *Lake Michigan, Man's Effects on Native Fish Stocks and other Biota,* Technical Report No. 20, Ann Arbor, Michigan, Great Lakes Fishery Commission, 1973, 1.

23. *Ibid.,* 25.

24. Gordon Lightfoot, "The Wreck of the Edmund Fitzgerald."

25. A. H. Lawrie and Jerold F. Rahrer, *Lake Superior, A Case History of the Lake and its Fisheries,* Technical Report No. 19, Ann Arbor, Michigan, Great Lakes Fishery Commission, 1973, 29.

26. *Ibid.,* 30.

27. *Ibid.,* 14.

28. *Ibid.,* 48.

29. *Ibid.,* 49.

30. Hubert R. Gallagher, A. G. Hunstsman, D. J. Taylor, John Van Oosten, *International Board of Inquiry for the Great Lakes Fisheries,* Washington, D.C., U.S. Government Printing Office, 1943, 32.

31. John Van Oosten, "Fisheries Facing Extermination," *The Fisherman,* November, 1936, 5:11, 1.

32. Gallagher, *et al.,* 38.

33. *Ibid.,* 96.

34. *Ibid.*

35. *Ibid.,* 99.

36. "Sportsmen versus Commercial Fishermen," *The Fisherman,* November, 1936, 5: 11, 2.

Section 2

1. Personal interview with Claude VerDuin, editor of *The Fisherman,* May 1978, commenting on receipt of an article by Dr. Charles Creaser, "The Parasitic Lampreys of the Lakes," *The Fisherman,* June, 1933, 2:6, 4.

1a. Vernon Applegate, "Menace of the Sea Lamprey," *Michigan Conservation,* May 1947, 10:4, 6.

2. W. J. Christie, *A Review of the Changes in the Fish Species Composition of Lake Ontario,* Technical Report No. 23, Ann Arbor, Michigan, Great Lakes Fishery Commission, 1973, 28-30.

3. Telephone interview with Dr. Vernon Applegate, July, 1978.

4. "Too Little and Too Late," *The Fisherman,* November, 1948, 5.

5. "The Trout are Gone," *The Fisherman,* Late Fall, 1951, 5.

6. "Hordes of Sea Lamprey Invade Waters of Green Bay," *The Fisherman,* Fall, 1953, 13.

7. Vernon Applegate, "The Sea Lamprey in Michigan," *Michigan Conservation,* July-August, 1949, 14.

8. *Ibid.,* 15.

9. J. W. Moffett, "Attack on the Sea Lamprey," *Michigan Conservation,* May-June, 1958, 25.

10. *Ibid.*

11. Applegate, "The Sea Lamprey in Michigan," 15.

12. *Ibid.*

13. "Find More Marked Trout," *The Fisherman,* Late Fall, 1952, 14.

14. Applegate, Interview, July, 1978.

15. Moffett, 26.

16. Vernon C. Applegate, John Howell, James W. Moffett, B. G. H. Johnson, and Manning A. Smith, *Use of 3-Trifluormethyl-4-nitrophenol as a Selective Sea Lamprey Larvicide,* Technical Report No. 1, Ann Arbor, Michigan, Great Lakes Fishery Commission, 1961, 15-16.

17. Vernon C. Applegate, Manning A. Smith, and Bennet R. Willeford, "Molecular Characteristics Versus Biological Activity," *Chemistry,* October, 1967, 40:30.

18. A. H. Berst and G. R. Spangler, Lake Huron, *The Ecology of the Fish Community and Man's Effects on It,* Technical Report No. 21, Great Lakes Fishery Commission, Ann Arbor, Michigan, 1973, 32.

19. Christie, 28.

20. Edward E. Schultz, "Three New Fish," *Michigan Conservation,* March-April, 1963, 33.

21. Howard Tanner, "Great Lakes, Sport Fishing Frontier," *Michigan Conservation,* November-December, 1965, 5.

22. There are indications that alewife populations reached maximum abundance in their initial explosion, then stabilized at a lower, but still dominant level.

APPENDIX

23. Wilbur L. Hartman, *Effects of Exploitation, Environmental Changes, and New Species on the Fish Habitats and Resources of Lake Erie,* Technical Report No. 22, Ann Arbor, Michigan, Great Lakes Fishery Commission, 1973, 27.

24. *Ibid.,* 13-15.

25. A. H. Lawrie, Jerold F. Rahrer, *Lake Superior, A Case History of the Lake and Its Fisheries,* Technical Report No. 19, Ann Arbor, Michigan, Great Lakes Fishery Commission, 1973, 53.

Section 3

1. John A. Scott, "Great! Lakers are Back," *Michigan Natural Resources,* May-June, 1971, 26.

2. Henry A. Regier and Vernon C. Applegate, "Historical Review of the Management Approach to Exploitation and Introduction in SCOL Lakes," *Journal of the Fisheries Research Board of Canada,* 1972, 29:6, 683.

3. Personal Interview with Nino Green, Attorney (Green, Renner, Weisse, Rettig, Rademacher, and Clark), Escanaba, Michigan, May, 1978.

3a. "Adson Casey, Commercial Fisherman," *Michigan Conservation,* July-August, 18.

3b. Justin W. Leonard, "Our Stake in the Great Lakes," *Michigan Conservation,* September-October, 13.

4. Justin W. Leonard, "The Questionable Sea Lamprey . . . And Some Answers," *Michigan Conservation,* January-February, 1957, 21.

5. Walter R. Crowe, "The Lake Trout are Back," *Michigan Conservation,* July-August, 1965, 3-4.

6. Howard A. Tanner, "Great Lakes, Sport Fishing Frontier," *Michigan Conservation,* November-December, 1965, 2-4.

7. *Ibid.,* 4.

8. *Ibid.,* 6-7.

9. *Ibid.,* 7.

10. Wayne H. Tody, "Great Lakes Victory," *Michigan Conservation,* November-December, 1966, 4.

11. Dave Borgeson, "Log of the Chinook," *Michigan Natural Resources,* September-October, 1970, 5.

12. David Richey, "Salmon Surprise," *Michigan Natural Resources,* March-April, 1976, 36.

13. Telephone Interview with C. R. Burrows, Minnesota Department of Natural Resources, July, 1978.

14. K. H. Loftus, "Science for Canada's Fisheries Rehabilitation Needs," *Journal of the Fisheries Research Board of Canada,* 1976, 33:8, 1832.

15. Burrows interview (See note 13).

16. *Ibid.*

17. Wayne Tody, ''The World's Finest Fishery?'' *Michigan Conservation*, May-June, 1967, 6.

18. *Ibid.*, 7.

19. Green interview (See note 3).

20. Personal Interview with Claude VerDuin, *Commissioner*, Great Lake Fishery Commission, *Publisher*, The Fisherman, May, 1978.

21. Wayne H. Tody, ''Zones for the Big Lakes,'' *Michigan Natural Resources*, March-April, 1970, 7.

22. Linda Weimer, ''Wisconsin Fishery Administrator and Biologist Support Gill Nets in Open Hearings,'' *The Fisherman*, April, 1976, 28:4, 5.

23. *Ibid.*, 10.

24. Joe Fellegy, Jr., ''Minnesota Sportsmen Use Gill Nets for Tullibees and Whitefish Fishing,'' *The Fisherman*, February, 1975, 27:2, 11.

25. ''Governor Milliken Favors Payments or Modified Rules for Michigan Fishermen,'' *The Fisherman*, 27:4, 5.

26. ''Michigan Begins Compensating Gill Net Fishermen,'' *The Fisherman*, May, 1976, 28:5, 3.

27. ''Lake Fisheries Threatened by New Regulations in Illinois,'' *The Fisherman*, 27:3.

28. ''Legality of Administrative Orders Being Tested in Illinois,'' *The Fisherman*, 27:5, 3.

29. *Ibid.*

30. Item: ''The News in Review,'' *The Fisherman*, March, 1976, 28:3, 6.

31. Vernon C. Applegate and Harry D. Van Meter, *A Brief History of Commercial Fishing in Lake Erie*, Fishery Leaflet 630, Washington, D.C., Bureau of Commercial Fisheries, April, 1970, 23.

32. Item: ''The News in Review,'' *The Fisherman*, March, 1976, 28:3, 6.

33 General Accounting Office, *The U.S. Great Lakes Commercial Fishing Industry—Past, Present, and Potential*, Washington, D.C. (CED-77-96), September 30, 1977, 18.

33b. Ohio Department of Natural Resources, Division of Wildlife, *Lake Erie Fisheries Investigations*, Creel Census, Annual Report (I-35-R-16), December 15, 1977, 1.

33c. ''Lt. Governor Martin J. Schreiber Testifies at Public Hearing on Proposed Changes in Wisconsin Regulations,'' *The Fisherman*, December, 1974, 26:3, 3.

33d. *Ibid.*, 4.

34. ''Wisconsin Task Force Recommends New Policy for the Administration of the Great Lakes Fisheries,'' *The Fisherman*, 27:3, 7.

35. ''Commercial Fisheries Compare Favorably with Sport Fisheries in New Economic Study Conducted by University of Wisconsin Sea Grant People,'' *The Fisherman*, 27:4, 3.

36. *Ibid.*

37. General Accounting Office Report, 19. (See Note 33a).

38. Keta Steebs (Quoting Tom MacMillan, past president of the Northeastern Wisconsin Great Lakes Sports Fishermen), ''Bad Apples pertain to Commercial Fishermen Too,'' *The Door County Advocate*, August 2, 1977, Section 2, 2.

39. Keta Steebs (Quoting Elaine Johnson, Secretary of Northeastern Wisconsin Consumer Fisheries Association), ''Commercial Fishing Views Expressed,'' *The Door County Advocate*, July 28, 1977, Section 1, 1.

41. C. W. Burrows interview (See note 13).

42. *Ibid.*

43. *Ibid.*

44. ''Minnesota Fishermen and Department of Natural Resources Cooperate in Stocking Lake Herring,'' *The Fisherman*, 27:7, 11.

45. *Ibid.*

46. C. W. Burrows interview (See note 13).

47. Telephone Interview with Indiana Resource official, July 1, 1978.

48. Telephone Interview with Bob Koch, Indiana Department of Natural Resources, August, 1978.

49. Jack D. Bails, ''Who Owns the Great Lakes,'' *Michigan Natural Resources*, May-June, 1975, 6.

50. *Ibid.*

51. *Ibid.*, 7.

52. ''Strong Resolution on Indian Fishing Adopted by Michigan's Natural Resources Commission,'' *The Fisherman*, 29:6, 2, 13.

53. *''Opposing Views Aired at Congressional Hearing on Indian Fishing,'' The Fisherman,* February, 1978, 30:2, 18.

54. *Ibid.*, 10.

55. *Ibid.*, 11.

56. *Ibid.*

57. Telephone Interview with Tom Washington, Michigan United Conservation Clubs, June, 1978.

58. Green interview (See note 3).

58a. *Nylund vs. Michigan Department of Natural Resources et al.,* Michigan Circuit Court for the County of Delta, File No. 77-3601-AA, 1978, 9.

59. *Ibid.*, 3.

60. *Ibid.*, (Footnote 1).

61. *Ibid.*, 5 (Footnote).

62. Green interview (See note 3).

63. Personal interview with Asa Wright, Michigan Department of Natural Resources, June, 1978.

64. Telephone interview with Carl Parker, New York Department of Environmental Conser-

vation, August, 1978.

65. Telephone interview with Delano Graff, Pennsylvania Fish Commission, August, 1978.

66. *Ibid.*

67. Telephone Interview with Bill Shepherd, New York Department of Environmental Conservation, August, 1978.

68. G. F. Adams and D. P. Kolensoky, *Out of the Water,* Ontario, Ministry of Natural Resources, 1974, 65.

69. *Ibid.,* 37.

70. H. D. Howell, *The Development of a Bulk Handling Technique for Smelt on Lake Erie,* Ontario, Ministry of Natural Resources, 1972, 4-8.

71. General Accounting Office Report, 51 (See note 33a).

72. Personal Interview with K. H. Loftus, Ontario Ministry of Natural Resources, Fisheries Branch, Toronto, April, 1978.

Section 4

1. Stanford Smith, "Factors of Ecologic Succession in Oligotrophic Fish Communities of the Laurentian Great Lakes," *Journal of the Fisheries Research Board of Canada,* June, 1972, 29:6, 726.

2. R. H. Millest, comment in *Workshop on Environmental Mapping of the Great Lakes,* (Proceedings of a Symposium held in Windsor, Ontario, November 8-10, 1976), ed. by D. R. Rosenberger and A. Robertson, Windsor, International Joint Commission (IJC), 1976, 195.

3. Common Complaint.

4. International Joint Commission (IJC), *Great Lakes Water Quality 1976, Appendix B, Surveillance Subcommittee Report,* Windsor, Ontario, June, 1977, 76.

5. J. H. Judd and R. A. Sweeney, "The Distribution and Role of Aquatic Macrophytes and Cladaphora in the Great Lakes," in *Workshop* (See note 2).

6. D. McNaught, Comment in *Great Lakes Surveillance and Monitoring* (Proceedings of a Workshop held on January 20-21, 1976), ed. by Norma Gibson MacDonald, Windsor, International Joint Commission (IJC), 1977, 34.

7. C. Schelske, Comment in *Surveillance* (See note 6).

8. A. M. Beeton and W. T. Edmondson, "The Eutrophication Problem," *Journal of the Fisheries Research Board of Canada,* June, 1972, 29:6, 675.

9. *Ibid.*

10. IJC, *Surveillance,* 69 (See note 6).

11. A. H. Lawrie and Jerold F. Rahrer, *Lake Superior, A Case History of the Lake and its Fisheries,* Technical Report No. 19, Ann Arbor, Michigan, Great Lakes Fishery Commission, 1973, 22-23.

12. International Joint Commission, *Asbestos in the Great Lakes Basin,* Windsor, Research Advisory Board, 1975, 25.

13. IJC, *Appendix B,* 73 (See note 4).

14. LaRue Wells and Alberton L. McLain, *Lake Michigan, Man's Effects on Native Fish Stocks and other Biota,* Technical Report No. 20, Ann Arbor, Michigan, Great Lakes Fishery Commission, 1973, 18.

15. *Ibid.*

16. IJC, *Appendix B,* 73 (See note 4).

17. *Ibid.,* 36.

18. *Ibid.,* 18.

19. Wells, et. al., 19.

20. Judd et. al., 136.

21. Great Lakes Basin Commission, *Great Lakes Basin Study, Appendix 8,* 141.

22. A. H. Berst and G. R. Spangler, Lake Huron, *The Ecology of the Fish Community and Man's Effects on It,* Technical Report No. 21, Ann Arbor, Michigan, Great Lakes Fishery Commission, 1973, 10-11.

23. Beeton et. al., 676.

24. IJC, *Appendix B,* 40.

25. Beeton et. al., 674.

26. Wilbur L. Hartman, *Effects of Exploitation, Environmental Changes, and New Species On the Fish Habitats and Resources of Lake Erie,* Technical Report No. 22, Ann Arbor, Michigan, 1973, Great Lakes Fishery Commission, 9.

27. Beeton et. al., 679.

28. Hartman, 9.

29. International Joint Commission, *Great Lakes Water Quality 1976 Annual Report,* Windsor, Ontario, Great Lakes Water Quality Board, 1977, 24.

30. *Ibid.,* 36.

31. *Ibid.*

32. Judd et al., 138.

33. McNaught, 34 (See note 6).

34. IJC, *Appendix B,* 95.

35. *Ibid.,* 57.

36. Judd et. al., 138-139.

37. Irma S. Rombauer and Marion Rombauer, *Joy of Cooking,* Indianapolis, Bobbs-Merrill Co., 1976.

38. Eleanor Ward, "The PBB Affair: how disaster is not only created, but perpetuated," *MacLeans,* February, 1977, 90:4, 56.

39. Ralph A. MacMullen, "The Case Against Hard Pesticides," *Michigan Natural Resources,* January-February, 1968, 4.

40. *Ibid.,* 5.

41. IJC, *Appendix B,* 82 (See note 4).

42. International Joint Commission, *Great Lakes Water Quality Appendix E, Status Report on the Persistent Toxic Pollutants in the Lake Ontario Basin,* Windsor, Ontario, December, 1976, 21.

43. "What Can Pesticides Do?" *Michigan Conservation,* January-Feburary, 1968, 8.

44. IJC, *Appendix B* (See note 4).

45. Richard Morscheck, "Minding Our PCB's," *Michigan Natural Resources,* March-April, 1976, 4.

46. *Ibid.,* 5.

47. *Ibid.,* 6.

48. J. E. Amson, Discussion, in *Structure-Activity Correlations in Studies of Toxicity and Biocentration with Aquatic Organisms,* (Proceedings of a Symposium held at Burlington, Ontario, March 11-13, 1975), ed. by Gilman D. Vieth and Dennis E. Konasewich, Windsor, International Joint Commission, 1975, 302.

49. IJC, Appendix B, 83 (See note 4).

50. IJC, *Appendix E,* 93 (See note 42).

51. *Ibid.,* 85-86.

52. *Ibid.,* 86.

53. *Ibid.,* 87.

54. IJC, *Surveillance,* 82 (See note 6).

55. *Ibid.,* 82.

56. Morscheck, 6.

57. Keta Steebs, "Why are Fish Unfit to Eat Still Being Planted?" *The Door County Advocate,* October 13, 1977, Section 1, 14.

58. *Ibid.*

59. *Ibid.*

60. *Ibid.*

61. IJC, *Appendix B,* 79 (See note 4).

62. IJC, *Appendix E* (See note 42).

63. IJC, *1976 Report,* 62 (See note 29).

Section 5

1. Steve Hannah, "PBB Costs Still Rising," *The Milwaukee Journal,* April 22, 1978.

2. "Oozing Chemicals Scare Niagara Falls," *New York Times-UPI,* August 3, 1978.

3. Paul G. Hayes, "State Produces Tons of Dangerous Waste," *Milwaukee Journal,* September 3, 1978.

4. Thomas J. Hagerty, "Dioxin in Herbicide 2,4,5-T Far Deadlier Than Thought," *The Milwaukee Journal,* October 1, 1978.

5. Nathaniel P. Reed, remarks delivered at the Environmental Protection Agency's Conference on Polychlorinated Biphenyls, Chicago, Illinois, November 21, 1975.

6. International Joint Commission, *Great Lakes Water Quality 1976 Annual Report,* Windsor, Ontario, Great Lakes Water Quality Board, 1977, 58-61.

7. Discussion, R. H. Hall, Proctor and Gamble Company in *Structure-Activity Correlations and Bioconcentration with Aquatic Organisms,* (Proceedings of a Symposium held at Burlington, Ontario, March 11-13, 1975), ed. by Gilman D. Vieth and Dennis E. Konasewich, Windsor, International Joint Commission, 1975, 324.

8. Discussion, Dr. Gilman Vieth, National Water Quality Laboratory, Duluth, Minnesota, Professor Perry D. Anderson, Dept. of Biology, Sir George Williams University, Quebec, Dr. Anthony S. DeFreitas, National Research Council, Division of Biological Science, Ottawa, Ontario, in *Structure-Activity,* 320, (See note 7).

9. J. E. Amson, Environmental Protection Agency, Washington, D.C., in *Structure-Activity,* 290-291, (See note 7).

10. Discussion, Amson and Anderson, in *Structure-Activity,* 325, (See note 7).

11. Personal Interview with Dr. Harold Harvey, Zoology Dept., University of Toronto, Toronto, Ontario, June, 1978.

12. *Ibid.*

13. *Ibid.*

14. Harold Harvey, "Aquatic Environmental Quality: Problems and Proposals," *Journal of the Fisheries Research Board of Canada,* 1976, 33:11, 2656-57.

15. Harvey interview, (See note 11).

16. Telephone Interview with Dr. David Schindler, Fresh Water Institutes of Canada, August, 1978.

17. Stanford H. Smith, "Responses of Fish Communities to Early Ecologic Changes in the Laurentian Great Lakes and their Relation to the Invasion and Establishment of the Alewife and the Sea Lamprey," Unpublished, 13-14.

18. There have been a number of efforts to pull together scattered data to construct a picture of earlier lake conditions. This process has been termed "retrospective monitoring."

19. Stanford H. Smith, "Long Term Management Strategies if Consumptive Use of Great Lakes Fish is Curtailed During the Next 25 Years," delivered at Sea Grant Workshop, University of Wisconsin, December 13-15, 1977.

20. Stanford H. Smith, "Application of Theory and Research in Fishery Management of the Laurentian Great Lakes," *Transactions of the American Fisheries Society,* 1973, 102:1, 157.

21. *Ibid.,* 158.

22. *Ibid.,* 159.

23. Stanford H. Smith, "Environmental Stress and Survival of Fish in the Great Lakes," unpublished.

24. W. J. Christie and N. M. Burns, ''Present Lake Conditions and What Caused Them,'' in *Feasibility Study: Great Lakes Ecosystems Rehabilitation and Restoration,* (Preliminary Report), Great Lakes Fishery Commission, May, 1978, 3.17.

25. Smith, *Environmental Stress,* 8, (See note 23).

26. M. G. Johnson, ''Impact of Future Developments on Rehabilitation and Restoration Strategy,'' in *Feasibility Study,* 8.11, (See note 24).

27. Ralph Hile, Paul H. Eshmeyer, and George F. Lunger, *Decline of the Lake Trout Fishery in Lake Michigan,* Fishery Bulletin 60, 1951, 94.

28. J. W. Moffett, ''Attack on the Sea Lamprey,'' *Michigan Conservation,* May-June, 1958, 23.

29. John Scott, ''Great! Lakers are Back,'' *Michigan Natural Resources,* May-June, 1971, 24.

30. Henry Regier, ''Sequence of Exploitation of Stocks in Multispecies Fisheries in the Laurentian Great Lakes, *Journal of the Fisheries Research Board of Canada,* 1973, 30:12, 1996.

31. Exchange between Dr. Howard Tanner, Director, Michigan Department of Natural Resources, and Robert D. Thornton, Committee Counsel, Hearing before the Subcommittee on Fisheries and Wildlife Conservation and the Environment, January 13, 1978, Serial No. 95-27, Washington, U.S. Government Printing Office, 1978, 162.

32. Christie et. al., 3.12.

33. J. W. Bulkey and G. R. Francis, ''Institutional Arrangement for Rehabilitation and Restoration,'' in *Feasibility Study,* 9.2-3, (See note 24).

34. Smith, *Application,* 162, (See note 20).

35. D. E. Armstrong and D. Weininger, ''Role of Microcontaminants in Restoration of Great Lakes Ecosystems,'' in *Feasibility Study,* 7.22 (See note 24).

36. Johnson, 8.12.

37. W. C. Sonzong and S. C. Chopra, ''Pollutant Loads, Especially Phosphorous,'' in *Feasibility Study,* 7.11 (See note 24).

38. Harvey, ''Aquatic Environmental Quality,'' 2643-44, (See note 14).

Appendix *The Native Species*

The whitefish have declined to near oblivion in Lake Ontario. The slide started in the 30's but at first it was not particularly alarming. Harvests had been much lower at the turn of the century, perhaps due to sea lamprey predation. Moreover, the decline was irregular with occasional swings from a quarter to a half million pounds. The last good year was 1961 when 631 thousand pounds were produced by the lake fishery. A precipitous decline came in 1964, which led eventually to the 4 thousand pound catch of 1976, an amount which suggests that the whitefish has gone to join the sturgeon in Memory Bay.

What led to the final decline? One possibility is that the commercial fishery turned its full energy on the whitefish after the decline of the chubs and lake trout. Another is that the lamprey did the same thing. Lamprey scarring, high in the 20's and 30's rose sharply after 1953. Perhaps a combination of the two factors wiped out the fish.

There is, however, another consideration. The Bay of Quinte stock collapsed abruptly a number of years before that of the main lake. The obliteration of the Bay of Quinte whitefish corresponds with the invasion of the white perch. Yellow perch prey on whitefish eggs but their spawning run reduces feeding during the crucial spring development of the whitefish larvae. White perch, on the other hand, feed extensively in the spring. There is also the fact that pollution on the Bay of Quinte had become severe before such conditions affected other parts of the lake.

The whitefish have also disappeared from Lake Erie. The swift and seemingly irreversible decline is the more impressive when it is pointed out that the highest catch ever recorded in the lake, 7 million pounds, occurred in 1949. There had been a strong upsurge in the fishery after World War II. In 1950 production dropped by four million pounds. There was another drop from 2.7 million to 944 thousand from 1953 to 1954. A brief recovery in 1957 brought it back to 1.2 million, but subsequently the bottom fell out, and by 1960 only 36 thousand pounds were caught. The fishery never recovered.

Lake Erie was seriously affected by neither the lamprey nor the alewife and this rules out some of the typical villains. Whitefish decline does, however, coincide closely with the rise of the smelt. This interaction shows up in other areas often enough to suggest some connection.

Each of the SCOL series emphasizes certain characteristics of the lakes. The Lake Erie discussion points out that all of the coldwater species are operating at the southern limit of their natural range in Erie. Further, the lake has warmed by 1 degree C over the last fifty years. The temperature change might be crucial in marginal situations:

''. . . Price (1940) reporting on the embryonic development of whitefish to hatching at constant temperatures, stated that the optimum temperature range for incubation is rather narrow, extending from 0.5 to 6.0 C. Higher incubation temperatures reduced the length of fry at hatching, increased the percentage of abnormal embryos that hatched alive, and increased total mortality to hatching. For example, at 8 C only 19 percent of the eggs hatched, and 25 percent of these were abnormal; at 10 C only 1 percent of the eggs hatched and half of these were abnormal. Lawler (1965) found that strong year classes were produced only when certain favorable temperature conditions prevailed: (1) Fall temperatures should drop early to 43 F (6.1 C), the temperature below which most successful spawning occurs; (2) the temperature decrease to the optimum for development should be steady and not fluctuating; (3) the spring temperature should increase slowly and late, thus providing a prolonged incubation period at near optimum development temperatures. The strong year classes of 1926, 1936, and 1944 all developed under these favorable circumstances.'' (23)

If such precision is necessary for a successful year class to develop, it is easy to see that environmental warming produced by natural change, thermal pollution, and increasing urbanization may have had a combined lethal effect. It is also important to remember that the whitefish had earlier abandoned the western spawning grounds because of pollution. The overall impact of this had gradually spread eastward. The final collapse of the whitefish began after 1953. Something else also happened:

''Oxygen depletion in the western basin was apparently not serious before the critical year of 1953 . . . 28 days of calm, hot weather during the summer of 1953 caused sufficient stratification to prevent complete vertical circulation. . . . Oxygen demands of the water or bottom muds, or both, were great enough to reduce (dissolved oxygen) to less than 1.2 mg/1.''

''The changes in oxygen regimes in the central basin of Lake Erie are especially important because this region is a key area for certain fish populations. Before anoxic conditions set in, the hypolimnion served as a required oversummering sanctuary for such cold stenotherms as lake herring, lake whitefish, and some trout moving in from the deeper eastern basin. . . .''(24)

Lake Herring

Lake herring and chub statistics were combined in Lake Ontario until 1951, so comparison of relative abundance before that time is generally from the records of commercial fishermen. There was a series of strong years at the end of the 30's and through the war when combined catches were over a million pounds. The decline began in 1945 and reached 242 thousand pounds in 1951. Herring alone accounted for 135 thousand pounds in 1952, and thereafter the trend was downward with occasional small revivals. In 1976 the figure was 15 thousand.

Herring seemed to have reached the disappearing point in the lake. The lamprey may have turned on the fish as the trout disappeared. Their decline coincides closely with the rise of the smelt. The Bay of Quinte stock disappeared first and this raises the possibility that pollution was a crucial factor. It is possible that the three factors worked together.

In Erie the herring produced one last great comeback before their final disappearance. They had fallen to record lows of under a hundred thousand pounds per year in the early 40's when there was a single spectacular year class, that of 1944. In 1945, 9.2 million pounds came out of the nets and in 1946 an awesome 16.1 million, the greatest year of the fishery since 1924. This catch appears to have been heavily concentrated in the eastern waters, raising the possibility that even in good years the herring was forced to the less polluted waters of the eastern basin. Another possibility is that of climatic stress. In 1921, 1946, and 1947, March temperatures were abnormally high and the increase of temperature could have put hatching ahead of adequate supplies of plankton. Each spring was followed by a massive decline in the herring stocks. By 1960 the catch was down to 18 thousand pounds, in 1965 it was one thousand and thereafter the fish was a negligible part of the commercial fishery. The bulk of the great decline came with the increasing period of oxygen depletion and the rapid increase in smelt. The combinations of these factors makes it doubtful that the herring will be a significant part of the Erie population until conditions have changed.

In Huron the pattern is repeated. Production stayed over a million pounds per year from 1940 to 1954. In 1957 the figure fell below a hundred thousand and has since remained at a low level. The great smelt die-off seems to have some relationship with the stability of herring in the 1945-55 decade. Again the smelt and alewives rose to dominance with the decline of the herring. Saginaw Bay had been the center of strong production, and pollution there may have limited survival. It is important to point out that decline was simultaneous and lakewide.

The smelt collapse also reversed a decline in Lake Michigan waters. The recovery there was very strong. Herring went from 1.7 million in 1940 to over 5 million in 1946 and stayed above that mark for a decade. The 9.6 million of 1952 was a thirty-year record. The second disappearance of the herring again coincided with the recovery of the smelt and the rise of the alewives. The increasing pollution of Green Bay may also have been important.

Superior conforms to the patterns seen in the other lakes. Herring was the most important fish in tonnage for much of this century. In 1940 there was an all time record catch of 19.2 million pounds. Except for a single year, production was above 10 million pounds for the next twenty-three years. A slow, continuous fall began in 1964, which corresponds with the abrupt rise of the smelt. The decline came after the lamprey numbers had been reduced but also coincided with an increase in chubs. The herring is not yet at the oblivion point, as 1.7 million were taken in 1976.

There has been a shift in domination of the fishery through all of the surrounding jurisdictions. The sequence in this century has been Minnesota-Wisconsin-Michigan-Ontario. The fact that declines in these fisheries occurred at a time of declining fishing efforts led to an interesting conclusion:

''. . . Anderson and Smith (1971a) examined the commercial catch statistics from all western U.S. fisheries and demonstrated that for most statistical districts, not only yield, but abundance and effective effort have all been declining more or less steeply since 1949. On this basis they rejected overfishing as the primary cause of the post 1961 collapse and finding no deleterious abiotic factor of general significance, concluded that competition for food with the increasing populations of bloater . . . and particularly of the introduced smelt . . . was the most probable cause of the decline.''(25)

Blue Pike

The collapse of the blue pike fisheries of Lakes Erie and Ontario is the most stunning species disintegration in the history of the Great Lakes. As noted, the blue pike production fluctuated as erratically as that of the herring. In 1941 4.8 million pounds came out of Lake Erie. In 1944, just three years later, the harvest was 24.3 million pounds. A plunge to 4.8 million in 1947 was followed by 23.8 million in 1949. Thus when the final slide began, it caught almost everyone by surprise. The specifics are staggering:

Year	Number of Pounds
1955	19,685,000
1956	18,857,000
1957	10,370,000
1958	1,399,000
1959	79,000
1960	12,000
1961	2,000

The peak year for the blue pike on Lake Ontario was 1952 when 648 thousand pounds were harvested. In the 1950-54 period this fish constituted half the volume and dollar value of the lake catches. After 1961 it had virtually disappeared. The fish appeared to have been concentrated in the western part of the lake. The near simultaneous collapse of the population of both lakes and their position in western Lake Ontario have led some writers to speculate that the fish were actually part of the same stock, originating in Lake Erie.

There was another familiar event that occurred during the period—the rise of the smelt populations, particularly in Lake Erie. This fish once again appears at a period of declining abundance of both the blue pike and walleye. It overlapped their environment for periods of the year and may have put additional stress on species beset by an increasingly unfavorable environment.

In the U.S. waters of Erie alone the blue pike had constituted 38.7 percent of the total lake catch by weight in the years 1935-39. From 1950 to 1954 it had been 23.3 percent of the total volume and 25.9 percent of the dollar value of the commercial catch. In the period 1960-64 it was less than .1 percent of the volume and exactly .1 percent of the dollar value.

The blue pike were heavily dependent on strong year classes. Their fluctuation is reflected in the commercial statistics. The last year class of significance was that of 1954. After that there was an almost total failure of the fish to reproduce. The average age and size increased the chances they would be caught. The fish disappeared first in the central basin and persisted in the deeper eastern sections until the final collapse.

All of these events appeared suspiciously close to the years when dissolved oxygen was decreasing in summer waters of the central basin. The habitat had reached a point where the survival of fish, such as the pike, which preferred the colder waters, was no longer possible.

The fish may have been forced to the eastern basin and statistics indicate that this is what happened.